TEST PREPARATION

MTTC

Upper Elementary (3-6) Education (121-124) Secrets Study Guide Part 1 of 2

Dear Future Exam Success Story

First of all, **THANK YOU** for purchasing Mometrix study materials!

Second, congratulations! You are one of the few determined test-takers who are committed to doing whatever it takes to excel on your exam. **You have come to the right place.** We developed these study materials with one goal in mind: to deliver you the information you need in a format that's concise and easy to use.

In addition to optimizing your guide for the content of the test, we've outlined our recommended steps for breaking down the preparation process into small, attainable goals so you can make sure you stay on track.

We've also analyzed the entire test-taking process, identifying the most common pitfalls and showing how you can overcome them and be ready for any curveball the test throws you.

Standardized testing is one of the biggest obstacles on your road to success, which only increases the importance of doing well in the high-pressure, high-stakes environment of test day. Your results on this test could have a significant impact on your future, and this guide provides the information and practical advice to help you achieve your full potential on test day.

Your success is our success

We would love to hear from you! If you would like to share the story of your exam success or if you have any questions or comments in regard to our products, please contact us at **800-673-8175** or **support@mometrix.com**.

Thanks again for your business and we wish you continued success!

Sincerely,
The Mometrix Test Preparation Team

Need more help? Check out our flashcards at:
http://mometrixflashcards.com/MTTC

Written and edited by the Mometrix Exam Secrets Test Prep Team
Printed in the United States of America

TABLE OF CONTENTS

Introduction

Thank you for purchasing this resource! You have made the choice to prepare yourself for a test that could have a huge impact on your future, and this guide is designed to help you be fully ready for test day. Obviously, it's important to have a solid understanding of the test material, but you also need to be prepared for the unique environment and stressors of the test, so that you can perform to the best of your abilities.

For this purpose, the first section that appears in this guide is the **Secret Keys**. We've devoted countless hours to meticulously researching what works and what doesn't, and we've boiled down our findings to the five most impactful steps you can take to improve your performance on the test. We start at the beginning with study planning and move through the preparation process, all the way to the testing strategies that will help you get the most out of what you know when you're finally sitting in front of the test.

We recommend that you start preparing for your test as far in advance as possible. However, if you've bought this guide as a last-minute study resource and only have a few days before your test, we recommend that you skip over the first two Secret Keys since they address a long-term study plan.

If you struggle with **test anxiety**, we strongly encourage you to check out our recommendations for how you can overcome it. Test anxiety is a formidable foe, but it can be beaten, and we want to make sure you have the tools you need to defeat it.

Secret Key #1 – Plan Big, Study Small

There's a lot riding on your performance. If you want to ace this test, you're going to need to keep your skills sharp and the material fresh in your mind. You need a plan that lets you review everything you need to know while still fitting in your schedule. We'll break this strategy down into three categories.

Create Notebook With vocab

Information Organization

Start with the information you already have: the official test outline. From this, you can make a complete list of all the concepts you need to cover before the test. Organize these concepts into groups that can be studied together, and create a list of any related vocabulary you need to learn so you can brush up on any difficult terms. You'll want to keep this vocabulary list handy once you actually start studying since you may need to add to it along the way.

Time Management

Once you have your set of study concepts, decide how to spread them out over the time you have left before the test. Break your study plan into small, clear goals so you have a manageable task for each day and know exactly what you're doing. Then just focus on one small step at a time. When you manage your time this way, you don't need to spend hours at a time studying. Studying a small block of content for a short period each day helps you retain information better and avoid stressing over how much you have left to do. You can relax knowing that you have a plan to cover everything in time. In order for this strategy to be effective though, you have to start studying early and stick to your schedule. Avoid the exhaustion and futility that comes from last-minute cramming!

Study Environment

The environment you study in has a big impact on your learning. Studying in a coffee shop, while probably more enjoyable, is not likely to be as fruitful as studying in a quiet room. It's important to keep distractions to a minimum. You're only planning to study for a short block of time, so make the most of it. Don't pause to check your phone or get up to find a snack. It's also important to **avoid multitasking**. Research has consistently shown that multitasking will make your studying dramatically less effective. Your study area should also be comfortable and well-lit so you don't have the distraction of straining your eyes or sitting on an uncomfortable chair.

The time of day you study is also important. You want to be rested and alert. Don't wait until just before bedtime. Study when you'll be most likely to comprehend and remember. Even better, if you know what time of day your test will be, set that time aside for study. That way your brain will be used to working on that subject at that specific time and you'll have a better chance of recalling information.

Finally, it can be helpful to team up with others who are studying for the same test. Your actual studying should be done in as isolated an environment as possible, but the work of organizing the information and setting up the study plan can be divided up. In between study sessions, you can discuss with your teammates the concepts that you're all studying and quiz each other on the details. Just be sure that your teammates are as serious about the test as you are. If you find that your study time is being replaced with social time, you might need to find a new team.

Secret Key #2 – Make Your Studying Count

You're devoting a lot of time and effort to preparing for this test, so you want to be absolutely certain it will pay off. This means doing more than just reading the content and hoping you can remember it on test day. It's important to make every minute of study count. There are two main areas you can focus on to make your studying count.

Retention

It doesn't matter how much time you study if you can't remember the material. You need to make sure you are retaining the concepts. To check your retention of the information you're learning, try recalling it at later times with minimal prompting. Try carrying around flashcards and glance at one or two from time to time or ask a friend who's also studying for the test to quiz you.

To enhance your retention, look for ways to put the information into practice so that you can apply it rather than simply recalling it. If you're using the information in practical ways, it will be much easier to remember. Similarly, it helps to solidify a concept in your mind if you're not only reading it to yourself but also explaining it to someone else. Ask a friend to let you teach them about a concept you're a little shaky on (or speak aloud to an imaginary audience if necessary). As you try to summarize, define, give examples, and answer your friend's questions, you'll understand the concepts better and they will stay with you longer. Finally, step back for a big picture view and ask yourself how each piece of information fits with the whole subject. When you link the different concepts together and see them working together as a whole, it's easier to remember the individual components.

Finally, practice showing your work on any multi-step problems, even if you're just studying. Writing out each step you take to solve a problem will help solidify the process in your mind, and you'll be more likely to remember it during the test.

Modality

Modality simply refers to the means or method by which you study. Choosing a study modality that fits your own individual learning style is crucial. No two people learn best in exactly the same way, so it's important to know your strengths and use them to your advantage.

For example, if you learn best by visualization, focus on visualizing a concept in your mind and draw an image or a diagram. Try color-coding your notes, illustrating them, or creating symbols that will trigger your mind to recall a learned concept. If you learn best by hearing or discussing information, find a study partner who learns the same way or read aloud to yourself. Think about how to put the information in your own words. Imagine that you are giving a lecture on the topic and record yourself so you can listen to it later.

For any learning style, flashcards can be helpful. Organize the information so you can take advantage of spare moments to review. Underline key words or phrases. Use different colors for different categories. Mnemonic devices (such as creating a short list in which every item starts with the same letter) can also help with retention. Find what works best for you and use it to store the information in your mind most effectively and easily.

Secret Key #3 – Practice the Right Way

Your success on test day depends not only on how many hours you put into preparing, but also on whether you prepared the right way. It's good to check along the way to see if your studying is paying off. One of the most effective ways to do this is by taking practice tests to evaluate your progress. Practice tests are useful because they show exactly where you need to improve. Every time you take a practice test, pay special attention to these three groups of questions:

- The questions you got wrong
- The questions you had to guess on, even if you guessed right
- The questions you found difficult or slow to work through

This will show you exactly what your weak areas are, and where you need to devote more study time. Ask yourself why each of these questions gave you trouble. Was it because you didn't understand the material? Was it because you didn't remember the vocabulary? Do you need more repetitions on this type of question to build speed and confidence? Dig into those questions and figure out how you can strengthen your weak areas as you go back to review the material.

Additionally, many practice tests have a section explaining the answer choices. It can be tempting to read the explanation and think that you now have a good understanding of the concept. However, an explanation likely only covers part of the question's broader context. Even if the explanation makes perfect sense, **go back and investigate** every concept related to the question until you're positive you have a thorough understanding.

As you go along, keep in mind that the practice test is just that: practice. Memorizing these questions and answers will not be very helpful on the actual test because it is unlikely to have any of the same exact questions. If you only know the right answers to the sample questions, you won't be prepared for the real thing. **Study the concepts** until you understand them fully, and then you'll be able to answer any question that shows up on the test.

It's important to wait on the practice tests until you're ready. If you take a test on your first day of study, you may be overwhelmed by the amount of material covered and how much you need to learn. Work up to it gradually.

On test day, you'll need to be prepared for answering questions, managing your time, and using the test-taking strategies you've learned. It's a lot to balance, like a mental marathon that will have a big impact on your future. Like training for a marathon, you'll need to start slowly and work your way up. When test day arrives, you'll be ready.

Start with the strategies you've read in the first two Secret Keys—plan your course and study in the way that works best for you. If you have time, consider using multiple study resources to get different approaches to the same concepts. It can be helpful to see difficult concepts from more than one angle. Then find a good source for practice tests. Many times, the test website will suggest potential study resources or provide sample tests.

Practice Test Strategy

If you're able to find at least three practice tests, we recommend this strategy:

Untimed and Open-Book Practice

Take the first test with no time constraints and with your notes and study guide handy. Take your time and focus on applying the strategies you've learned.

Timed and Open-Book Practice

Take the second practice test open-book as well, but set a timer and practice pacing yourself to finish in time.

Timed and Closed-Book Practice

Take any other practice tests as if it were test day. Set a timer and put away your study materials. Sit at a table or desk in a quiet room, imagine yourself at the testing center, and answer questions as quickly and accurately as possible.

Keep repeating timed and closed-book tests on a regular basis until you run out of practice tests or it's time for the actual test. Your mind will be ready for the schedule and stress of test day, and you'll be able to focus on recalling the material you've learned.

Secret Key #4 – Pace Yourself

Once you're fully prepared for the material on the test, your biggest challenge on test day will be managing your time. Just knowing that the clock is ticking can make you panic even if you have plenty of time left. Work on pacing yourself so you can build confidence against the time constraints of the exam. Pacing is a difficult skill to master, especially in a high-pressure environment, so **practice is vital**.

Set time expectations for your pace based on how much time is available. For example, if a section has 60 questions and the time limit is 30 minutes, you know you have to average 30 seconds or less per question in order to answer them all. Although 30 seconds is the hard limit, set 25 seconds per question as your goal, so you reserve extra time to spend on harder questions. When you budget extra time for the harder questions, you no longer have any reason to stress when those questions take longer to answer.

Don't let this time expectation distract you from working through the test at a calm, steady pace, but keep it in mind so you don't spend too much time on any one question. Recognize that taking extra time on one question you don't understand may keep you from answering two that you do understand later in the test. If your time limit for a question is up and you're still not sure of the answer, mark it and move on, and come back to it later if the time and the test format allow. If the testing format doesn't allow you to return to earlier questions, just make an educated guess; then put it out of your mind and move on.

On the easier questions, be careful not to rush. It may seem wise to hurry through them so you have more time for the challenging ones, but it's not worth missing one if you know the concept and just didn't take the time to read the question fully. Work efficiently but make sure you understand the question and have looked at all of the answer choices, since more than one may seem right at first.

Even if you're paying attention to the time, you may find yourself a little behind at some point. You should speed up to get back on track, but do so wisely. Don't panic; just take a few seconds less on each question until you're caught up. Don't guess without thinking, but do look through the answer choices and eliminate any you know are wrong. If you can get down to two choices, it is often worthwhile to guess from those. Once you've chosen an answer, move on and don't dwell on any that you skipped or had to hurry through. If a question was taking too long, chances are it was one of the harder ones, so you weren't as likely to get it right anyway.

On the other hand, if you find yourself getting ahead of schedule, it may be beneficial to slow down a little. The more quickly you work, the more likely you are to make a careless mistake that will affect your score. You've budgeted time for each question, so don't be afraid to spend that time. Practice an efficient but careful pace to get the most out of the time you have.

Secret Key #5 – Have a Plan for Guessing

When you're taking the test, you may find yourself stuck on a question. Some of the answer choices seem better than others, but you don't see the one answer choice that is obviously correct. What do you do?

The scenario described above is very common, yet most test takers have not effectively prepared for it. Developing and practicing a plan for guessing may be one of the single most effective uses of your time as you get ready for the exam.

In developing your plan for guessing, there are three questions to address:

- When should you start the guessing process?
- How should you narrow down the choices?
- Which answer should you choose?

When to Start the Guessing Process

Unless your plan for guessing is to select C every time (which, despite its merits, is not what we recommend), you need to leave yourself enough time to apply your answer elimination strategies. Since you have a limited amount of time for each question, that means that if you're going to give yourself the best shot at guessing correctly, you have to decide quickly whether or not you will guess.

Of course, the best-case scenario is that you don't have to guess at all, so first, see if you can answer the question based on your knowledge of the subject and basic reasoning skills. Focus on the key words in the question and try to jog your memory of related topics. Give yourself a chance to bring the knowledge to mind, but once you realize that you don't have (or you can't access) the knowledge you need to answer the question, it's time to start the guessing process.

It's almost always better to start the guessing process too early than too late. It only takes a few seconds to remember something and answer the question from knowledge. Carefully eliminating wrong answer choices takes longer. Plus, going through the process of eliminating answer choices can actually help jog your memory.

Summary: Start the guessing process as soon as you decide that you can't answer the question based on your knowledge.

How to Narrow Down the Choices

The next chapter in this book (**Test-Taking Strategies**) includes a wide range of strategies for how to approach questions and how to look for answer choices to eliminate. You will definitely want to read those carefully, practice them, and figure out which ones work best for you. Here though, we're going to address a mindset rather than a particular strategy.

Your odds of guessing an answer correctly depend on how many options you are choosing from.

Number of options left	5	4	3	2	1
Odds of guessing correctly	20%	25%	33%	50%	100%

You can see from this chart just how valuable it is to be able to eliminate incorrect answers and make an educated guess, but there are two things that many test takers do that cause them to miss out on the benefits of guessing:

- Accidentally eliminating the correct answer
- Selecting an answer based on an impression

We'll look at the first one here, and the second one in the next section.

To avoid accidentally eliminating the correct answer, we recommend a thought exercise called **the $5 challenge**. In this challenge, you only eliminate an answer choice from contention if you are willing to bet $5 on it being wrong. Why $5? Five dollars is a small but not insignificant amount of money. It's an amount you could afford to lose but wouldn't want to throw away. And while losing $5 once might not hurt too much, doing it twenty times will set you back $100. In the same way, each small decision you make—eliminating a choice here, guessing on a question there—won't by itself impact your score very much, but when you put them all together, they can make a big difference. By holding each answer choice elimination decision to a higher standard, you can reduce the risk of accidentally eliminating the correct answer.

The $5 challenge can also be applied in a positive sense: If you are willing to bet $5 that an answer choice *is* correct, go ahead and mark it as correct.

Summary: Only eliminate an answer choice if you are willing to bet $5 that it is wrong.

Which Answer to Choose

You're taking the test. You've run into a hard question and decided you'll have to guess. You've eliminated all the answer choices you're willing to bet $5 on. Now you have to pick an answer. Why do we even need to talk about this? Why can't you just pick whichever one you feel like when the time comes?

The answer to these questions is that if you don't come into the test with a plan, you'll rely on your impression to select an answer choice, and if you do that, you risk falling into a trap. The test writers know that everyone who takes their test will be guessing on some of the questions, so they intentionally write wrong answer choices to seem plausible. You still have to pick an answer though, and if the wrong answer choices are designed to look right, how can you ever be sure that you're not falling for their trap? The best solution we've found to this dilemma is to take the decision out of your hands entirely. Here is the process we recommend:

Once you've eliminated any choices that you are confident (willing to bet $5) are wrong, select the first remaining choice as your answer.

Whether you choose to select the first remaining choice, the second, or the last, the important thing is that you use some preselected standard. Using this approach guarantees that you will not be enticed into selecting an answer choice that looks right, because you are not basing your decision on how the answer choices look.

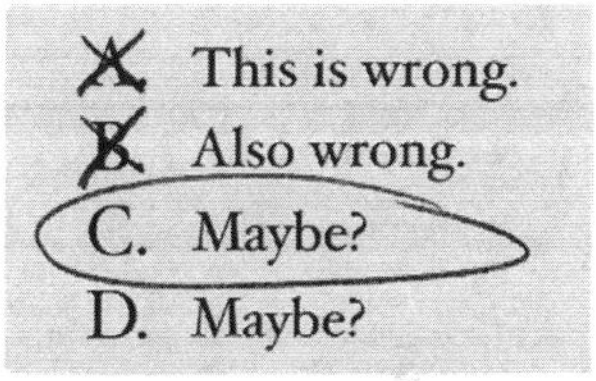

This is not meant to make you question your knowledge. Instead, it is to help you recognize the difference between your knowledge and your impressions. There's a huge difference between thinking an answer is right because of what you know, and thinking an answer is right because it looks or sounds like it should be right.

Summary: To ensure that your selection is appropriately random, make a predetermined selection from among all answer choices you have not eliminated.

Test-Taking Strategies

This section contains a list of test-taking strategies that you may find helpful as you work through the test. By taking what you know and applying logical thought, you can maximize your chances of answering any question correctly!

It is very important to realize that every question is different and every person is different: no single strategy will work on every question, and no single strategy will work for every person. That's why we've included all of them here, so you can try them out and determine which ones work best for different types of questions and which ones work best for you.

Question Strategies

✓ Read Carefully

Read the question and the answer choices carefully. Don't miss the question because you misread the terms. You have plenty of time to read each question thoroughly and make sure you understand what is being asked. Yet a happy medium must be attained, so don't waste too much time. You must read carefully and efficiently.

✓ Contextual Clues

Look for contextual clues. If the question includes a word you are not familiar with, look at the immediate context for some indication of what the word might mean. Contextual clues can often give you all the information you need to decipher the meaning of an unfamiliar word. Even if you can't determine the meaning, you may be able to narrow down the possibilities enough to make a solid guess at the answer to the question.

✓ Prefixes

If you're having trouble with a word in the question or answer choices, try dissecting it. Take advantage of every clue that the word might include. Prefixes can be a huge help. Usually, they allow you to determine a basic meaning. *Pre-* means before, *post-* means after, *pro-* is positive, *de-* is negative. From prefixes, you can get an idea of the general meaning of the word and try to put it into context.

✓ Hedge Words

Watch out for critical hedge words, such as *likely, may, can, sometimes, often, almost, mostly, usually, generally, rarely*, and *sometimes*. Question writers insert these hedge phrases to cover every possibility. Often an answer choice will be wrong simply because it leaves no room for exception. Be on guard for answer choices that have definitive words such as *exactly* and *always*.

✓ Switchback Words

Stay alert for *switchbacks*. These are the words and phrases frequently used to alert you to shifts in thought. The most common switchback words are *but*, *although*, and *however*. Others include *nevertheless, on the other hand, even though, while, in spite of, despite*, and *regardless of*. Switchback words are important to catch because they can change the direction of the question or an answer choice.

✓ Face Value

When in doubt, use common sense. Accept the situation in the problem at face value. Don't read too much into it. These problems will not require you to make wild assumptions. If you have to go beyond creativity and warp time or space in order to have an answer choice fit the question, then you should move on and consider the other answer choices. These are normal problems rooted in reality. The applicable relationship or explanation may not be readily apparent, but it is there for you to figure out. Use your common sense to interpret anything that isn't clear.

Answer Choice Strategies

⊘ Answer Selection

The most thorough way to pick an answer choice is to identify and eliminate wrong answers until only one is left, then confirm it is the correct answer. Sometimes an answer choice may immediately seem right, but be careful. The test writers will usually put more than one reasonable answer choice on each question, so take a second to read all of them and make sure that the other choices are not equally obvious. As long as you have time left, it is better to read every answer choice than to pick the first one that looks right without checking the others.

⊘ Answer Choice Families

An answer choice family consists of two (in rare cases, three) answer choices that are very similar in construction and cannot all be true at the same time. If you see two answer choices that are direct opposites or parallels, one of them is usually the correct answer. For instance, if one answer choice says that quantity *x* increases and another either says that quantity *x* decreases (opposite) or says that quantity *y* increases (parallel), then those answer choices would fall into the same family. An answer choice that doesn't match the construction of the answer choice family is more likely to be incorrect. Most questions will not have answer choice families, but when they do appear, you should be prepared to recognize them.

⊘ Eliminate Answers

Eliminate answer choices as soon as you realize they are wrong, but make sure you consider all possibilities. If you are eliminating answer choices and realize that the last one you are left with is also wrong, don't panic. Start over and consider each choice again. There may be something you missed the first time that you will realize on the second pass.

⊘ Avoid Fact Traps

Don't be distracted by an answer choice that is factually true but doesn't answer the question. You are looking for the choice that answers the question. Stay focused on what the question is asking for so you don't accidentally pick an answer that is true but incorrect. Always go back to the question and make sure the answer choice you've selected actually answers the question and is not merely a true statement.

⊘ Extreme Statements

In general, you should avoid answers that put forth extreme actions as standard practice or proclaim controversial ideas as established fact. An answer choice that states the "process should be used in certain situations, if…" is much more likely to be correct than one that states the "process should be discontinued completely." The first is a calm rational statement and doesn't even make a definitive, uncompromising stance, using a hedge word *if* to provide wiggle room, whereas the second choice is far more extreme.

⊘ Benchmark

As you read through the answer choices and you come across one that seems to answer the question well, mentally select that answer choice. This is not your final answer, but it's the one that will help you evaluate the other answer choices. The one that you selected is your benchmark or standard for judging each of the other answer choices. Every other answer choice must be compared to your benchmark. That choice is correct until proven otherwise by another answer choice beating it. If you find a better answer, then that one becomes your new benchmark. Once you've decided that no other choice answers the question as well as your benchmark, you have your final answer.

⊘ Predict the Answer

Before you even start looking at the answer choices, it is often best to try to predict the answer. When you come up with the answer on your own, it is easier to avoid distractions and traps because you will know exactly what to look for. The right answer choice is unlikely to be word-for-word what you came up with, but it should be a close match. Even if you are confident that you have the right answer, you should still take the time to read each option before moving on.

General Strategies

☑ Tough Questions

If you are stumped on a problem or it appears too hard or too difficult, don't waste time. Move on! Remember though, if you can quickly check for obviously incorrect answer choices, your chances of guessing correctly are greatly improved. Before you completely give up, at least try to knock out a couple of possible answers. Eliminate what you can and then guess at the remaining answer choices before moving on.

☑ Check Your Work

Since you will probably not know every term listed and the answer to every question, it is important that you get credit for the ones that you do know. Don't miss any questions through careless mistakes. If at all possible, try to take a second to look back over your answer selection and make sure you've selected the correct answer choice and haven't made a costly careless mistake (such as marking an answer choice that you didn't mean to mark). This quick double check should more than pay for itself in caught mistakes for the time it costs.

☑ Pace Yourself

It's easy to be overwhelmed when you're looking at a page full of questions; your mind is confused and full of random thoughts, and the clock is ticking down faster than you would like. Calm down and maintain the pace that you have set for yourself. Especially as you get down to the last few minutes of the test, don't let the small numbers on the clock make you panic. As long as you are on track by monitoring your pace, you are guaranteed to have time for each question.

☑ Don't Rush

It is very easy to make errors when you are in a hurry. Maintaining a fast pace in answering questions is pointless if it makes you miss questions that you would have gotten right otherwise. Test writers like to include distracting information and wrong answers that seem right. Taking a little extra time to avoid careless mistakes can make all the difference in your test score. Find a pace that allows you to be confident in the answers that you select.

☑ Keep Moving

Panicking will not help you pass the test, so do your best to stay calm and keep moving. Taking deep breaths and going through the answer elimination steps you practiced can help to break through a stress barrier and keep your pace.

Final Notes

The combination of a solid foundation of content knowledge and the confidence that comes from practicing your plan for applying that knowledge is the key to maximizing your performance on test day. As your foundation of content knowledge is built up and strengthened, you'll find that the strategies included in this chapter become more and more effective in helping you quickly sift through the distractions and traps of the test to isolate the correct answer.

Now that you're preparing to move forward into the test content chapters of this book, be sure to keep your goal in mind. As you read, think about how you will be able to apply this information on the test. If you've already seen sample questions for the test and you have an idea of the question format and style, try to come up with questions of your own that you can answer based on what you're reading. This will give you valuable practice applying your knowledge in the same ways you can expect to on test day.

Good luck and good studying!

Professional Knowledge and Skills

Student Development and Impacts on Learning

Piaget's Theory of Cognitive Development

Jean Piaget's theory of cognitive development consists of four stages that a child moves through throughout life. The four stages are the **sensorimotor stage** (birth-2 years), **preoperational stage** (2-7 years), **concrete operational stage** (7-11 years), and **formal operational stage** (12 years and beyond). Piaget believed that the way children think changes as they pass through these stages. In the **sensorimotor stage**, infants exist in the present moment and investigate their world for the first time through their five senses, reflexes, and actions. Key skills infants acquire during this stage include object permanence and self-recognition. In the **preoperational stage**, children learn to express ideas symbolically, including through language and pretend play. Markers of this stage include engaging in animism, egocentrism, and the inability to understand conservation (the knowledge that the quantity of something does not change when its appearance does). In the **concrete operational stage**, children develop logical thought and begin understanding conservation. The **formal operational stage** brings the ability to think abstractly and hypothetically. Piaget believed that children learn through experimenting and building upon knowledge from experiences. He asserted that educators should be highly qualified and trained to create experiences that support development in each of these stages.

Skills Typically Acquired at Each Stage of Cognitive Development

- **Sensorimotor:** As children in the sensorimotor stage gain an increasing awareness of their bodies and the world around them, a wide range of skills are acquired as they mature from infancy to toddlerhood. Early skills at this stage include sucking, tasting, smiling, basic vocalizations, and **gross motor skills** such as kicking and grasping. These skills increase in complexity over time and come to include abilities such as throwing and dropping objects, crawling, walking, and using simple words or phrases to communicate. As children near the end of this stage, they are typically able to exhibit such skills as stacking, basic problem solving, planning methods to achieve a task, and attempting to engage in daily routines such as dressing themselves or brushing their hair.
- **Preoperational:** This stage is marked by significant leaps in **cognition** and **gross motor skills**. Children in the preoperational stage are able to use increasingly complex language to communicate, and develop such skills as jumping, running, and climbing as they gain increasing control over their bodies. Preoperational children begin learning the basic categorization of alike objects, such as animals, flowers, or foods. This stage is also characterized by the development of pretend play and includes such skills as creating imaginary friends, role playing, and using toys or objects to symbolize something else, such as using a box as a pretend house.
- **Concrete Operational:** In this stage, children begin developing **logical reasoning** skills that allow them to perform increasingly complex tasks. Concrete operational children are able to distinguish subcategories, including types of animals, foods, or flowers, and can organize items in ascending or descending order based upon such characteristics as height, weight, or size. Children at this stage develop the understanding that altering the appearance of an object or substance does not change the amount of it. A classic example of this is the understanding that liquid transferred from one container to another retains its volume. This concept is known as **conservation**.
- **Formal Operational:** The formal operational stage is characterized by the development of **abstract** and **hypothetical** cognitive skills. Children at this stage are able to solve increasingly complex math equations, hypothesize and strategically devise a plan for engaging in science experiments, and develop creative solutions to problems. They are also able to theorize potential outcomes to hypothetical situations, as well as consider the nuances of differing values, beliefs, morals, and ethics.

Substages of the Sensorimotor Stage

Piaget's sensorimotor stage is divided into six substages. In each, infants develop new skills for representing and interacting with their world. In the first substage, infants interact **reflexively** and involuntarily to stimuli in the form of muscle jerking when startled, sucking, and gripping. Subsequent stages are circular, or repetitive, in nature, and are based on interactions with the self and, increasingly, the environment. **Primary circular reactions**, or intentionally repeated actions, comprise the second substage. Infants notice their actions and sounds and purposefully repeat them, but these actions do not extend past the infant's body. Interaction with the environment begins in the third substage as infants engage in **secondary circular reactions**. Here, infants learn that they can interact with and manipulate objects within their environment to create an effect, such as a sound from pressing a button. They then repeat the action and experience joy in this ability. In the fourth substage, secondary circular reactions become coordinated as infants begin planning movements and actions to create an effect. **Tertiary circular reactions** allow for exploration in the fifth substage, as infants start experimenting with cause and effect. In the sixth substage, infants begin engaging in **representational thought** and recall information from memory.

Examples of Primary, Secondary, and Tertiary Circular Reactions

The following are some common examples of primary, secondary, and tertiary circular reactions:

- **Primary:** Primary circular reactions are comprised of repeated **bodily** actions that the infant finds enjoyable. Such actions include thumb sucking, placing hands or feet in the mouth, kicking, and making basic vocalizations.
- **Secondary:** Secondary circular reactions refer to repeated enjoyable interactions between the infant and objects within their **environment** in order to elicit a specific response. Such actions include grasping objects, rattling toys, hitting buttons to hear specific sounds, banging two objects together, or reaching out to touch various items.
- **Tertiary:** Tertiary circular reactions are comprised of intentional and planned actions using objects within the environment to **achieve a particular outcome**. Examples include stacking blocks and knocking them down, taking toys out of a bin and putting them back, or engaging in a repeated behavior to gauge a caretaker's reaction each time.

Defining Characteristics of the Preoperational Stage of Development

The preoperational stage of development refers to the stage before a child can exercise operational thought and is associated with several defining characteristics including **pretend play**, **animism**, and **egocentrism**. As children learn to think and express themselves symbolically, they engage in pretend play as a means of organizing, understanding, and representing the world around them as they experience it. During this stage, children do not understand the difference between inanimate and animate objects, and thus demonstrate animism, or the attribution of lifelike qualities to inanimate objects. Egocentrism refers to the child's inability to understand the distinction between themselves and others, and consequentially, the inability to understand the thoughts, perspectives, and feelings of others. During the preoperational stage, the brain is not developed enough to understand **conservation**, which is the understanding that the quantity of something does not change just because its appearance changes. Thus, children in this stage exhibit **centration**, or the focusing on only one aspect of something at a time at. Additionally, children struggle with **classification** during this stage, as they are not cognitively developed enough to understand that an object can be classified in multiple ways.

Milestones Achieved During the Concrete Operational Stage of Development

The concrete operational stage marks the beginning of a child's ability to think logically about the concrete world. In this stage, children develop many of the skills they lacked in the preoperational phase. For example, egocentrism fades as children in this stage begin to develop empathy and understand others' perspectives. Additionally, they develop an understanding of conservation, or the idea that the quantity of something does not change with its appearance. Children in this stage begin to learn to classify objects in more than one way and can categorize them based on a variety of characteristics. This allows them to practice **seriation**, or the arranging of objects based on quantitative measures.

Development of Cognitive Abilities in the Formal Operational Stage

In the formal operational stage, children can think beyond the concrete world and in terms of abstract thoughts and hypothetical situations. They develop the ability to consider various outcomes of events and can think more creatively about solutions to problems than in previous stages. This advanced cognitive ability contributes to the development of personal identity. In considering abstract and hypothetical ideas, children begin to formulate opinions and develop personal stances on intangible concepts, thus establishing individual character. The formal operational stage continues to develop through adulthood as individuals gain knowledge and experience.

Lev Vygotsky's Theory of Cognitive Development

Lev Vygotsky's theory on cognitive development is heavily rooted in a **sociocultural** perspective. He argued that the most important factors for a child's cognitive development reside in the cultural context in which the child grows up and social interactions that they have with adults, mentors, and more advanced peers. He believed that children learn best from the people around them, as their social interactions, even basic ones such as smiling, waving, or facial expressions, foster the beginning of more complex cognitive development. He is well-known for his concept of the **Zone of Proximal Development (ZPD)**, which is the idea that as children mature, there are tasks they can perform when they receive help from a more advanced individual. He believed that children could move through the ZPD and complete increasingly complicated tasks when receiving assistance from more cognitively advanced mentors. According to Vygotsky, children develop the most when passing through the ZPD. Vygotsky's contributions are heavily embedded in modern education, and often take the form of teacher-led instruction and scaffolding to assist learners as they move through the ZPD.

Zone of Proximal Development

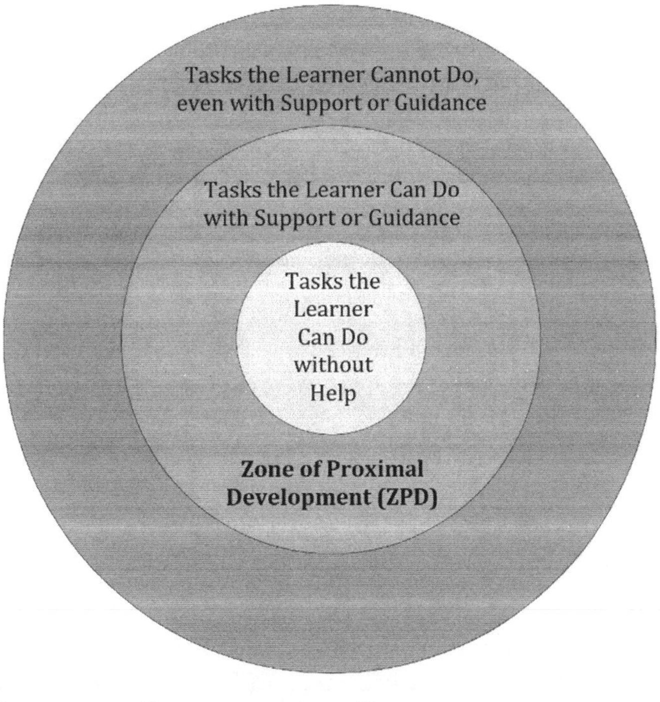

Erik Erikson's Eight Stages of Psychosocial Development

Erik Erikson defined eight predetermined stages of psychosocial development from birth to late adulthood in which an individual encounters a crisis that must be resolved to successfully transition to the next stage. The first is **trust vs. mistrust** (0-18 months), where the infant learns that the world around them is safe and they can trust caregivers to tend to their basic needs. The next stage is **autonomy vs. shame** (18 months-3 years), where children learn to control their actions and establish independence. In the **initiative vs. guilt stage** (3-5 years), children acquire a sense of purpose and initiative through social interactions. Next, children enter the

industry vs. inferiority stage (6-11 years), where they develop mastery and pride in completing a task. The next stage is **identity vs. role confusion** (12-18 years), in which children explore and develop characteristics that will comprise their identity and determine their role in society. The sixth stage is **intimacy vs. isolation** (19-40 years), where one forms relationships by sharing the identity developed in the previous stage with others. **Generativity vs. stagnation** (40-65 years) occurs in middle adulthood and focuses on contributing to society's next generation through finding one's life purpose. The last stage is **ego integrity vs. despair** (65 to death), in which one reflects on the productivity and success of their life.

Expected Behaviors at Each Stage of Psychosocial Development

Stage	Examples of expected behaviors
Trust vs. mistrust	In this stage, the infant's primary goal is ensuring the fulfillment of their **basic needs**. Infants will cry or make other vocalizations to indicate to caregivers when they want something, such as to be fed or picked up. Separation anxiety from parents is also typical during this stage.
Autonomy vs. shame	Children in this stage begin attempting to perform daily tasks **independently**, such as making food, dressing themselves, bathing, or combing their hair. As children in this stage begin to realize they have a separate identity, they often begin attempting to assert themselves to parents and caregivers.
Initiative vs. guilt	Children at this stage often begin actively engaging and playing with other children. In play settings, these children will often assume **leadership roles** among a group of peers, create new games or activities, and devise their own rules for them. The initiative vs. guilt stage is also characterized by the development of feelings of sadness or guilt when making a mistake or hurting another's feelings.
Industry vs. inferiority	In this stage, children begin attempting to master concepts or skills with the intention of seeking **approval** and **acceptance** from others, particularly those older than themselves, in order to secure a feeling of competency. Children in this stage often become more involved in striving to succeed academically, extracurricular activities, and competitive sports.
Identity vs. role confusion	This stage is characterized by experimentation and uncertainty as young adolescents strive to establish an **independent identity**. Typical behaviors include interacting with new peer groups, trying new styles of dress, engaging in new activities, and considering new beliefs, values, and morals. As young adolescents in this stage are impressionable, they may potentially engage in risky or rebellious behavior as a result of peer pressure.
Intimacy vs. isolation	Individuals in this stage have typically established their identities and are ready to seek **long-term relationships**. This stage marks the development of a social network comprised of close friends and long-term romantic partners.
Generativity vs. stagnation	During this stage, individuals begin engaging in **productive** activities to benefit others and elicit personal fulfillment. Such activities include advancing in a career, parenting, or participating in community service projects.
Integrity vs. despair	This stage occurs at the end of one's life and is characterized by **reflection** upon lifetime accomplishments and positive contributions to society. Doing so allows the individual to assess whether their life purpose was fulfilled and begin accepting death.

Incorporating Life Skills into Curriculum

In addition to academic achievement, the ultimate goal of education is to develop the whole child and provide a successful transition to independence and adulthood. Incorporating such valuable life skills as decision-making, goal setting, organization, self-direction, and workplace communication in early childhood through grade 12 curriculum is vital in ensuring students become productive contributors to society. Furthermore, the implementation of these life skills in early childhood is integral in allowing children to successfully progress in independence and maturity. The acquisition of such skills instills in students the self-motivation and ability to set goals, make decisions on how to effectively organize and manage time to complete them, and overcome obstacles. Additionally, teaching students to apply these skills promotes effective communication when working with others toward a goal. Through incorporating life skills into curriculum, teachers instill a growth mindset and foster self-empowered, confident lifelong learners with the necessary tools to navigate real-life situations and achieve success as they transition to adulthood. In the classroom, activities that promote leadership skills, cooperative learning, goal setting, self-monitoring, and social interaction foster an increasing sense of independence as children develop.

Developmental Changes Experienced in Early Adolescence

Early adolescence is a time of considerable development in all domains. Physically, children enter puberty, and must learn to deal with its emotional, social, and academic impacts. Consequently, children at this stage are impressionable, and begin developing habits that influence success as they transition to adulthood. Thus, early adolescents have specific developmental needs, and an accommodating approach to instruction is required. As the goal of education is providing the necessary skills to successfully transition into adulthood and increasing independence, it must be recognized that the shift from elementary to high school is drastic, and high school curriculum is not developmentally appropriate for early adolescence. The shift from elementary to high school is stressful and may negatively impact a child's attitude toward acquiring necessary life skills for success. Thus, middle-level education is integral in providing a developmentally responsive curriculum that eases this transition yet allows for increasing personal and academic independence. Middle-level education considers the physical developmental changes of early adolescents and fosters cognitive, social, and emotional growth through engaging instruction that encourages self-direction and responsibility, and positive social relationships. Middle-level curriculum instills skills such as organization, time management, and goal setting that promote success in high school and ultimately, adulthood.

Risks Faced by Students When Experiencing Challenges

As students in later childhood, adolescence, and young adulthood reconcile with rapid physical, cognitive, emotional, and social developments, they inevitably encounter challenges as they develop habits, beliefs, and relationships that will comprise their identity and future decisions. Such challenges as self-image, changing physical appearance, eating disorders, rebelliousness, identity formation, and educational and career decisions pose emotional, social, behavioral, and academic risks with long-term consequences if not addressed. Students may respond to challenges by engaging in risky behavior, or developing social and emotional issues such as depression, anxiety, or aggression. Such challenges may induce apathy toward academics and extracurricular activities and declining academic performance. These risks threaten the successful transition to adulthood and success throughout life in that they potentially hinder the educational and career choices that would lead to a successful future. Early intervention is imperative to provide supports for students facing challenges to try and prevent the consequences associated with them. Some supports include fostering and encouraging positive social relationships with peers and mentors, encouraging participation in extracurricular activities within the school and community, providing access to guidance counselors, and providing adequate health education to help students understand the challenges they are facing as they develop.

Indicators and Negative Impacts of Risky Behaviors in Students

The likelihood that students will engage in risky behaviors, such as drug and alcohol use, gang involvement, or other dangerous activities, increases as they approach adolescence. Such behaviors pose serious negative consequences on development and learning. Cognitively, risky behaviors harm brain function and development, and lead to trouble sleeping, focusing, and learning. Socially, these students may have trouble maintaining positive relationships and are more likely to associate with others engaging in the same behaviors. Emotionally, these behaviors could cause depression, anxiety, and low self-esteem. Physically, negative impacts include injury, illness, or long-term health consequences. Furthermore, risky behaviors are detrimental to learning. Students participating in these behaviors have trouble focusing, grasping new concepts, and become apathetic toward academics. It is important to recognize indicators of risky behavior to intervene as early as possible and prevent long-term negative consequences. Indicators include being withdrawn, poor grades, poor appearance, hygiene, sleeping and eating habits, and lack of interest in academics or extracurricular activities. Schools and communities must do their best to prevent students from engaging in risky behaviors through encouraging positive social relationships, participation in extracurricular activities, providing access to guidance counselors, and providing access to proper health education.

Roles of Peers, Acceptance, and Conformity During Adolescent Development

Adolescence is an insecure and impressionable time as students navigate rapid physical, emotional, social, and cognitive development. This stage introduces an increased sense of independence as adolescents begin developing the opinions, beliefs, values, and social relationships that will comprise their identity and establish the foundation for their future as they transition to adulthood. Social relationships are a vital part of identity formation during this stage, as adolescents engage with different peer groups, norms, and expectations, and seek acceptance in desired crowds. Adolescents will often conform their behavior to the social norms of a desired peer group for fear of rejection, and thus, the nature of the peer group has significant implications for teaching and learning. Involvement with unhealthy peer groups may lead to engaging in risky behaviors in seeking social acceptance, and a disinterest in learning and academic success. In contrast, association with healthy peer groups fosters the development of positive and supportive social relationships that encourage constructive behavior. Consequently, engaging in healthy peer groups increases the likelihood that the adolescent will be interested in academic involvement, achievement, and success.

Factors that Affect Development

Physical Changes Occurring in Early Childhood Through Adolescence

As children pass through stages of development from early childhood through middle childhood and adolescence, they experience significant physical changes. Children in early childhood experience rapid growth in height and weight as they transition away from physical characteristics of infancy. In this stage, children begin to gain independence as they develop and improve upon gross and fine motor skills. By early childhood, children develop the ability to walk, run, hop, and as they mature through this stage, learn to throw, catch, and climb. They learn to hold and manipulate small objects such as zippers and buttons, and can grasp writing utensils to create shapes, letters, and drawings with increasing accuracy. Physical growth varies for individual children in middle childhood as some children begin experiencing prepubescent bodily changes. Children in middle childhood experience further improvements and refinements of gross and fine motor skills and coordination. Significant physical and appearance changes occur in adolescence as children enter puberty. These changes often occur quickly, resulting in a period of awkwardness and lack of coordination as adolescents adjust to this rapid development.

Impact of External Factors on Physical Development

As children pass through physical development stages from early childhood to adolescence, it is important that environmental factors are supportive of proper growth and health. Physical development can be hindered by external factors, such as poor nutrition, lack of sleep, prenatal exposure to drugs, and abuse, as these can cause significant and long-lasting negative consequences. Exposure to such factors can lead to stunted physical growth, impaired brain development and function, poor bone and muscle development, and obesity. Furthermore, the negative impacts from such external factors ultimately impedes cognitive, social, and emotional development. Impaired brain development and function negatively affect cognitive development by impacting the ability to concentrate and grasp new concepts. In terms of emotional development, physical impairments due to external factors can cause a child to become depressed, withdrawn, aggressive, have low self-esteem, and unable to self-regulate. Improper physical growth and health impacts social development in that physical limitations could hinder a child's ability to properly interact with and play with others. Impacted brain development and function can limit a child's ability to understand social cues and norms.

Effect of External Environmental Factors on Social and Emotional Development

Social and emotional development is heavily influenced by a child's home environment. Children learn social and emotional skills such as self-regulation, self-awareness, coping, and relationship building through modeling from parents and caregivers. A positive and supportive home environment is integral for proper social and emotional development. External factors, including lack of affection and attention, parental divorce, and homelessness, pose profound negative impacts on this development. In terms of social development, such external factors could lead to attachment or abandonment issues, as well as distrust. Furthermore, children exposed to negative environmental factors could struggle forging relationships, cooperating, and following societal rules. Emotionally, negative impacts on development cause aggression, poor self-regulation, insecurity, anxiety, isolation, and depression. Since developmental domains are interconnected, the impacts that external factors have on social and emotional development ultimately damage cognitive and physical development. Underdeveloped social skills impair cognitive development because the inability to properly interact with peers impedes the ability to learn from them. Additionally, inadequate emotional skills can inhibit concentration and understanding in school, thus inhibiting cognitive development. Physically, struggling to interact with others leads to impaired development of gross and fine motor skills as well as large muscle development that would be achieved through play.

Individual Developmental Differences Implications for Instructional Planning

Developmental Differences Encountered and Strategies to Address Them

Cognitive, physical, social, and emotional milestones through which children pass as they mature are approximate, and development in any domain depends on the individual child as well as countless environmental factors that comprise each child's unique situation. Therefore, a teacher will encounter multiple variations in cognitive, physical, social, and emotional development in students that pose significant implications for instructional planning. Cognitively, a teacher will encounter several intelligences and learning styles. They will encounter students with various learning disabilities, gifted and talented students, or English Language Learners. Physically, students grow and develop at individual rates, and a teacher will encounter students with varying physical abilities or limitations. Social developmental differences vary as well and are heavily influenced by environmental factors. Variances in social cues, norms, relationship building, and communication are based on a child's culture and environment. Emotional development such as self-regulation and coping are impacted by environment also. Such an array of differences requires a teacher to be trained to recognize individual prior knowledge and learning needs to effectively teach to those differences. Strategies to achieve this include adjusting curriculum, activities, and assessments to match individual student needs, providing necessary scaffolds, and differentiating instruction to access learners of all abilities.

Effect of Developmental Delays on Learning Experiences and Assessments

Developmental delays in any domain pose significant potential impacts on learning experiences and assessments through affecting comprehension and participation. A delay in cognitive development could impact information processing times, information retention, and the ability to understand complex ideas, thus hindering comprehension and ultimately impacting the willingness to participate. A student with a physical developmental delay may struggle with fine and gross motor skills that prevent effective participation in class activities that would improve comprehension of new instruction. Students with social developmental delays may have difficulty properly expressing a need for assistance, thus potentially discouraging participation and overall comprehension. Furthermore, students with social or emotional developmental delays may be withdrawn, depressed, anxious, or have behavioral issues that impede their self-motivation and ability to focus, thus affecting comprehension and willingness to participate. These potential impacts can have long-lasting consequences on students' overall learning experience, and early recognition is imperative for instilling the proper accommodations for each student.

Accommodations to Assist Students with Developmental Delays

In order to create an equitable and inclusive environment, the teacher must have an understanding of the developmental characteristics of each student. Furthermore, the teacher must be able to use this knowledge to make the proper accommodations to the curriculum, instruction, and assessments in such a way that addresses individual needs and abilities across the domains of development. Modifications should be specific to the student depending on their individual need and should provide the necessary support to allow for success in learning. Such accommodations may include scaffolding to break instruction into smaller, more manageable pieces, extended work time for assignments and assessments, shorter work periods with frequent breaks, reduced ratio of students to teacher, individualized instruction, and preferential seating based on the student's need for proximity. Additionally, students may require accommodations to address physical developmental delays, including scribes, text to speech for assignments, or enlarged fonts. Providing accommodations to address individual needs in the four areas of development allows for the teacher to effectively assess student progress and ultimately allows for success in learning.

Recognizing Signs of Developmental Delays or Impairments

Although each child develops at their own pace, there are often indicators that a student is not developing at a generally similar rate as their peers. Developmental delays or impairments can be cognitive, physical, emotional, or social. Some common indicators of developmental delays include but are not limited to lower-than-average assessment scores, difficulty concentrating and retaining new information, difficulty socializing or communicating with others, limited vocabulary compared to others in the same age group, clumsiness, and difficulty holding small objects. Delays can be difficult to detect, but a teacher can recognize signs through observation of the student and analyzing their progress across subject areas generally compared to their peers. Early recognition and detection are beneficial in allowing for early intervention to develop a treatment plan for the child that could improve their progress both inside and outside of the classroom.

Planning Developmentally Appropriate Instruction and Assessment

Developmentally Appropriate Practice

Developmentally Appropriate Practice **(DAP)** is an approach to teaching grounded in theories of child development. It is derived from the belief that children are naturally curious to learn, and when provided a stimulating environment, are encouraged to take initiative in their own learning. This approach allows for a great deal of choice in learning experiences. The teacher's role is to facilitate active learning by creating developmentally appropriate activities based on the awareness of similarities between children in various developmental stages and the knowledge that each child develops at their own rate. With this knowledge, the teacher can then adjust the curriculum, activities, and assessments to fit the needs of individual students based on an awareness of age, cultural, social, and individual expectations.

Using Knowledge of Cognitive Changes to Create Instruction

A developmentally responsive teacher understands that the needs of students change as they mature through the stages of cognitive development. Furthermore, an effective teacher uses this knowledge to plan instruction that coincides with each developmental level. The early childhood teacher understands the needs and abilities of preoperational children, and designs instruction that focuses on interacting with the world around them through hands-on activities and pretend play. Such activities foster exploration of the environment, roles, and connections. Developmentally responsive elementary school teachers are aware of the logical thinking patterns that occur during the concrete operational stage. Thus, they create instruction that allows children to interact with tangible materials to help them draw logical conclusions about their environment and understand abstract ideas. As children reach adolescence, a developmentally responsive teacher understands the increased ability to think abstractly, hypothetically, and reflectively in the formal operational stage. They use this knowledge to create instruction that encourages discussion, debate, creative problem solving, and opportunities to develop opinions, beliefs, and values.

Appropriate Instructional Activities

The following are some examples of appropriate instructional activities for early childhood, middle-level, and high school students:

- **Early childhood:** Activities that allow for exploration, play, and movement while teaching young children to function and cooperate in a group setting are most valuable in early childhood classrooms. **Movement activities** such as dancing, jumping rope, using outdoor play equipment, as well as structured and unstructured play, are beneficial in developing gross motor skills and teaching young children to properly interact with others. **Whole-group** activities such as circle time, class songs, and read-aloud sessions are also valuable in teaching young children appropriate communication skills within a group. **Thematic learning stations**, such as a science center, dramatic play area, library corner, block area, art center, and technology center, allow young children to explore their own interests on a variety of topics while developing creative and imaginative skills. **Sensory play** stations that include such items as a sand box or water table, are beneficial in further developing motor skills and allowing young children to explore and experiment with a variety of textures. Young children also require opportunities for quiet activities, such as naptime, self-selected reading, or meditation throughout the day in order to process information, reflect, and rest after active movement.

- **Middle-level**: Students at this age are best supported by the implementation of **hands-on** learning activities that develop **logical reasoning** and **collaboration** skills. Collaborative activities such as science experiments, mathematical word problems, the use of manipulatives, and projects that allow opportunities for building, creating, disassembling, and exploring, are beneficial in facilitating such a learning experience. Social and emotional learning activities are also important in developing middle school students' skills in these domains. Incorporating such activities as class meetings, community building activities, and self-reflection activities, are valuable methods for teaching social and emotional skills. In addition, cooperative learning opportunities should be implemented frequently across subject areas to further develop students' ability to work productively with others. Examples include literacy circles, creating teams for class review games, or group presentations.
- **High School:** Instructional activities for high school students should be designed to foster the development of **abstract** and **hypothetical** thinking abilities while preparing them to become productive members of society as they enter adulthood. Activities such as debates, class discussions, and mock trials are beneficial in providing high school students the opportunity to employ abstract reasoning, consider solutions to hypothetical situations, and develop empathy for opposing viewpoints. Assignments that require students to engage in the research process are valuable opportunities for developing higher-order thinking skills, as they encourage students to analyze, compare, and interpret information, as well as seek evidence to support their claims. In addition, incorporating activities that benefit the community, such as fundraisers or food and clothing drives, are beneficial in teaching high school students the importance of positively contributing to society.

Effective and Developmentally Appropriate Learning Experiences and Assessments

Effective developmentally appropriate instruction requires careful consideration when planning to ensure that students' individual needs across domains are supported to facilitate growth and a positive learning experience. The teacher must consider the developmental stage of their students based upon their age group, as well as students' individual differences. With this knowledge in mind, teachers must ensure that they provide an inclusive learning environment that fosters growth and development by creating challenging, yet attainable activities based on students' needs. Likewise, teachers must evaluate whether learning experiences and assessments are age, developmentally, and culturally appropriate while ensuring that they are tailored to students' unique learning differences. Learning experiences must provide opportunities for hands-on, cooperative, and self-directed learning, exploration, and participation to allow students to interact with their environment and build experiences. Additionally, lessons and activities should be flexible in nature to allow for inquiry and build upon students' prior experiences. Effective developmentally appropriate assessments are aimed at monitoring student progress and allow for flexibility based on students' learning differences. They should be intended to provide feedback to the teacher on how to better adapt instruction to meet students' individual needs and foster developmental growth.

Facilitating Development of Life Skills and Attitudes in Middle School-Age Children

Middle school-age children are at a pivotal development point in which they experience rapid and profound change. In this transition, they often demonstrate characteristics of younger and older children and are therefore at a critical stage for developing the beliefs, attitudes, and habits that will be the foundation for their future. Teachers must understand the implications of these changes and design instruction that addresses students' learning needs and facilitates the development of such important life skills as working and getting along with others, appreciating diversity, and committing to continued schooling. Cooperative learning and team building strategies instill the importance of working together positively to problem solve, building on one another's strengths, and valuing other's perspectives. These strategies also teach students to appreciate diversity through encouraging them to work with peers with different backgrounds and experiences. Additionally, teachers can teach students to embrace diversity through creating a culturally responsive classroom environment that models acceptance and incorporates elements of students' differences into instruction to demonstrate the value of diverse perspectives. Teachers promote positive attitudes toward academics that encourage a commitment to continued schooling by teaching organization, time management, and goal-setting skills that instill a growth mindset and provide a foundation for success.

Impact of Student Characteristics on Teaching and Learning

Young Children

The developmental level of young children is characterized by defining attributes that impact teaching and learning, and for which several considerations must be made to design and implement effective instruction. As the attention span of young children is limited, the teacher must think about how to effectively act as a facilitator for learning more often than directly instructing students. **Direct instruction** must be delivered in small, manageable chunks to accommodate students' attention spans and ensure they retain and understand new concepts. Thus, the teacher must evaluate which elements of the curriculum require structured learning, while allowing for flexibility within instruction to accommodate student inquiry. Young children also need frequent **movement**, **physical activity**, and **social interaction**, as they learn and build experiences concretely through moving, playing, interacting with, and exploring their environment. To create a learning environment that accommodates these characteristics, the teacher must consider the physical arrangement of the classroom, and whether it adequately allows for movement. Additionally, teachers must incorporate **structured** and **unstructured activities** that foster and promote exploration, inquiry, play, cooperative learning, and hands-on interactions with the learning environment. With these considerations in mind, the teacher enhances students' learning experience by tailoring instruction to their developmental characteristics.

Middle School Aged Children

As middle school-age children transition from childhood to adolescence, they experience vast changes across all developmental domains. Consequently, they exhibit characteristics that affect teaching and learning that require careful consideration when adapting instruction to their unique learning needs. While these students require increasing independence as they mature, they still need a structured, predictable environment to ease the transition into high school. The teacher must create a balance between fostering independence and growth while providing a schedule and routine. Opportunities for self-directed learning and student choice, as well as strategies for self-assessment and reflection foster autonomy and self-responsibility over learning while the teacher facilitates and monitors progress. Strategies to teach effective organizational and time management skills further promote independence and prepare students for success upon entering high school. As middle school-age students develop, the importance of peers becomes increasingly prevalent as they begin to search for their identity and shape their own values and beliefs. Teachers must ensure to provide opportunities for cooperative and small group learning to facilitate students' social development while considering the importance of promoting positive peer relationships at this impressionable developmental level.

Adolescent Children

The developmental changes that occur in adolescence result in distinct characteristics as students in this age group transition into young adulthood. During this stage, students are discovering their identities, values, and beliefs and begin to explore long-term career and life choices. As they navigate their development and shape the person they will become, social relationships come to be increasingly important. Teachers must consider the impact of these characteristics when developing instruction to effectively address the unique needs of this age group and establish foundational attitudes, habits, and skills necessary for success in life. Effective instruction encourages adolescents to consider different perspectives, morals, and values to broaden their worldview and foster the development of their own beliefs. Lessons and activities should allow for exploration of personal interests, skills, and abilities as students shape their personalities and begin to consider long-term life goals. Moreover, the teacher should incorporate strategies that assist adolescents in goal setting to successfully foster a growth mindset and provide a foundation for success. Additionally, as socialization is highly influential at this stage, teachers must consider the importance of incorporating cooperative learning strategies and opportunities for socialization within instruction to encourage healthy peer relationships and foster positive identity development.

Interconnection of Developmental Domains

Developmental domains are deeply interconnected. If one area of a child's development is negatively impacted, it is likely to pose negative consequences on other developmental areas. Proper physical development is key to developing cognitively, socially, and emotionally in that physical development allows children to acquire the necessary gross and fine motor skills to explore and experiment with the world around them, as well as interact with others. Physical development includes development of the brain, and factors such as poor nutrition, sleep, or prenatal exposure to drugs potentially hinder brain development. Consequentially, this may result in cognitive delays, and ultimately lead to social or emotional developmental delays through negatively impacting the child's ability to interact with others, build relationships, emotionally regulate, or communicate effectively.

Characteristics of the Developmental Play Stages

As children develop, so do their styles of play. Developmental play stages are divided into five primary phases: **solitary play** (Birth-2 years), **onlooker play** (2 years), **parallel play** (2-3 years), **associative play** (3-4 years) and **cooperative play** (4 years and beyond). During the **solitary play** stage, children play alone and are uninterested in playing with others, or what other children around them are doing. When they reach the **onlooker play** stage, children will watch other children play, but will not actively engage in playing with others. In **parallel play**, children do not play with one another, but will often play next to each other and will use similar materials. They may be curious about what other children are doing, and may copy them, but will not directly play with them. Children begin to intentionally play with others in the **associative play** stage, but the play is unorganized and still largely individual in its goals. In **cooperative play**, children begin to intentionally play and share materials in organized groups, and often have a common purpose or goal when playing.

Purposes and Benefits of Play in Early Childhood Education

Purposeful play is an integral part of learning and development in the early childhood classroom. Its purpose is to aid and allow children to incorporate all aspects of development and thus provides cognitive, social, emotional, and physical benefits. Purposeful play deepens children's understanding of new concepts through allowing them to explore and experiment in the world around them using imagination and creativity. Integrating purposeful play into the early childhood classroom is further beneficial in that it allows children to construct and build on knowledge through experiences and helps develop divergent and convergent thinking. The socialization children get from play strengthens their language skills through speaking to one another, using new vocabulary, and listening to others. Purposeful play strengthens physical-motor development in that it calls for children to move their bodies in games, running, jumping, etc. Play is necessary for building important emotional and social skills that are necessary for being a successful member of society later in life.

Factors to Consider When Selecting Materials for Learning and Play

To plan meaningful, integrated, and active learning and play experiences, the teacher must have a deep understanding of both the developmental stage of the students and an understanding of students' individual needs. With this knowledge in mind, there are several factors that the teacher must consider when choosing materials that support active learning and play experiences, and ultimately, the development of the whole child. Materials should be adaptable in use to facilitate development in multiple areas. Versatility is also important in fostering imagination and creativity. The teacher must consider how the chosen materials will support understanding of concepts covered in instruction, as well as how they will support conceptual, perceptual, and language development. Furthermore, the teacher must ensure that materials are age-appropriate, stimulating, and encourage active participation both independently and cooperatively.

Equality vs. Equity

Equality refers to providing everyone with the same resources when working toward a goal, regardless of the unique needs or situation of the individual. **Equity** means considering an individual's needs and circumstances to provide the proper supports that allow them a fair opportunity to achieve a common goal. In the classroom, creating an equitable environment requires the consideration of students' individual learning styles, needs, and personal situations, and using this knowledge to instill necessary supports to help each student achieve the same objectives relative to their peers. Equity in the classroom is especially important for closing the achievement gap, particularly in low socioeconomic areas, because many of these students come from disadvantaged situations and need additional help to gain a fair opportunity for academic success.

Supports Utilized to Provide an Equitable Learning Environment

The nature of academic, physical, and behavioral supports depends largely on the needs of the individual student. However, some common supports are effective in addressing an array of needs to facilitate an equitable learning environment. Students with **learning disabilities** may benefit from such academic supports as preferential seating near the front of the room and minimized distractions to enhance focus. Modified test questions or alternate assignments, graphic organizers, scaffolded texts, extra copies of class notes, and individualized instruction as necessary are also valuable in enhancing focus, preventing overwhelm, and ensuring learning activities are aligned with students' capabilities. Students with **physical disabilities** may require wheelchair access, a sign language interpreter or scribe, braille text, enlarged fonts, or the use of technology devices to aid in reading and writing. Common **behavioral supports** in the classroom include opportunities for frequent breaks or movement as needed, a daily check-in with a caseworker or other dedicated staff member, or a behavior chart to allow students to self-monitor.

Characteristics of a Developmentally Responsive Classroom

A developmentally responsive classroom is one in which the teacher understands the cognitive, physical, social, and emotional developmental stages of students while recognizing nuances and individual developmental differences within these stages. The teacher understands that developmental domains are interconnected, and effectively responds to unique developmental differences by designing a learner-centered curriculum and classroom environment that caters to each students' abilities, needs, and developmental levels to develop the whole child. The developmentally responsive classroom is engaging, supportive, and provides challenging learning opportunities based on individual learner abilities. There are several factors the teacher must consider in the developmentally responsive classroom when planning an appropriate, engaging, and challenging learning experience. The teacher must have a deep understanding of which teaching strategies will most effectively appeal to students of varying developmental levels and be prepared to teach content in multiple ways. Furthermore, the teacher must consider how to plan and organize activities, lessons, breaks, and the overall classroom environment. This would include considering how to arrange the classroom, which activity areas to include, spacing, and classroom equipment. The developmentally responsive classroom should promote positivity and productivity through creating a supportive yet challenging learning atmosphere that welcomes and respects differences, thus encouraging students' curiosity and excitement for learning.

Establishing High Academic Expectations

In any classroom, establishing high academic standards is imperative for motivating and empowering students to succeed. By communicating high expectations clearly and frequently, the teacher demonstrates belief that each student can overcome obstacles and excel academically, thus inspiring student engagement, curiosity for learning, and an overall positive and productive learning environment. To create an environment of high academic standards, the teachers' expectations must be apparent in instruction. The teacher must provide lessons and activities that are rigorous but not so challenging that students are unable to complete them without assistance, as this would disempower and disengage students from learning. The teacher must set achievable learning goals based on knowledge of student abilities and encourage self-reflection. Additionally, the teacher must utilize knowledge of students' individual needs to instill necessary supports to help students in achieving tasks and create an equitable environment for learning. This will ultimately empower students to overcome obstacles and motivate them for academic success.

Student Diversity and Equity

Implications for Teaching, Learning, and Assessment in Diverse Classrooms

In any classroom, a teacher will encounter a wide range of variances among individual students that inevitably will influence teaching, learning, and assessment. Diversities in ethnicity, gender, language background, and learning exceptionality will likely exist simultaneously in a single classroom. Educators must be prepared to teach to these diversities while concurrently teaching students the value and importance of diversity. The curriculum and classroom environment must be adjusted to meet individual student needs and create an **inclusive**, **respectful**, and **equitable** environment that welcomes differences and allows for success in learning. This begins with the teacher developing an understanding of the unique diversities that exist within their students and using this knowledge to **differentiate** curriculum, materials, activities, and assessments in such a way that students of all needs, interests, backgrounds, and abilities feel encouraged and included. Furthermore, the teacher must understand how to instill appropriate supports to accommodate the diverse needs of students, as well as how to modify the classroom environment in such a way that is reflective of the diversity of the students.

Considerations for Teaching in Diverse Classrooms

Ethnically-Diverse Classrooms

As society becomes increasingly diverse, teachers will certainly encounter classrooms with students of multiple ethnicities. Thus, to create an accepting and respectful classroom environment that allows for success in learning for all students, there are several factors to consider. Teachers must educate themselves on the various ethnicities within their classroom. This includes being mindful of **social norms, values, beliefs, traditions,** and **lifestyles** of different ethnic groups, and learning to communicate with students and families in a respectful, culturally sensitive manner. Additionally, the teacher must make a conscious effort to incorporate aspects of each ethnicity into the curriculum, activities, and classroom environment to create an inclusive atmosphere that teaches the acceptance, respect for, and celebration of differences. Teachers must be **culturally competent** and ensure that all materials are accurate, relevant, authentic, and portray the different ethnicities within the classroom in a respectful, unbiased manner. Furthermore, teachers must consider how their own ethnicity impacts their teaching style and interactions with students, how they may be perceived by other ethnic groups, and how to respond in a manner that fosters respect and inclusivity.

Gender-Diverse Classrooms

When approaching a gender-diverse classroom, teachers need to consider their perceptions, interactions with, and expectations of different genders, as well as how the classroom environment and materials portray gender differences. Teachers must work to eliminate possible stereotypical beliefs so all students feel respected, accepted, and encouraged to participate. Furthermore, teachers must consider how their behavior acts as a model for how students perceive gender roles and should act in a way that eliminates gender divisiveness. Teachers should use gender-neutral language when addressing students and ensure that all students receive equal attention. Teachers must maintain equal academic and behavioral expectations between genders and be sure to equally praise and discipline students so that neither gender feels superior or inferior to another. Regarding curriculum and classroom materials, teachers must ensure that the classroom environment encourages equal participation in, access to, and choice of all activities and procedures. Activities and materials should provide equal opportunities and foster collaboration between genders. Furthermore, teachers must ensure that curriculum materials avoid gender stereotypes, and highlight each gender equally in order to create an accepting and respectful learning environment that provides equal opportunities for students of all genders to develop their individual identities and abilities.

Linguistically Diverse Classrooms

In a **linguistically diverse** classroom, teachers must consider how to effectively demonstrate value for students' native languages while simultaneously supporting the development of necessary language skills to thrive in the school setting. By accepting and encouraging students to use their native languages, teachers can establish an inclusive learning environment that celebrates linguistic differences, and therefore, encourages students to want to build upon their language skills. Through this, teachers create an equitable learning environment that allows for academic success. To develop English language skills, the teacher must first consider each students' language ability and level of exposure to English prior to entering the classroom, as well as the level of language learning support each student has at home. Teachers can then implement effective instructional strategies and supports to modify curriculum in a way that addresses students' language needs. Teachers must also consider the implications of the classroom environment on language acquisition. By creating an atmosphere that encourages language acquisition through **literacy-rich resources** and **cooperative learning**, teachers promote the use of language skills and ultimately provide opportunities for success for all students.

Linguistic Supports and Instructional Strategies Promoting English Language Proficiency

Incorporating a variety of linguistic aids and instructional strategies is beneficial in supporting ELL students of varying levels of English language proficiency. **Visual representations** to accompany instruction, such as posters, charts, pictures, slide shows, videos, tables, or anchor charts, are valuable in providing clarification and reference while promoting vocabulary acquisition. When delivering instruction, **body language** such as hand gestures, eye contact, and movement to mimic verbal directions and explanations can provide clarification to enhance understanding. These students may also require **translation devices** for clarification, an interpreter to help with understanding instructions and new concepts, alternate assignments with simplified language, or **individualized instruction** from an ESL teacher. Frequently checking for understanding and providing clarification as necessary throughout instruction are necessary to ensuring ELL students understand learning materials, instructions, and assessments. In addition, creating a print and literacy-rich environment by including word walls for new vocabulary, reading materials that vary in complexity, labels, and opportunities for speaking, reading, and writing within instruction are valuable in promoting English language acquisition.

Learning Disabilities and Other Exceptionalities

In a classroom where learning disabilities and exceptionalities are present, teachers must consider accommodations for students of various learning needs while fostering an atmosphere of respect and acceptance. Teachers must understand the individual learning needs of each student and differentiate instruction accordingly to create an equitable and inclusive learning atmosphere. For **learning disabled** students, teachers must consider accommodations that allow for inclusion in all areas of curriculum and instruction. Such considerations may include extended work time, individualized instruction, and cooperative learning activities to ensure that learning disabled students are provided the necessary supports to achieve academic success. For students with other exceptionalities, such as **gifted and talented** students, teachers need to consider ways to provide challenging and stimulating opportunities for expansion and enrichment of curriculum. Furthermore, the teacher must be aware of their own interactions with students in order to demonstrate and encourage respect and acceptance among students. By providing supports for individual student success, teachers can effectively highlight students' strengths and therefore, teach students to accept and celebrate differences in learning abilities.

Goals of Teaching Diversity in the Classroom

Teaching diversity in the classroom aims to establish a welcoming and inclusive classroom environment that encourages academic achievement and whole-child development. Diversity education works to develop students' understanding, acceptance, and respect for others' perspectives while instilling the concept that people are ultimately more alike than different, and that diversities should be celebrated. Teaching the importance of differences creates a positive, inclusive classroom atmosphere in which all students feel respected, safe, and valued by their teacher and peers. Such an environment promotes academic achievement among students in that it encourages participation in learning and builds the self-esteem necessary for positive growth and development. Furthermore, teaching diversity has a significant role in **whole-child development** in that it instills the ability to understand and respect multiple frames of reference, thus increasing their ability to problem solve, cooperate with others, and develop a broader global perspective. Additionally, it allows for the development of cultural competency and ultimately creates accepting and respectful contributors to society.

Recognizing and Eliminating Personal Biases

Personal biases are often subtle and unconscious, yet it is essential that teachers work to recognize and eliminate them to create an accepting and respectful classroom environment. Personal biases may negatively impact teaching style, interactions with students, and ultimately, student learning and self-esteem. In eliminating personal bias, teachers ensure that they establish an inclusive classroom environment where each student is treated fairly. Furthermore, students' beliefs toward diversity are influenced by the attitudes and behaviors modeled by their teacher, and therefore, eradicating personal bias is vital in positively influencing students to accept and respect differences. To eliminate personal bias, teachers must **reflect** on their own culture's attitudes toward diversity, as well as how these attitudes influence their interactions toward other groups, and work to make positive changes. Teachers must **educate** themselves on the diversities among their students and work to deepen their understanding of different groups through **communicating** with families, **integrating** themselves into students' communities, and participating in **professional development** that focuses on **cultural competency** and the importance of teaching diversity. Through making positive changes against personal biases, teachers foster a classroom environment that promotes diversity and empowers all students to be successful.

Impact of Diverse Cultural Climate in the Classroom

Creating a diverse cultural climate in the classroom results in an empowering and engaging learning environment that facilitates academic success. An atmosphere that respects and accepts differences fosters a sense of inclusivity and welcoming among teachers and students, which allows students to feel comfortable with differences, safe in their own identities, and consequently, comfortable to engage in learning. This fosters a positive attitude toward learning that promotes academic achievement. Additionally, when students accept one another's differences in a diverse cultural climate, they are better able to work together and adopt creative problem-solving solutions through others' perspectives, which results in success in learning. Furthermore, a successfully diverse cultural climate reflects the diversity of the students within it, which ultimately creates a more engaging and relevant academic environment that sparks motivation and curiosity toward learning. Learning environments that reflect students' diversity create a sense of unity and belonging in the classroom and positively contribute to success in learning through building students' self-esteem and self-concept to empower them in believing they can achieve academic success.

Authentic Classroom Materials

Authentic classroom materials are artifacts from various cultures, events, or periods of time. These items enhance the relevancy of instruction by promoting students' real-world connection to learning and may also be used to incorporate students' backgrounds and experiences into the classroom to increase engagement. Such materials include magazines, newspapers, advertisements, restaurant menus, and recipes. In addition, resources such as video clips, films, television shows, documentaries, news segments, and music serve as authentic media sources to incorporate into instruction. Original works or documents, including art pieces, literature, poetry, maps, or historical records, are also valuable authentic resources for providing students with a real-world learning experience.

Locating and Implementing

Authentic classroom materials and resources are integral in creating a classroom environment that fosters engaging, relevant, and positive learning experiences. Teachers must work to develop an understanding of the diversities among their students and use this knowledge to locate and implement authentic classroom materials into daily instruction. In doing so, teachers create a positive learning environment that accepts and respects differences through incorporating **relevant** and **familiar** materials that make students from all backgrounds feel valued and included in instruction. When students can see aspects of their culture reflected in authentic learning materials, they can make **personal connections** between what they are learning and their own lives, and learning becomes more valuable, engaging, and relevant, thereby promoting success in learning.

Incorporating Diversity Education into the Classroom

Incorporating diversity into the classroom maximizes student opportunities for academic success through creating a welcoming, empowering, and inclusive atmosphere. Teachers can implement multiple strategies to incorporate **diversity education** into the curriculum both as its own unit and woven into content instruction once they develop an understanding of the diversities among their own students. Through **building relationships** with students, teachers can use their knowledge of students' lives to incorporate aspects of their backgrounds into the curriculum by creating specific **cultural lessons** on food, music, language, art, and history. Additionally, **cultural comparison** studies are an effective method of teaching students the value of diversity, as well as highlighting the fact that people from different backgrounds often have more similarities than differences. Teachers can further implement diversity education by encouraging students to participate in learning through having them share elements of their culture and background with the class through activities such as show and tell or hosting family nights. Furthermore, integrating **cooperative learning** activities into instruction allow and encourage students from different backgrounds to work together and gain an understanding of the perspectives and backgrounds of others.

Incorporating Diversity in the Entire Classroom Environment

Incorporating diversity into the curriculum is vital for teaching the value and importance of differences and for contributing to a respectful and accepting environment. Additionally, it is imperative that diversity education extend from the curriculum to the entire classroom environment to maximize student growth and opportunity to reach potential. When students learn in an atmosphere that celebrates diversity and identifies strengths in differences, they feel a sense of belonging and confidence that encourages them to engage in learning, thus maximizing the potential for academic success. Teachers can effectively integrate diversity into the classroom environment through making authentic cultural materials such as texts, music, and art readily accessible for students. Additionally, providing several opportunities for students to collaborate and socialize in a natural setting allows them to gain an understanding and respect for their peers' backgrounds. By encouraging students to share aspects of their own lives and backgrounds with the class through cultural activities, teachers facilitate a diverse climate that celebrates differences.

Understanding Students' Diverse Backgrounds and Needs

Self-Education

Educating oneself on students' diverse backgrounds and needs enhances one's overall understanding of their students and creates a culturally sensitive, accepting classroom environment tailored to students' individual needs. There are several avenues through which teachers should educate themselves in an effort to build an accepting and respectful classroom climate. Communication is key for learning about diversities; thus, it is important for teachers to foster and maintain positive communications with students' families to deepen understanding of cultures, beliefs, lifestyles, and needs that exist within their classroom. This could include learning some language of students with different cultural backgrounds, attending family nights at school, or participating in social events within their students' communities to integrate themselves into the culture. Furthermore, teachers can learn more about their students' backgrounds and needs through gaining an understanding of student differences, incorporating these diversities into the curriculum, and encouraging students to participate in learning by sharing aspects of their lives with the class.

Teaching, Learning, and Classroom Climate Benefits

A deep understanding of students' diverse backgrounds and needs provides multiple benefits for teaching, learning, and overall classroom climate. Knowledge of students' diversities allows teachers to understand the individual needs and abilities of their students, and tailor instruction accordingly to maximize student development and achievement. Additionally, it allows teachers to know which authentic materials to incorporate in lessons and instructions to best create an engaging, relevant, and respectful learning experience that fosters student interest in learning and promotes success. Furthermore, by enhancing understanding of students' diverse backgrounds and needs, teachers consequently begin to model an attitude of inclusivity, acceptance, and respect for differences, which is then reflected by students and achieves a positive, welcoming classroom climate that promotes diversity.

The Role of Assessment in Education

Roles of Assessment

Instructional Planning for Individuals and Groups

Effective assessments provide valuable feedback to teachers on how to design and adjust instruction for individuals and groups. Both **formative** and **summative** assessments give insight into student understanding and needs before and after content material is taught. As instruction should be designed based on students' individual needs, assessment provides the information necessary to effectively do so. **Diagnostic** assessments provide teachers with pertinent information about students' individual background knowledge, experiences, and learning needs, thus allowing them to understand students' skills and abilities to focus and plan future instruction accordingly. Additionally, assessments provide teachers with feedback on student progress and areas of individual need that drive instructional planning in allowing teachers to more effectively plan curriculum that is tailored to students' individual needs, skills, and abilities. Assessments inform future instruction through highlighting concepts that students are not understanding for reteaching. Furthermore, it allows them to group students more effectively in future planning to provide scaffolding and ensure that all students are supported in achieving academic standards.

Providing Teacher Accountability and Evaluating Teacher Effectiveness

Teachers are responsible for ensuring that all students are properly supported in achieving lesson objectives, instructional goals, and state academic standards. Thus, they are responsible for effectively designing and implementing instruction, lessons, and activities that are tailored to meet individual students' needs as they work to achieve learning outcomes. Assessments provide feedback regarding student mastery of academic standards and are reflective of the effectiveness of the instructional practices and strategies implemented to support them in their achievement. Consequently, student achievement on assessments reflects and measures the effectiveness of the teacher in designing instructional materials that meet individual students' needs, foster engagement and understanding, and facilitate desired learning outcomes. When the teacher is evaluated based on student assessment results, they are held accountable for developing effective instruction and identifying areas for improvement in their teaching practice.

Assessment Methods and Applications for Analyzing Students' Strengths and Needs

Instructional assessment takes many forms, and each method has different applications and provides distinct feedback for analyzing students' strengths and needs. All forms of assessment should be incorporated in order to develop comprehensive instruction that is tailored to students' individual strengths and needs. **Formative assessments** are an informal, ongoing method of measuring student understanding throughout a lesson. They are valuable in allowing the teacher to adjust and adapt instructional practices and strategies to individual student needs as necessary as they move through a lesson. **Summative assessments** generally occur at the end of a lesson or unit and are intended to measure student achievement of a particular objective or instructional goal. These assessments allow teachers to identify students' individual strengths and needs, and influence future instruction by highlighting areas of understanding or misconception for reteaching. **Standardized assessments** reflect student mastery of state academic standards and illustrate whether students have met academic benchmarks for their grade level. The results of these assessments can be applied to identify students' strengths and needs to determine the starting point of future instruction and proper grouping of students based on skills, needs, and abilities.

Use of State Standards and Assessments

Instruction Development

Effective instruction is driven by state standards and assessment. State academic standards serve as a framework for grade level academic benchmarks that students are expected to achieve during the school year. From these, teachers derive instructional goals and objectives, and ultimately, determine instruction, activities, and materials that will support students in academic achievement. Additionally, teachers use state standards as assessment criteria to monitor student progress and evaluate how successfully students are reaching them.

These assessments provide feedback to teachers that influence future instruction through allowing them to identify areas of misconception that require reteaching or individual student need. State standardized assessments influence the development of instruction in that student achievement on these assessments indicates their level of success in meeting academic targets. They highlight areas of strength and need among students, providing teachers with a framework for effectively designing instruction to address these needs and support students in meeting academic goals.

EVALUATING STUDENT PROGRESS, STRENGTHS, AND NEEDS

State and classroom assessments provide data that allow the teacher to effectively analyze whole-class and individual student performance in meeting learning targets to determine further instructional planning. Whole-class achievement on assessments is indicative of the effectiveness of learning objectives, instructional strategies, and lesson activities in supporting students' achievement of academic standards. Whole-class assessments also provide insight on areas for improvement and reteaching. Individually, in analyzing where students fall on a bell curve for assessment, teachers can effectively identify specific strengths and needs of students to determine instructional planning. This information indicates student progress and where they may need additional support, which allows teachers to better meet students' individual needs in planning future instruction by implementing strategies which are tailored to their skills and abilities.

Instructional Planning

Designing and Sequencing Lesson Plans and Units to Align with Instructional Goals

The effective sequencing of units and lesson plans is key to developing coherent, comprehensible instruction that aligns with instructional goals and fosters success in learning. The teacher must first determine the instructional goals that students will be expected to achieve based on state academic standards as a framework, as well as students' individual needs, knowledge, and abilities. The teacher must then logically arrange specific units of instruction aimed toward achieving the determined instructional goals. Each unit should build upon knowledge from the prior unit. Within each unit, the teacher must determine what students must achieve as they work toward instructional goals and determine objectives that facilitate success based on individual need and ability. Once objectives are defined, teachers must design lesson plans in a logical sequence that will facilitate students in reaching these objectives and increasingly build upon knowledge as students work toward achieving the learning goal. When planning lessons, teachers must decide which activities, procedures, and materials are necessary for successfully completing lesson objectives while ensuring that individual learning needs are met. The teacher must also decide what will be assessed at the end of each lesson and unit to determine student success in achieving instructional goals.

Creating Developmentally Appropriate Learning Experiences and Assessments

Multiple factors must be considered when designing developmentally appropriate learning experiences and assessments that effectively facilitate student growth and achievement. Teachers must consider the general cognitive, physical, social, and emotional developmental levels of students, as well as individual differences in background, skill, knowledge, and learning needs. With this understanding, teachers must then evaluate whether learning experiences are simultaneously appropriate to students' developmental levels and individual needs. This includes ensuring that learning activities and teaching strategies are varied in approach, tailored to students' interests and incorporate student choice in learning. Learning experiences must build upon students' background knowledge and experiences and provide challenging, yet attainable learning opportunities based on individual skills and abilities. Additionally, the teacher must consider whether learning experiences promote student participation and engagement as well as cooperative learning to ensure development across domains. Just as with learning experiences, the developmental appropriateness of assessments must also be evaluated. The teacher must consider whether assessments allow for choice in how students demonstrate their learning so as to address individual learning needs. Furthermore, it is important that teachers consider the purpose of each assessment regarding the feedback they are seeking and how it can help determine further instruction.

Role of Learning Theory in Instructional Process and Student Learning

Multiple learning theories exist to explain how people acquire knowledge, abilities, and skills. Each theory proposes its own approach for best practices in teaching and learning, and therefore, each is most effective and applicable based on the context of learning and individual student needs. Thus, learning theory has a significant role as the framework for the instructional process and facilitating student learning. The teacher must understand the principles of various learning philosophies as well as their students' unique learning needs to effectively design and implement instruction from the perspective of the most applicable theory. Learning theories serve as a context from which, upon identifying desired learning outcomes, teachers can make informed decisions about designing instruction, activities, and assessments that are most effective based on their students' learning styles, skills, and abilities. In developing an understanding of students' learning needs, teachers can determine which learning theory is appropriate in order to design the most effective instruction possible. This facilitates student learning in that it allows for the implementation of student-centered methodologies tailored to students' learning needs and preferences and enhances instruction through allowing the teacher to implement methods from the theory most relevant to students' needs.

The following are examples of some common learning theories that can be used as a framework in the instructional process:

- **Constructivism (Jean Piaget):** This theory proposes that students learn by interacting with the learning environment and connecting new information to their background knowledge to build understanding. This active process allows students to personalize their learning and construct their own perceptions of the world through the lens of their previous experiences.
- **Humanism (Carl Rogers):** This theory proposes that everyone seeks the fulfillment of a hierarchy of basic needs. This begins with physiological needs, such as food and water, and extends to the need for safety, love and belonging, esteem, and ultimately, self-actualization. In the classroom, teachers can create a learning environment that strives to meet these needs by establishing a safe, accepting learning environment, celebrating students' differences, and praising academic and personal achievement.
- **Connectivism (George Siemens, Stephen Downes):** This theory proposes that learning occurs by making a series of connections across pieces of information, ideas, concepts, and perspectives. Connectivism is rooted in the notion that learning occurs externally, and technology resources facilitate connections, as learners have access to several outlets for acquiring and processing new information.
- **Experiential Learning (David Kolb):** This theory proposes that students learn and retain information best through physical exploration and interaction with the learning environment. In the classroom, teachers can facilitate this student-led approach by providing students with varying relevant experiences and opportunities for hands-on learning, such as projects or learning centers.
- **Multiple Intelligences (Howard Gardner):** Gardner's theory proposes there are several versions of intelligence, and as such, the process of learning differs among individuals. Some learners may have a stronger intelligence in one domain, but perhaps have difficulty in another, and therefore, learn best when instruction is presented through the lens of their dominant intelligence. Intelligences are categorized as logical-mathematical, verbal-linguistic, visual-spatial, bodily-kinesthetic, interpersonal, intrapersonal, musical, and naturalistic.

Connecting New Information and Ideas to Prior Knowledge

When students connect new information to prior knowledge, learning becomes relevant and engaging. Effective instruction encourages students to connect learning to background knowledge and experiences, which increases retainment, deepens understanding, and enhances the effectiveness of the overall learning experience. Fostering personal connections to learning is achieved through incorporating an array of strategies and technologies into instruction. Activities including KWL charts, anticipatory guides, graphic organizers, and brainstorming encourage students to consider what they know before learning new concepts, thus allowing them to build upon their prior knowledge and ability to make connections that strengthen learning. Cooperative learning strategies promote sharing and building prior knowledge with other students, thus increasing students' connections to new information. Numerous technologies exist to enhance the learning experience by fostering connections between prior knowledge and new information. Teachers can incorporate a wide range of apps and games across subject areas that build upon prior knowledge by providing activities with increasing levels of difficulty. Online polls, surveys, and word association websites allow students to demonstrate prior understanding of a topic to begin making connections. Self-reflection and closure opportunities at the end of instruction further strengthen learning by encouraging students to connect new material to prior knowledge and experiences.

Making Learning Meaningful and Relevant

Effective instruction occurs when learning is meaningful and relevant. When the purpose of learning is clear, students are engaged, motivated, and retain new information. Instruction must be student-centered, foster personal connections, and be applicable to real-life situations to create meaningful and relevant instruction. Teachers achieve this through an array of methods and technologies that are tailored to students' learning needs. Through forging positive relationships with students, teachers learn their unique interests, preferences, and experiences. Activities such as interest inventories, surveys, and community building develop a positive rapport between teachers and students. This allows teachers to make learning meaningful by creating learner-centered instruction that facilitates personal connections and builds upon prior knowledge. Field trips and community outreach programs are effective in enhancing relevancy through demonstrating the real-world applications of instruction. Additionally, technologies including virtual field trips and tours, videos, and documentaries, assist in increasing students' understanding the purpose of learning by illustrating the real-world applications of instruction. Self-assessments make learning meaningful and relevant through encouraging student ownership and responsibility over learning as students seek areas for improvement. Moreover, closure activities serve to demonstrate overall purpose for learning through encouraging students to connect learning to the lesson's objective and their prior knowledge.

INTRADISCIPLINARY AND INTERDISCIPLINARY INSTRUCTION

Intradisciplinary and interdisciplinary instruction are both valuable strategies for teaching and learning. In **intradisciplinary** instruction, several elements of a single broad subject area are incorporated into the lesson. For example, in a science lesson, the teacher could incorporate elements of chemistry, biology, and physics into instruction. This method of instruction is beneficial in deepening students' understanding of the nuances of a particular subject area through demonstrating the various components that comprise the overarching discipline. **Interdisciplinary** instruction refers to the simultaneous integration of ideas, knowledge, and skills from several subject areas when approaching an idea, problem, or theme, and applying principles of one subject area to another. For example, in an interdisciplinary unit on food, the teacher could incorporate elements of math by teaching students to measure ingredients, language arts by teaching them to read or write a recipe, science through examining chemical reactions of the cooking process, and social studies through having students explore the impact of food agriculture on economy and society. Interdisciplinary instruction is beneficial in deepening students' understanding across subject areas and developing real-world critical thinking skills by encouraging them to make connections between disciplines and teaching them to consider an idea or problem from multiple perspectives.

EXAMPLES OF INTRADISCIPLINARY INSTRUCTION

- **Language Arts:** A single language arts lesson can incorporate components of reading, writing, grammar, and listening skills. For example, a lesson on a particular poem can include a close reading of the poet's use of grammar, symbolism, imagery, and other literary techniques, as well as an audio recording of the poet reading aloud. At the end of the unit, students can be assigned to use what they learned to compose their own original poems.
- **Social Studies:** Social studies units can incorporate elements of history, anthropology, archaeology, sociology, psychology, or any other field that involves the study of humans, civilizations, cultures, and historical events. For example, a unit on the Aztec people may include an examination of their religious beliefs, customs, architecture, and agricultural practices.
- **Science:** Intradisciplinary units in science can include several branches within the field, such as chemistry, biology, physics, earth science, botany, or geology. For example, a unit on volcanoes may incorporate lessons on plate tectonics, the Earth's layers, chemicals released during a volcanic eruption, islands formed from cooled volcanic rock, as well as plants that grow best near volcanoes.
- **Mathematics:** An intradisciplinary math lesson may simultaneously include several branches within the field, such as arithmetic, algebra, or geometry. For example, in a geometry lesson on the Pythagorean theorem, students must utilize algebraic equations and arithmetic to determine the length of the sides of a right triangle.

EXAMPLES OF INTERDISCIPLINARY INSTRUCTION

- **Language Arts:** A unit based in language arts may also incorporate several other disciplines, such as social studies, art, or music. For example, a unit on William Shakespeare's *Romeo and Juliet* may include a reading of the play and an analysis of the use of literary techniques within it, as well as a study of William Shakespeare's life and the society in which he lived to incorporate social studies. Students can also act out the play to incorporate the arts and participate in a rhythmic study on iambic pentameter to incorporate music.
- **Social Studies:** Units based in social studies can include lessons focused on multiple disciplines, including language arts, music, science, and math. For example, an interdisciplinary unit on Ancient Egypt may include a historical study of the culture, religion, architecture, and practices of the Ancient Egyptians while integrating other subject areas, such as a study of hieroglyphics to incorporate language arts and creating Egyptian masks to incorporate art. Students can also study the scientific advancements of the Ancient Egyptians, as well as incorporate math to study how the ancient pyramids were constructed.
- **Science:** Scientific units can also incorporate elements of art, math, social studies, and language arts in order to become interdisciplinary. For example, a unit on Punnett squares focuses on biology and genetics but can also include several other subject areas. Math can be incorporated by integrating lessons on probability, students can be assigned to research their genetics, create a family tree, and write a report on their findings to incorporate language arts and social studies. Art can also be incorporated by having students create portraits of the potential outcomes from Punnett squares.
- **Mathematics:** Interdisciplinary units in mathematics can also include lessons focused on such disciplines as art, social studies, science, and music. For example, a geometry unit on measuring triangles may also incorporate songs to memorize equations, lessons on the pyramids of Ancient Egypt to incorporate social studies, as well as an art project in which students use only triangles to create an original piece.

INCORPORATING COOPERATIVE LEARNING ALLOWING CONSIDERATION FROM MULTIPLE VIEWPOINTS

In any classroom, teachers will encounter a wide range of diversities among students' backgrounds, cultures, interests, skills, and abilities. Thus, providing students with several opportunities for cooperative learning gives them access to others' perspectives and is highly valuable in teaching students to consider ideas from multiple viewpoints. As each student has different experiences and background knowledge, collaborative learning allows them to share their views on ideas with others. Additionally, in working together, students have the opportunity to work with others from different backgrounds that they may have otherwise never encountered and gain exposure to approaching ideas from multiple viewpoints. Cooperative learning opportunities allow students to understand and appreciate others' perspectives and teaches them that there are multiple approaches to problem solving and ideas.

LEARNING EXPERIENCES THAT DEVELOP REAL-WORLD LIFE SKILLS

The ultimate goal of education is to develop the whole child and ensure that students develop into productive, contributing members of society once they leave the classroom. Therefore, it is imperative to provide learning experiences that will develop life skills that are applicable and beneficial in the real world. In an increasingly fast-paced global society, students must be prepared to enter the professional and societal world as confident, independent, responsible, and adaptive individuals. They must have the leadership skills necessary to compete in the professional arena. Students must be able to work cooperatively with others, respect and value multiple perspectives, and be effective problem solvers and critical thinkers in order to be successful outside of the classroom. Teachers must also aim to help students develop the skills necessary to become lifelong learners to ensure continuous growth and development as they enter society. Therefore, learning experiences that promote the development of real-world life skills in addition to academic skills are necessary in adequately preparing students for success.

Cross-Curricular Instruction for Exploring Content from Varied Perspectives

Cross-curricular instruction allows teachers to demonstrate that elements from one subject area can be applied to ideas or problem solving in another. Thus, this instructional strategy is highly valuable in developing students' abilities to explore content from varied perspectives. As this method incorporates several disciplines in approaching a topic, it deepens students' understanding that there are several perspectives that one can take when solving a problem, and that elements of one subject area are relevant in another. In addition, cross-curricular instruction prepares students for the real world through developing critical thinking skills and allowing them to make connections between disciplines, thus allowing them to understand how to successfully approach ideas from varied perspectives.

Benefits of Multicultural Learning Experiences

Multicultural learning experiences demonstrate to students the array of diversities that exist both inside and outside of the classroom. Just as each culture has its own values, norms, and traditions, each has its own perspectives and approaches to ideas and problem solving. Incorporating multicultural experiences in the classroom exposes students to cultures and groups that they may have otherwise never encountered and teaches them to respect and value perspectives outside of their own. As students learn other cultures' beliefs, customs, and attitudes, they develop the understanding that each culture solves problems and considers ideas from multiple viewpoints and that each approach is valuable. As students learn other perspectives, they can apply this knowledge, and ultimately build problem solving and critical thinking skills that will be beneficial in developing successful lifelong learning habits.

Incorporating Multiple Disciplines into a Thematic Unit

In **cross-curricular**, or **interdisciplinary** instruction, multiple disciplines are incorporated into a thematic unit in order to deepen students' understanding through fostering connections and demonstrating multiple perspectives and methods of problem solving. Effective interdisciplinary instruction requires careful planning to ensure that all activities are relevant to the overall lesson theme and effectively support students in achieving desired learning outcomes. The teacher must first select a thematic unit based on state academic standards and then determine desired learning outcomes. Then, the teacher must design lessons and activities for students to reach learning goals and objectives. When integrating multiple disciplines into a thematic unit, the teacher must seek out materials, resources, and activities from various subject areas that are applicable to the main topic and reinforce lesson objectives. The teacher can then integrate these elements into lesson planning to create multifaceted instruction. Additionally, the teacher can create activities that approach the overarching lesson theme from the perspective of different subject areas. The activities and materials should be coordinated and relate to one another in order to deepen students' understanding of the overall concept.

Effectively Allocating Time When Creating Lessons and Units

Effective time management is vital for successful teaching and learning. To ensure that all academic standards are covered within a school year, teachers must consider how to best allocate specific amounts of time for units and lessons that allow for review, enrichment, and reteaching. A unit plan for the school year is an effective strategy in allowing the teacher to visualize and plan the amount of content that must be covered. A unit plan can also be utilized on a smaller scale, as a framework for designing and allotting time for instructional goals, objectives, and lessons within each unit. By setting learning goals and daily objectives within individual units, the teacher can determine the amount of time available for completing each unit, thus ensuring more effective lesson planning by allowing the teacher to develop a daily schedule with dedicated time for teaching and learning. When planning lessons, the teacher must consider how much instructional time is necessary to cover each topic and the time students will need to complete lesson activities. Additionally, teachers must ensure that they allow time at the end of each lesson for reteaching if students have misconceptions, as extra time can be utilized for enrichment if reteaching is unnecessary.

Opportunities for Reflection

Opportunities for reflection within lesson plans are beneficial in enhancing learning experiences through strengthening student understanding and influencing further instruction. When students are given the opportunity to reflect, they are able to connect their learning back to the original objective and better understand the overall purpose for learning, thus fostering engagement. Reflection deepens students' understanding by allowing them to connect new concepts to their own personal experiences, which ultimately helps in comprehension and retainment through making learning relevant. Reflecting on performance empowers students to become self-motivated lifelong learners by allowing them to analyze what they understood and did well, as well as encouraging them to identify areas for improvement. Teachers can utilize students' reflections to influence and drive further instruction. Students' reflections also allow teachers to identify areas in which students excelled, areas for improvement, and can aid them in tailoring future lesson plans to adapt to students' needs and interests.

Opportunities for Self-Assessment

Self-assessments within lessons are a valuable formative assessment strategy that enriches student learning and provides insight to the teacher. Providing students with the opportunity to monitor their progress and assess their learning supports them in developing a wide range of skills that are beneficial both inside and outside of the classroom. Self-assessments empower students in their learning by creating a sense of ownership and responsibility over their own learning, thus fostering self-motivation and engagement. They also serve to foster a sense of independence and objectivity within students to effectively review their own work and identify areas of improvement, which is a vital skill needed to becoming a lifelong learner. When students evaluate their own performance, the teacher is able to effectively assess student understanding, thus allowing them to identify areas of weakness or misconception for reteaching.

Opportunities for Closure Activities

Closure activities at the end of each lesson or topic are beneficial for both students and teachers. These short activities allow teachers to formatively assess student understanding of content covered within a lesson and identify areas of misconception for reteaching. Additionally, closure activities are valuable in measuring whether the intended lesson objective was achieved before moving to the next topic. For students, closures at the end of a lesson provide structure and organization to learning, as well as emphasize the purpose for instruction by allowing them to connect what they learned back to the original objective. Moreover, in having students restate what they have learned in a closure activity, learning is strengthened by giving students the opportunity to internalize new information. In demonstrating their understanding, they can better make personal connections between their own learning, background knowledge, and experiences.

Factors that Impact Student Learning

Culturally Responsive Teaching

Culturally responsive teaching is an instructional approach in which the teacher practices awareness, inclusivity, and sensitivity regarding the social and cultural diversities that are present within the classroom. With this awareness in mind, the culturally responsive teacher designs curriculum, instruction, activities, and assessments that are inclusive and reflective of students' social and cultural backgrounds and experiences. When planning instruction and learning experiences, the teacher can demonstrate awareness of social and cultural norms through consciously educating themselves on the beliefs, values, and norms of their students. This is achieved through connecting with students and building positive relationships to learn about their individual backgrounds and locate authentic learning materials that are reflective of their experiences. Through communicating with students' parents, family members, and members of the community, the teacher can practice and build awareness of the diverse social and cultural norms of their students to gain an understanding of how to design culturally responsive instruction. By educating themselves on the social and cultural norms of their students, the teacher can effectively ensure that students' diversities are reflected in all areas of instruction in a culturally sensitive manner to create an empowering learning environment that engages all students.

Practices for Culturally Responsive Teaching	
1	Create an inclusive classroom environment
2	Recognize personal biases and work to eliminate them
3	Self-educate on the community and students' social and cultural backgrounds
4	Use curriculum that reflects students' diversities using authentic materials
5	Frequently communicate with students' families
6	Build positive interpersonal relationships with students
7	Be involved in the community

Home and Community Factors Impacting Student Learning

Students are exposed to multiple social and cultural factors from their homes and communities that significantly impact learning, so it is imperative that the teacher is conscious of these factors to effectively adapt instruction and assessment to enhance students' learning. Students are often held to different academic and behavioral expectations by their parents, depending on their social and cultural background, that affect self-motivation, engagement, and academic performance. When adapting instruction and assessment, teachers must ensure that all students are held to high expectations while providing individual students with the necessary supports for success. Teachers must also consider the availability of community resources that offer support and enhance learning, as this differs among social and cultural groups. Students from low sociocultural backgrounds may lack quality resources such as libraries, tutoring, or after-school activities, so teachers must adapt to include time outside of instruction for completing assignments, additional support, and use of school resources. Community problems pose obstacles that hinder students' motivation, self-concept, and attitude toward learning. It is important that teachers establish a safe, welcoming, and engaging classroom while providing the necessary academic and behavioral supports to foster equity and promote a growth mindset.

Importance of Self-Directed Learning

In a **self-directed learning** environment, students are given a sense of agency that enhances self-motivation, feelings of ownership and responsibility for their own learning. By choosing what and how they learn based on their individual interests, learning styles, and preferences, students have the ability to explore and inquire freely, thus increasing their natural curiosity and motivation to do so. In choosing their own learning, students determine their own learning goals, thus creating a sense of ownership and self-responsibility. This sentiment is also increased when students can tailor their learning according to their own needs and challenge themselves based upon their skills and abilities. Furthermore, when students achieve self-decided goals, they develop a sense of ownership over their learning. In order to foster a self-guided environment in which students are fully engaged in their own learning, teachers must adopt a facilitator role in instruction and offer support when necessary. Instruction and assessment must allow multiple opportunities for student choice in how learning is determined and demonstrated. By providing opportunities for self-evaluation and reflection, teachers further facilitate self-motivation, ownership, and responsibility over students' own learning through encouraging them to make personal connections, reflect on accomplishments, and seek areas for self-improvement.

Impact of Teacher Roles on Student Learning

The teacher's role is multifaceted in nature, and teachers must often adopt multiple roles within a single lesson to effectively facilitate learning and accommodate individual students' needs. The role of the **lecturer**, **model**, and **facilitator** are applicable to different learning situations and have varying impacts on learning. As the lecturer, the teacher delivers direct instruction to students. This role is most appropriate when introducing a new concept, providing instructions for an upcoming activity, or reviewing material. In addition, teachers can effectively communicate new skills, ideas, and thought processes through modeling to students, as this is a highly influential method of instruction. When teachers serve as facilitators, they guide students in learning while offering support, scaffolding, and assistance when necessary. This role is effective in active and open-ended learning situations in which students are encouraged to explore, practice, and engage in creative problem solving. Through this method, teachers allow students to adopt a self-directed approach that encourages ownership over their own learning, thus creating an engaging, empowering learning experience.

Impact of Student Roles on Learning

Students adopt multiple roles in the learning process, and teachers must be cognizant of individual learning styles and specific learning situations to determine which role is most applicable and effective for enhancing learning. As **active learners**, students participate and interact throughout the learning process. In this role, students are encouraged to implement higher-order thinking skills through exploration, inquiry, and problem solving, thus creating an engaging learning environment that promotes the retainment of information. This role is particularly effective in learning situations in which students are practicing new skills, testing hypotheses, and exploring new concepts. The opportunity to actively participate in learning allows them to better internalize new information and formulate creative solutions to problems. Active learning also occurs in effectively designed collaborative learning situations. As **group participants**, students can build upon one another's skills, abilities, and experiences to solve problems, explore new information, and understand new perspectives to enhance the overall learning experience. When students are learning new skills, behaviors, or thought processes, they often adopt the role of the observer. Modeling is an influential instructional strategy, and in **observing** the teacher or another more experienced individual, students learn to utilize and implement new information in learning situations.

Using Multiple Modalities of Instruction to Address Different Learning Styles

When determining instruction, activities, and assessment, teachers must consider and incorporate students' various approaches to learning. Every student learns differently and has unique needs, and thus, teachers must ensure that auditory, visual, kinesthetic, and tactile learning styles are addressed in all areas of curriculum to maximize students' learning potential. Through incorporating multiple modalities using Howard Gardner's **theory of multiple intelligences** as a framework, teachers can design content and activities that deliver instruction in a variety of ways simultaneously (visual-spatial, linguistic, musical, naturalistic, interpersonal, intrapersonal, logical-mathematical, bodily-kinesthetic). Through this approach, student understanding is reinforced, and each student is provided the opportunity to learn in the way that best suits their individual needs. By differentiating instruction with these modalities, teachers can incorporate several strategies simultaneously when teaching a concept, such as independent practice, cooperative learning, music, art, problem solving, and movement. Opportunities for student choice in learning further allows the integration of multiple modalities in instruction, as it lets students decide the method of learning that is best tailored to their individual learning style and needs.

Howard Gardner's Theory of Multiple Intelligences

Visual/Spatial	Prefers visual representations, able to visualize with the mind's eye, excels in activities that incorporate drawing, building, creative expression, and manipulatives.
Logical-Mathematical	Prefers activities that require order, analysis, and problem-solving using logical reasoning. Excels in solving math equations, conducting science experiments, puzzles, and analyzing data.
Verbal-Linguistic	Prefers learning through reading, writing, speaking, and listening. Often skilled in acquiring foreign languages. Excels in activities that incorporate discussion, debate, oral presentations, and written assignments.
Bodily-Kinesthetic	Prefers hands-on learning experiences that involve movement and physical interaction with the learning environment. Excels in activities that involve sports, dance, building, and hands-on projects.
Interpersonal	Prefers learning opportunities that involve communicating and collaborating with others. Excels in partner, small group, and whole-group learning activities.
Intrapersonal	Prefers to learn and work independently. Usually possesses a strong sense of self-awareness. Excels in activities that allow for independent, self-paced learning and self-reflection.
Musical	Learns best when music is incorporated into instruction. Prefers using songs, mnemonic devices and rhythms to learn concepts and retain information.
Naturalistic	Learns best when opportunities to connect with nature are incorporated into instruction. Prefers activities such as nature walks, identifying and classifying elements of nature, and working outside.

Creating Equitable Learning Environment for ELLs Using Linguistic Supports

To create an equitable learning environment, ELL students must be provided with linguistic supports that are applicable across content areas in order to ensure they are provided with an equal opportunity for success in learning. Teachers can implement varying supports appropriate to students' levels of English language proficiency that are beneficial in facilitating both English language and content-specific learning. Such supports include incorporating verbal cues, gestures, and visual representations into instruction to provide context and build background knowledge. The use of environmental print, word walls, and labels are also effective in supporting English language skills while simultaneously providing context for facilitating learning in the content area. Teachers should model speaking and listening skills, and practice slow speech or repetition when necessary to ensure understanding. Scaffolding instruction and activities across content areas through such supports as graphic organizers, outlines, and cooperative learning opportunities serve to assist ELL students in building English language proficiency skills across content areas at a pace appropriate for their ability level. By implementing the proper supports, teachers can effectively foster English language learning in all subject areas while ensuring that students simultaneously learn content-specific material.

Instructional Strategies for English Language Learning in All Subject Areas

Language acquisition occurs across content areas for ELL students, as each subject is comprised of different vocabulary, grammatical patterns, and methods of expressing ideas. Thus, it is important that teachers provide these students with learning strategies that are applicable in all subject areas in order to effectively support English language acquisition and content-specific learning. Through a metacognitive approach, teachers can facilitate ELL students in thinking about how they learn, reflecting on their strengths and weaknesses, and applying useful learning strategies from one content area to another to develop their English language skills in all subjects. This strategy enhances learning through teaching students how to apply learning strategies from one instructional context to another when developing language skills. By activating students' prior knowledge when introducing new material in a given subject area, teachers promote English language learning through providing context and encouraging students to consider what they may already know about a new concept.

Such methods as pre-teaching, anticipatory guides, graphic organizers, and brainstorming allow ELL students to make connections that build their language abilities across content areas.

Adapting Instruction for Varying Levels of English Language Proficiency

When encountering ELL students with varying English language skills, it is imperative to adapt instruction to accommodate these differences and ensure that all students receive appropriate linguistic support. Instruction must be communicated, sequenced, and scaffolded to support learners with different English proficiency abilities. The teacher must communicate instruction clearly while allowing time for repetition or slowed speech as necessary. In addition, teachers must supplement instruction with linguistic supports such as verbal cues, gestures, and visual representations as needed to provide assistance and context appropriate to individual ability levels. Instruction must also be sequenced logically and clearly communicate the expectations and steps of learning experiences. This is achieved by indicating an explicit beginning, middle, and end to activities through transition words and actions appropriate to students' levels of English proficiency. Teachers must scaffold instruction, activities, and assessments to meet individual students' language learning needs. Supports such as word walls, graphic organizers, charts, labels, and pairing students with others who can provide assistance are effective means of scaffolding learning to accommodate varying ability. By communicating, sequencing, and scaffolding instruction in a way that is tailored to ELL students' individual language needs, teachers effectively foster an equitable environment that promotes success in learning.

Cognitive Development

Importance in Design of Appropriate Learning Experiences That Facilitate Growth

The teacher must understand their students' cognitive developmental ability relative to their grade level in order to create effective, engaging learning experiences that facilitate growth. This understanding allows teachers to develop age-appropriate instruction, activities, and assessment that challenges students based on their skills and abilities but is attainable based on their cognitive developmental level. In knowing how students in a given grade level think and learn, the teacher can develop instruction that effectively facilitates learning and growth, such as creating opportunities for purposeful play with young children, opportunities for middle-school aged students to engage in logical problem solving, or activities that promote the development of abstract thinking and reasoning with adolescents. In addition, understanding students' cognitive abilities of each developmental level allow the teacher to better understand the nuances that exist within them, as students ultimately develop at their own pace and have individual learning needs.

Impact on Teaching and Learning

Students' thinking and learning develops as they mature, as their thought processes and worldview changes. Consequently, teaching and learning must adapt to accommodate these changes and facilitate growth. In the early years of cognitive development, children learn through interacting with the surrounding environment using their physical senses and engage in independent play. To facilitate this, young children need learning experiences that stimulate their development through exploration. As children reach early elementary school, they begin to think symbolically and play with others. Purposeful play and interaction with learning materials becomes an important part of learning at this stage. Teachers should act as facilitators and provide multiple opportunities for children to engage in purposeful, self-directed play with interactive materials as they learn to categorize the world around them. By later childhood, children think concretely and logically, and thus, need hands-on learning experiences that provide opportunities for classification, experimentation, and problem-solving skills to facilitate their level of cognition and promote development. As children reach adolescence, they are increasingly able to think abstractly and consider hypothetical situations beyond what is concretely present. To enhance learning, teachers must provide opportunities for exploring different perspectives, values, and synthesizing information to engage in creative problem solving.

The Learning Environment

Establishing a Positive, Productive Classroom Environment

Unique Characteristics and Needs of Students at Varying Developmental Levels

Students at each developmental level possess unique characteristics and needs that must be met in the classroom to ensure productivity and a positive classroom environment. For successful learning, the teacher must recognize the nuances of varying developmental levels to properly understand their students' abilities and design instruction accordingly. When the teacher is attuned to the distinct characteristics and needs of their students, they can align **curriculum, instructional strategies**, **activities**, and **assessments** in a way that is accessible and comprehensible to all students. This understanding enables the teacher to deliver instruction at a **pace** appropriate to students' developmental stage while ensuring they are challenged across domains based upon their ability for continuous whole-child development. In addition, knowledge of the general characteristics and needs of developmental stages enables the teacher to effectively identify and accommodate individual variances that occur within these stages for **student-centered** learning. When instruction is tailored to address the needs of varying developmental stages and individual differences, students feel supported in their learning. This ultimately fosters increased self-esteem, student engagement, and positive attitudes toward learning that contribute to an overall productive and successful classroom environment.

Addressing Developmental Characteristics and Needs of Younger Students

A positive and productive classroom environment for younger children requires the teacher to understand the intricacies of this developmental stage and implement strategies accordingly to promote success in learning. Younger students learn by **exploring** and **interacting** with the world around them and must be provided with multiple opportunities to do so. **Play** is integral to young students' development across domains. Therefore, both planned and free play should be incorporated throughout instruction. Play enables students to explore their environment and make connections that strengthen their learning while promoting the development of problem-solving and higher-order thinking skills. In addition, allowing frequent opportunities for play facilitates the acquisition of important social and emotional skills, such as cooperation, conflict resolution, and sharing. Likewise, incorporating frequent **movement** throughout lessons allows young students to explore their physical space and actively engage in learning for deeper understanding. Additionally, **cooperative learning** strategies encourage the development of necessary social and emotional skills and are important in teaching young children how to effectively work with others to solve a problem. When the teacher implements strategies appropriate to younger students' developmental levels, it enhances motivation, active engagement, and promotes positive attitudes toward learning for a productive classroom environment.

Collaborative Opportunities in Addressing Developmental Characteristics and Needs of Middle-Level Students

Middle-level students experience significant developmental changes as they approach adolescence and therefore, have unique characteristics and needs that must be met to ensure a positive and productive learning environment. **Collaborative opportunities** are beneficial in supporting the development of cognitive, social, and emotional skills of middle-level students and should be implemented frequently. This strategy enables these students to work productively with others and promotes the development of positive **interpersonal** and **communication** skills. This is especially important in middle-level education, as students at this developmental stage begin forming their identities, attitudes toward learning, and influential peer relationships. Middle-level students build **self-confidence** through collaborative learning, as it enables them to develop positive leadership skills. Additionally, collaborative opportunities expose students to the varying backgrounds and perspectives of their classmates, thus fostering appreciation for individual differences and contributing to a positive classroom climate. Collaborative learning is also beneficial for **cognitive development**, as it allows students to build upon one another's background knowledge for enhanced learning and encourages critical and higher-order thinking while working together to solve a problem. Providing middle-level students with collaborative opportunities increases overall engagement for a positive and productive classroom environment, as well as develops necessary skills for successful transition into adolescence.

Promoting Respect for the Community and People in It Among Older Students

As older students prepare for adulthood, it is important that they develop a respect for their community and the people in it. Implementing strategies to facilitate this is vital in equipping older students with **real-world skills** necessary to become productive contributors to society. By self-educating and modeling respect for the community and its people, the teacher can influence students to adopt the same sentiment. Establishing a positive community within the classroom through such activities as class meetings, discussions, and cultural activities promotes respect for others that extends to real-world situations. Strategies that demonstrate connection to the community strengthen students' overall respect and responsibility for it. This can be achieved by incorporating **authentic materials**, including news stories, art, music, and relevant speakers, to develop students' understanding and insight regarding the characteristics and needs of the community. Encouraging students to bring items from home to share fosters appreciation for their community by exposing them to the backgrounds and perspectives within it. **Community service** projects such as fundraisers, food drives, and service field trips further promote students' respect for their community while demonstrating the real-world applications of their learning. This ultimately makes learning meaningful and contributes to a positive, productive learning environment.

Positive Classroom Climate

Classroom climate refers to the overall atmosphere that the teacher establishes and is powerful in determining the nature of the learning experience. Students are most successful in their learning when the climate is positive, encouraging, and focused on creating a collaborative, supportive community. A positive classroom climate is **welcoming**, **inclusive**, and **respectful** of all individuals. Instruction is delivered in an engaging, comprehensible way in a structured, orderly, and safe environment. The atmosphere is **visually appealing** and stimulating, yet not overwhelming, and is physically arranged in a way that maximizes learning. **Collaboration** and **supportive interactions** are encouraged throughout the learning process to enhance engagement and develop positive social and emotional skills. Such an environment builds students' self-esteem and confidence by ensuring they feel safe and empowered to participate and work with others in the learning process. In addition, it encourages positive attitudes toward learning that are necessary for active student engagement and productivity. When the classroom climate is positive, students are more self-motivated, thus strengthening their learning and promoting academic achievement.

Collaboration and Supportive Interactions

Collaboration and **supportive interactions** are key components of a positive classroom climate and should be integrated throughout instruction to promote active engagement and success in learning for all students. To achieve this, the teacher must establish a classroom community focused on respect, inclusiveness, and open dialogue. This ensures students feel safe and empowered to express themselves and interact constructively. By teaching and **modeling** active listening skills, the teacher can demonstrate and influence respectful communication in the classroom. **Team-building activities**, including class meetings, games, and discussions, are valuable strategies for creating a community that encourages productive collaboration and supportive interactions. In addition, establishing **clear expectations** for positive communication and involving students in their creation instills a sense of personal responsibility to adhere to them when working with others. Once expectations are understood, students must be provided with multiple and varied **collaborative learning** opportunities to continuously practice developing positive interpersonal skills. As students participate in learning, the teacher must be sure to consistently praise cooperation and positive interactions to reinforce the standards of communication. When the teacher promotes collaboration and supportive interactions, they create a positive classroom climate that increases students' productivity and self-motivation to actively participate in learning for maximized achievement.

Respect for Diversity and Individual Differences

An emphasis on respect for **diversity** and **individual differences** in the classroom is necessary to establish a positive, productive learning atmosphere. Teaching and modeling this sentiment to students instills the notion that everyone has unique and valuable experiences, perspectives, and characteristics to contribute to the classroom community. Emphasizing respect for all individuals ensures students feel validated and secure in their own identities while teaching them to appreciate diversities among their classmates. Such an environment promotes collaboration and supportive interactions, as it is built on a foundation of welcoming, inclusiveness, and acceptance that empowers students to confidently interact with peers as they engage in learning. When students feel respected, it increases their self-esteem and positive self-concept. Students that feel confident in the classroom are more likely to develop positive attitudes toward learning. This ultimately fosters a positive classroom climate in which students are motivated to actively engage in instruction and achieve academic success.

Impact of Interactions on Classroom Climate

Teacher-Student Interactions

Interactions between teachers and their students play a significant role in determining overall classroom climate and the quality of the learning experience. The way in which the teacher interacts with students influences their **social**, **emotional**, and **cognitive development**, as well as sets the tone for how students interact with each other. This ultimately shapes students' **self-esteem** and contributes to their level of engagement, attitude toward learning, and academic achievement. Therefore, it is important that the teacher ensure all interactions with students on a whole-class and individual level are positive, unbiased, encouraging, and respectful of each individual. Working to build relationships with students demonstrates a genuine interest in their lives that contributes to a positive, productive classroom climate in which students feel welcomed, accepted, and empowered to actively engage in learning. Positive interactions between the teacher and students support a healthy sense of self-esteem as well as positive social and emotional skills that contribute to cognitive development. Students with greater self-esteem are more likely to develop positive attitudes toward learning that foster increased self-motivation to actively participate in learning, thus contributing to enhanced academic achievement.

Students' Interactions with One Another

The classroom climate is dependent on the nature of **students' interactions** with one another. These interactions largely determine the quality of student learning as well as development across domains. Positive communication facilitates the development of healthy **social** and emotional skills that serve to enhance cognitive development. Students with strong social and **emotional skills** are often more motivated to actively participate in learning and are more productive in collaborative situations, as they can build upon one another's knowledge. Therefore, the teacher must implement a variety of strategies to ensure interactions among students are positive, respectful, and supportive to establish a classroom climate focused on productive learning. **Community building** exercises establish a climate built on positive and supportive communication while demonstrating the benefits of productive cooperation in achieving a goal. Teaching and **modeling** positive communication skills sets the tone and expectations for how students will interact with one another. Students should be given **frequent opportunities** to interact both during and outside of instructional time to promote the development of necessary interpersonal skills for healthy social development. In addition, **strategic student groupings** during collaborative work and consistent monitoring help ensure maximized productivity and that the standards for communication are reinforced.

Communicating an Enthusiasm for Learning

Establishing Environments Promoting Positive Attitudes Toward Learning

The nature of the classroom environment is reliant on the **efforts**, **behaviors**, and **attitudes** of the teacher. The teacher is responsible for setting the tone of the classroom, which determines the overall climate and has significant impacts on the quality and effectiveness of the learning experience. The classroom environment influences students' engagement, positive communication, and attitudes toward learning, which contribute to their overall academic achievement. Successful teaching and learning require the teacher to intentionally take measures to establish a welcoming, accepting, and encouraging classroom environment that promotes excitement and positive attitudes toward learning. Teachers must model genuine respect for their students and enthusiasm for learning, as well as present instruction in a way that is engaging, comprehensible, and responsive to students' needs and interests. The physical classroom must be arranged in such a way that is visually appealing, safe, and facilitative of productive learning. It is also important that the teacher establish and consistently reinforce structured routines, procedures, and behavioral expectations to contribute to an overall positive climate and ensure students feel secure and willing to participate in learning. When the classroom environment is exciting, positive, and engaging, it encourages positive attitudes toward learning that increase motivation to succeed.

Influence on Students' Motivation, Productivity, and Academic Achievement

Modeling is perhaps one of the most powerful strategies in influencing students' attitudes, behaviors, and actions in the classroom. As students spend a great deal of time with their teachers, the level of enthusiasm for learning demonstrated by the teacher inevitably influences their own excitement in the classroom. Therefore, the teacher must conscientiously model enthusiasm for teaching and learning to positively influence students' internal motivation for productivity, learning, and achievement. Students are highly perceptive, and as such, if the teacher appears unmotivated in their practice or disinterested in the content, students will likely adopt the same sentiment and become disengaged or apathetic toward learning. The enthusiasm modeled by the teacher must be **authentic** to elicit the same genuine interest in learning from students. When the teacher demonstrates sincere excitement about the content they are teaching, it prompts curiosity for learning among students that enhances their motivation and attitudes toward learning. In addition, modeling enthusiasm for teaching and learning enhances the relationship between the teacher and students, thus contributing to a positive classroom climate that makes students excited to learn. When students have a positive attitude toward learning, they are more motivated to productively engage in learning and achieve academic success.

Methods and Impact on Classroom Climate and Student Engagement

Communicating sincere enthusiasm for teaching and learning is essential to establishing a positive, productive classroom climate focused on student engagement and achievement. Students' interest and excitement for learning are directly reflective of the sentiments exhibited by the teacher. As such, it is important that the teacher intentionally and consistently communicate excitement for their practice and content. To achieve this, the teacher must ensure that their **behaviors**, **actions**, **language**, **tone of voice**, and **interactions** with students are positive in nature. By working to build positive **interpersonal relationships** with students and demonstrating genuine interest in their lives, experiences, interests, and needs, the teacher can effectively communicate enthusiasm for their practice that motivates students to engage in learning. This is further reflected in the physical **classroom arrangement**. A classroom that is visually appealing, stimulating, and reflective of students' interests and achievements illustrates the teacher's enthusiasm and promotes a positive classroom climate in which students are excited and motivated to engage in learning.

Conveying High Expectations for All Students

Significance in Promoting Productivity, Active Engagement, and Success in Learning

Communicating **high academic** and **behavioral expectations** is necessary for establishing a classroom climate focused on productivity, active engagement, and achievement. Students are heavily influenced by the teacher's expectations for them, and therefore, when high learning standards are set, students will more likely strive to achieve them. High expectations increase the **relevancy** of learning by focusing instruction and providing a clear purpose that motivates students to participate. In addition, by conveying high expectations, the teacher demonstrates a **belief in their students' abilities** to overcome personal challenges and achieve success. This notion promotes a **growth mindset** among students, which is the belief that intelligence is not inherent, but rather, can be attained and consistently improved upon. This enhances students' self-esteem and confidence, which promotes positive attitudes toward learning that foster active engagement, productivity, and success. Communicating high expectations while providing necessary supports motivates students to challenge themselves academically and gives them a sense of self-responsibility over their learning that encourages them to work to their highest potential. This ultimately creates a positive classroom climate in which students feel supported and empowered to productively engage in learning and achieve success.

Strategies and Impact on Classroom Climate and Student Achievement

Communicating **high academic** and **behavioral expectations** is most effective when done so through a variety of means. This ensures that students are aware of the teacher's expectations of them and consistently reinforces high standards to establish a positive classroom climate focused on student motivation, productivity, and achievement. Expectations must always be **clear** and **visible** in the classroom, and the teacher must frequently remind students by restating them throughout instruction. Establishing learning goals and objectives that are challenging, yet attainable based on students' abilities effectively communicates high expectations and the teacher's belief that students can achieve them. This is further iterated when students encounter challenges and rather than lowering expectations, the teacher maintains the same high standards while providing necessary supports for achievement. The teacher can also communicate high expectations by ensuring they provide students with timely, clear, and constructive **feedback** on their progress and ways in which they can improve to meet them. Frequent **communication with families** is beneficial in reinforcing academic and behavioral expectations at home to ensure student awareness and maximize their effectiveness in the classroom.

Physical Characteristics of a Safe and Productive Learning Environment

A classroom environment that is **safe** and facilitates **productivity** in learning is essential to fostering student motivation, engagement, and achievement. The physical space must be **clean, well-organized**, and **orderly**. All equipment, furniture, and materials must be in usable condition, well-maintained, and free of damage. This ensures that students are safe when engaging with the learning environment, as well as provides an appealing space that encourages participation. Furniture and equipment must be arranged in a way that facilitates safety and ease of movement as students transition between activities. Likewise, all furniture, materials, and equipment must be appropriate to the students' **age group** in terms of level of difficulty, height, and size to enable students to properly interact with them for productive learning. Students must have access to a **variety** of learning materials to promote interest and engagement for productive learning, including areas for individual and collaborative learning. The classroom should be decorated in such a way that is welcoming, stimulating without being overwhelming, and reflective of students' diversities and interests. When the physical environment is inviting, safe, and tailored to students' developmental levels, it creates a positive classroom climate in which students are motivated to productively engage in learning.

Significance of Effective Classroom Arrangement

A thoughtfully arranged classroom has significant and positive impacts on the nature of the learning atmosphere. Effective classroom arrangement creates an inviting learning environment in which students are motivated to engage in learning actively and productively. The manner in which the teacher organizes furniture, equipment, and learning materials influences students' **focus**, **access** to resources, and **behavior**, as well as the teacher's ability to effectively implement **classroom management** strategies. An organized, orderly classroom in which necessary resources are easily accessible enables students to properly focus on instruction, thus promoting active engagement and productivity in learning. This reinforces positive behavior, as students are less likely to be disruptive when their learning environment is free of unnecessary distractions. The classroom arrangement determines the flow and ease of movement and should be strategically planned to facilitate productive learning while enabling the teacher to easily monitor and assist all students for effective classroom management. Effective arrangement allows the teacher to control the level of student movement and prevent potential distractions while ensuring students can easily transition from one learning activity to the next to promote efficiency, active engagement, and productivity.

Establishing Safe, Productive, and Successful Learning Environments

Establishing a safe, productive, and successful learning environment requires the teacher to thoughtfully consider several factors when determining the most effective classroom arrangement for meeting desired learning outcomes and students' needs. Students' **age group, size**, and **developmental levels** influence which arrangement best facilitates safety and productivity in learning. For example, younger students learn through interaction with their environment and therefore need ample space for movement and play to support their development. A more structured arrangement that enables direct instruction while also facilitating hands-on, collaborative learning meets the needs of middle-level and older students. In addition, students' **individual needs** must be considered when determining classroom arrangement in order to ensure equitable access to instruction and learning materials. The teacher must also consider the **size** and **layout** of the classroom, including the location of learning resources such as the projector screen, computers, and chalkboard. With this in mind, teachers must determine the **style** of teaching and learning taking place, how they want students to move, what information must be visible, as well as which materials must be accessible to create a safe, productive learning environment that meets students' needs in achieving learning outcomes.

Considerations for Desk Arrangement

There are numerous possibilities for desk arrangements in the classroom, each with advantages and limitations that must be considered and addressed. **Desired learning outcomes**, as well as the style of teaching and learning, influence which arrangement is most effective. Arrangements that facilitate individual focus, limited distraction, and clear teacher-student visibility are suited to **direct instruction**. However, these arrangements often limit collaborative learning. To address this, the teacher can designate an area in the classroom for group work, utilize common areas such as the library, or move students' desks for collaborative activities. Variations of group arrangements facilitate **collaborative learning**, as students can easily face one another and work together. However, grouped seating may cause student distraction during individual work and limit teacher-student visibility. It is therefore important that the teacher establish clear expectations and frequently monitor students' progress to ensure they remain on task. The **classroom size** must be considered, as the space may not allow for certain desk arrangements and still facilitate ease of movement, visibility, and student learning. **Individual learning needs** must also be considered when determining seating arrangements. Some students require specific accommodations, such as preferential seating, an individual learning space for limited distractions, or a physical accommodation.

Various types of seating arrangements are described below:

- **Stadium Seating**—Desks in this classroom are situated in lines at a slight angle with the students facing directly toward the teacher. This seating method is useful for lectures and individual work, as the teacher can easily monitor whether each student is on task. This arrangement is generally unsuited for group work, as students are not able to easily face one another, and may limit the teacher's ease of movement between students to provide individual assistance.
- **Cluster Seating**—Desks in this classroom are arranged in groups of 3-5 throughout the classroom. This method is beneficial for supporting collaborative work and pairing students that need support with others that can provide scaffolding. However, this arrangement may be distracting during individual work and limit teacher-student visibility.
- **Rows and Columns**—Desks are individually spaced apart with the students facing directly toward the teacher and front of the room. This arrangement is useful for presentations, direct instruction, and individual work, as it limits distractions from other students. The teacher can easily see whether individual students are on task. However, this arrangement is not facilitative of group work, as students cannot easily face each other. This arrangement also limits the teacher's ability to move between students to provide assistance.
- **Horseshoe**—Desks in this classroom are arranged in a large "U" shape with students facing the teacher at the front of the room. This arrangement is useful for individual instruction, as it ensures teacher-student visibility and equal view of the chalkboard and projector screen during direct instruction. This method also facilitates whole-class discussions. However, this arrangement inhibits students' ability to work collaboratively in groups and, depending on classroom size, may limit ease of teacher and student movement.

- **Miniature Horseshoes**—Desks in this classroom are arranged in 2-5 miniature horseshoes with students facing the front of the room. This arrangement is beneficial for both individual and collaborative work, as the teacher can clearly monitor whether students are on task and can move between groups to provide individual assistance, while enabling students to easily face one another for group activities. However, this method may lend itself to student distraction during individual work, and the physical size of the classroom may limit the possibility for this arrangement.
- **Pairs**—Desks in this classroom are arranged two-by-two in rows with students facing the front of the classroom. This arrangement is useful for partner work and pairing students that need support with others that provide scaffolding, while limiting distractions during individual work. This method is not suitable for group work or whole-class activities, as students cannot easily face each other, and movement may be limited.
- **Combination**—This classroom incorporates a variety of desk arrangements, including individual seats, pairs, groups, and the "horseshoe" arrangements. This method is useful for accommodating varying learning styles and needs, as it can facilitate individual and collaborative work. However, this arrangement utilizes a great deal of space and may impede ease of movement and visibility for the teacher and students.
- **Flexible**—This classroom provides students with a variety of options for seating choices throughout the classroom, such as bean bag chairs, exercise balls, or floor seating. This option is beneficial for supporting students' individual learning needs, as they can choose to sit where they learn best. Flexible seating also supports collaborative learning and contributes to a welcoming, positive classroom climate. However, unstructured seating may lend itself to student distraction and limit student-teacher visibility during direct instruction.
- **Runway**—Desks in this classroom are arranged in rows on either side of the room with students facing the center, leaving the middle space clear for the teacher. This is useful for direct instruction, as students can easily see the teacher and class presentations, and the teacher can monitor whether each student is on task. This method also facilitates whole-class discussions. This arrangement is generally not suited for collaborative work, as students cannot easily face those seated near them, and it may limit the teacher's ability to provide individual assistance.
- **Conference**—All desks in this classroom are arranged in a large, two-by-two rectangle situated in the middle of the room with students facing one another. This arrangement is beneficial for collaborative work, whole-class activities, and class discussions, as students can easily face one another. The teacher can generally provide individual assistance and can easily monitor whether students are on task. However, the physical size of the classroom may not facilitate this arrangement. In addition, this method may lead to student distraction during individual work.

Classroom Seating Arrangements

Stadium Seating	Cluster Seating
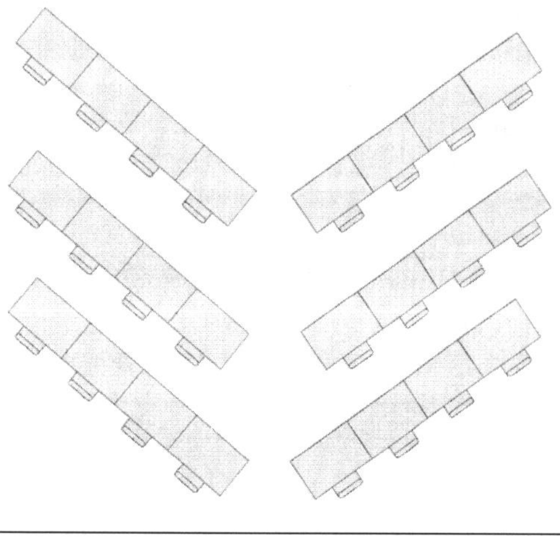	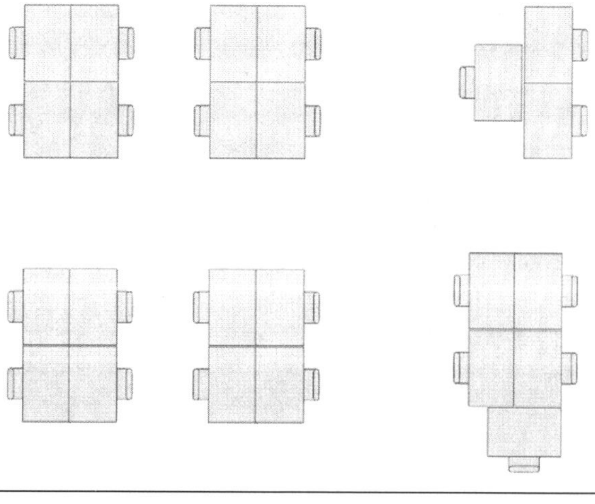

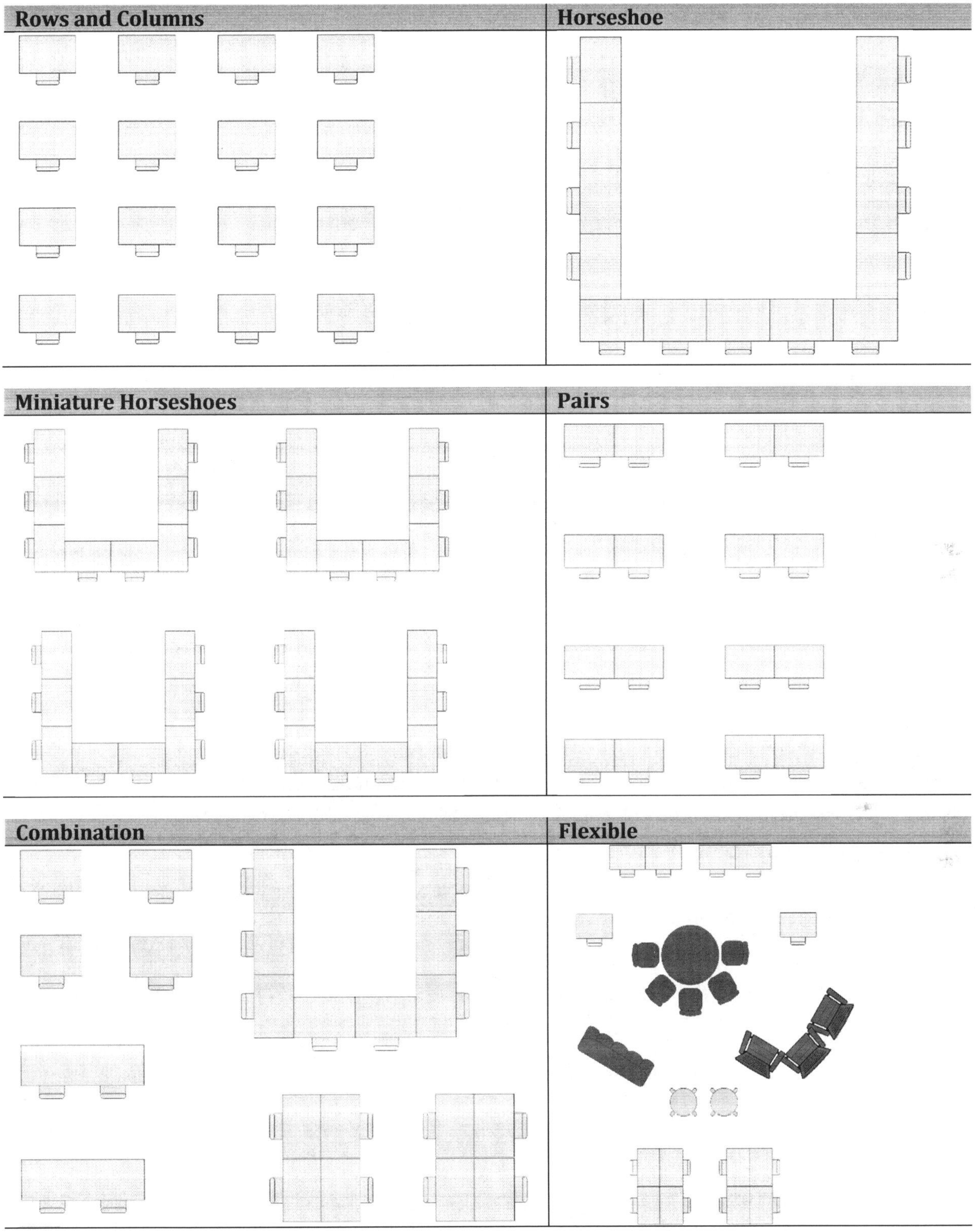
Rows and Columns
Horseshoe
Miniature Horseshoes
Pairs
Combination
Flexible

Runway	Conference
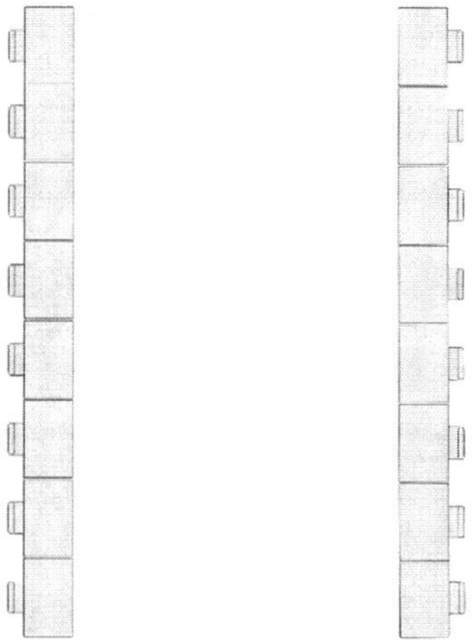	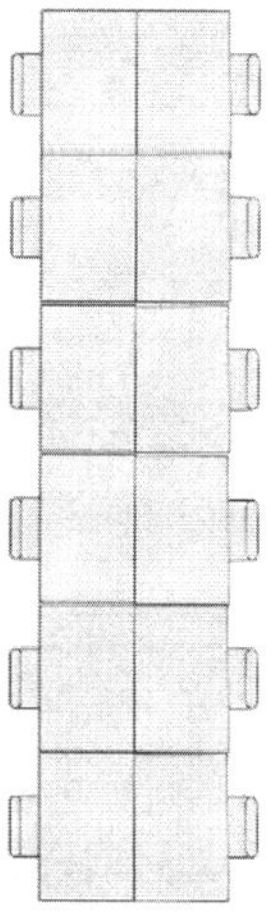

Classroom Organization Ensuring Accessibility and Facilitates Learning

Strategic classroom organization is necessary to ensure physical accessibility for all students and facilitating learning across instructional contexts. Students' **height, size**, and **special needs** must be considered and addressed when determining physical classroom arrangement. All furniture, equipment, and necessary materials must be equally accessible and facilitate ease of movement for all students as they participate in learning activities. Some students may require individualized **physical accommodations** to support their learning, such as preferential seating, special furniture arrangements to enable physical accessibility, or access to technology. By instilling these supports into the organization of the classroom, the teacher establishes an equitable environment that supports learning across instructional contexts. The classroom must be arranged to ensure all students have **visibility** and access to the teacher, as well as pertinent instructional information and resources, including the projector screen, chalk board, and computers. The physical environment must be aligned to and facilitative of the style of instruction taking place while supporting students' individual needs in achieving learning goals. When the teacher ensures that the classroom environment is physically accessible to all students, they empower students to engage in learning across instructional contexts successfully.

Literacy-Rich Environment

A **literacy-rich** classroom focuses on the development of all literacy components by immersing students in reading, writing, speaking, and listening skills across subject areas. While all students benefit from such an environment, it is especially important for **ELL students** and students with **developmental disabilities** in acquiring the literacy and language skills necessary for success. In a literacy-rich environment, the teacher provides multiple opportunities to engage in teacher-led and student-selected reading, writing, speaking, and listening activities in all areas of instruction. Students may be asked to solve word problems in math, write a report on a famous artist in art, or keep an observation log in science to encourage literacy development across content areas. Students are provided with multiple print and digital literacy materials on a variety of topics with varying levels of complexity to accommodate individual developmental levels while encouraging reading, vocabulary acquisition, and listening skills. Additionally, the teacher surrounds students with **print-rich** materials, including posters, word walls, labels, and bulletin boards on a variety of topics to further promote literacy development. A literacy-rich environment continuously promotes and emphasizes the importance of literacy skills in all areas of life that serve as a necessary foundation for academic and real-world success.

Review Video: Characteristics of Literacy-Rich, Content-Area Classrooms
Visit mometrix.com/academy and enter code: 571455

Safe, Nurturing, and Inclusive Classroom Environment

A safe, nurturing, and inclusive classroom environment focuses on meeting students' emotional needs for healthy development in this domain. The overall climate in such an environment is welcoming and emphasizes **respect**, **acceptance**, and **positive communication** among the teacher and students. The classroom is brightly decorated and reflective of students' diversities, interests, and achievements to promote a sense of security and inclusivity that motivates active participation in learning. Instructional activities are also reflective of students' differences, learning styles, and interests, with necessary supports instilled to accommodate individual learning needs. This establishes an **equitable environment** that ensures all students feel respected, nurtured, and supported both academically and emotionally. Such an environment is **structured** and orderly with clear expectations, procedures, and routines to foster a sense of security as students engage in learning. Collaboration and supportive interactions among students are encouraged to create a positive, productive classroom community in which students feel confident to express themselves and participate in learning. A classroom environment that is safe, nurturing, and inclusive develops students' sense of self-concept that contributes to positive communication, relationships, and attitudes necessary for emotional development.

Developing Students' Emotional Intelligence

Emotional intelligence refers to the ability to recognize and regulate one's own emotions as well as identify and empathetically respond to the emotions of others. Developing this skill through a variety of strategies is integral to successful development across other domains. By **modeling** such skills as empathy and active listening, the teacher can influence students' abilities to identify and properly respond to their own and other's emotions. Teaching **coping strategies**, including journaling, breathing, or counting techniques, promotes students' self-regulation to manage emotions when faced with a conflict or challenge. Teaching emotional intelligence can also be integrated throughout instruction, such as prompting students to describe the feelings of a character in a book, or discuss emotions evoked from a painting. Students with strong emotional intelligence are likely to develop positive interpersonal relationships for healthy social development. This contributes to improved cognitive development in that when students collaborate productively, they build upon one another's knowledge. Emotionally intelligent students are also likely to have positive attitudes toward learning, as they have the capacity to self-regulate when faced with obstacles and properly engage in instruction for enhanced cognitive development.

Meeting and Respecting Students' Emotional Needs, Individual Rights, and Dignity

Successful learning and **whole-child** development are reliant on the degree to which students' emotional needs, individual rights, and dignity are met and respected in the classroom. This establishes the tone of the overall classroom climate that determines students' sense of safety, nurturing, and inclusion when interacting with others and engaging in learning. By taking measures to prioritize students' emotional needs and create a respectful, accepting classroom community, the teacher establishes a positive learning atmosphere that promotes cognitive, social, and emotional growth for whole-child development. When students feel emotionally supported and respected in their identities, they develop a healthy sense of self-esteem that positively influences their attitude toward learning and motivation to participate. This ultimately impacts **cognitive development**, as students that actively and confidently engage in learning are more likely to be academically successful. These students are also more effectively able to develop important interpersonal communication skills necessary for healthy **social development**, as students that feel secure and accepted are more likely to be supportive of others. By meeting students' emotional needs and respecting their individual rights and dignities, the teacher effectively prepares students with the skills necessary for academic and real-world success.

Classroom Management, Routines, and Procedures

Classroom Routines and Procedures

Influence on Classroom Climate, Productivity, Student Behavior, and Learning

A well-managed classroom focused on productivity, positive behavior, and success in learning relies on the effectiveness and consistency of **routines** and **procedures** instilled for daily activities. By implementing these at the beginning of the school year and continuously reinforcing them throughout, the teacher establishes an orderly, efficient classroom that facilitates students' ability to productively engage in learning. Classroom management, and therefore, student behavior and productivity, is enhanced by structured routines and procedures, as students that are clear on expectations are more inclined to follow them. Such structure provides students with a sense of predictability and security in their environment that contributes to their willingness to participate in learning. Routines and procedures simplify daily tasks and allow for smooth transitions between activities. This minimizes opportunities for student distraction or disruption, thus promoting positive behavior, increasing instructional time, and enhancing students' ability to focus on learning in an orderly, productive classroom climate.

Review Video: Classroom Management - Rhythms of Teaching
Visit mometrix.com/academy and enter code: 809399

Considerations Regarding Age-Appropriateness to Ensure Effectiveness

Classroom procedures and routines must reflect the characteristics and capabilities of the students' **age group**. It is important that the teacher understand and apply their knowledge of students' **developmental levels** across domains when considering which routines and procedures to establish in their classroom. In doing so, the teacher ensures that expectations are age-appropriate, realistic, and effective in creating an orderly, productive environment. Procedures and routines must always be clear, succinct, and limited in number to avoid overwhelming students. However, in communicating them, the teacher must use comprehensible language relative to students' age-group. The nature of learning must be considered when determining age-appropriate routines and procedures. For young children, procedures for cleaning up toys after playtime is appropriate, whereas procedures for turning in homework and taking assessments applies to older students. The degree to which students are expected to perform routines and procedures independently must also be considered and reflective of their capabilities. Young children may need a great deal of assistance, whereas older students can perform certain tasks independently. Consequences for not following expectations must be appropriate to students' age group. Losing free play time may be appropriate for young children, whereas parent communication may be effective for older students.

Examples of Age-Appropriate Routines and Procedures

Young children: Young children can reasonably be expected to perform **basic daily routines** independently, although they likely will need frequent reminders. Daily procedures may include having young children hang up their coats, put away lunchboxes, and unpack their backpacks at the beginning of the day as they prepare to begin morning work. Similarly, young children can be expected to independently follow end-of-day procedures and routines, such as packing up their backpacks, cleaning up learning materials, and lining up at the door for dismissal. Young children should be able to follow simple behavioral procedures as well, such as keeping hands to themselves, responding to attention signals from the teacher, and cleaning up learning materials before transitioning between activities. Young children also benefit from being assigned classroom "jobs," such as line leader, paper collector, or teacher assistant, as these routines instill a sense of accountability and self-responsibility.

Middle-level: Middle-level students can be expected to follow a variety of routines and procedures with **increasing levels of independence**. These students can reasonably be expected to enter the classroom on time and prepared with necessary learning materials. In addition, middle-level students can be held responsible for independently turning in homework according to the procedures for doing so and beginning their morning work. Middle-level students should be able to follow procedures for accessing learning materials, transitioning to cooperative learning activities, cleaning up their own materials before moving to a new activity, and non-instructional tasks, such as sharpening pencils, using the restroom, or throwing away trash with minimal reminders from the teacher.

High school: Routines and procedures in the high school classroom should **reflect** students' level of **maturity and increasing capabilities for independence** as they approach adulthood. These students can reasonably be expected to independently come to class on time, prepared, and follow procedures for turning in homework and beginning morning work. In addition, high school students can be expected to follow procedures for direct instruction, cooperative learning activities, and independently transitioning between activities. High school students can be held to a greater degree of accountability regarding grading procedures, tardiness and attendance, and procedures for turning in late assignments.

Facilitating an Organized, Productive Environment that Maximizes Student Learning

Clear routines and procedures for daily classroom activities are necessary to create an organized, productive environment that maximizes student learning. In order to be effective, routines and procedures must be reflective of the teacher's **instructional** and **classroom management** style, explicitly stated, and consistently reinforced. This ensures expectations are relevant, realistic, and that students are continuously aware of them as they engage in learning. Procedures for entering and exiting the classroom, as well as how students will begin and end their day, establish a structured, **predictable** routine that enhances focus on instruction. Smooth **transition procedures** maintain order and enhance efficiency when moving between activities, as they eliminate idle time, minimize student distraction, and allow for increased time dedicated to productive teaching and learning. Such transition procedures include how and when to access and clean up materials, move from independent to collaborative group work, or move between learning stations. The teacher must also consider procedures for performing non-instructional activities, such as sharpening pencils or going to the restroom, as these further avoid disruptions to instructional time. Procedures and routines establish organization and efficiency in the classroom by simplifying tasks to allow for increased productive instructional time and enhanced student learning.

Procedures and routines are necessary for establishing a well-managed and productive classroom environment. While the specifics of routines may vary depending upon the teacher's classroom management style and students' learning needs, many common procedures and routines share similar guidelines.

- **Entering the classroom/morning routine:** A procedure for the beginning of class ensures that students enter the room in an orderly manner with a clear understanding of what is expected of them. This routine should include entering the room quietly, unpacking necessary items for class, turning in homework, and working on an opening activity while the teacher takes attendance.
- **Leaving the classroom/packing up routine:** A procedure for packing up and leaving the classroom at the end of class or the school day ensures that students have all of their necessary materials, leave the room clean and organized, and exit in an orderly manner. Such a routine may include cleaning up learning materials, putting away assignments or papers, straightening desks, throwing away trash, packing up backpacks, and lining up by the door prior to dismissal. Students may be assigned specific jobs for cleaning up and organizing the room.
- **Turning in work:** Procedures for turning in classwork and homework allow for smoother transitions between activities and limit interruptions to instruction. This should occur at a specific time during the class period and can include designating a "turn in" box in the classroom for students to hand in assignments, or having students pass their papers to the front in a specific order. A student may be designated to collect papers at the end of an activity as well.

- **Using the restroom:** Restroom procedures limit student distraction and interruptions to instruction. Restroom breaks should generally not occur during direct instruction, and students should be permitted to go one at a time to avoid misbehavior. Students should be given a restroom pass, sign out before leaving the room, and sign back in upon returning to ensure that the teacher is always aware of students' whereabouts. Specific hand signals in which students can silently request permission to use the restroom are beneficial in further minimizing disruptions.
- **Transitions between activities:** Procedures for transitions allow for an orderly learning environment in that they indicate to students when and how to move between activities in the classroom. These procedures should include an attention signal and a clear explanation of the steps for transitioning, such as cleaning up materials from the previous activity, and a signal to indicate when students are permitted to move. Students should be expected to transition between activities quickly, quietly, and without disruption.
- **Non-instructional tasks:** Procedures for non-instructional tasks limit interruptions to instructional time for more focused learning. Activities such as getting a tissue, sharpening pencils, and throwing away trash should occur during specific times when the teacher is not directly instructing and should be done quietly and without disruption.
- **Managing student behavior:** Clear procedures for misbehavior establish a predictable, orderly learning environment. These procedures should be explicit, consistent, and follow a logical sequence. They may include a verbal warning, seating change, loss of privileges, or communication with home.
- **Accessing and using materials, supplies, and technology:** Procedures for these activities are beneficial in limiting disruption, maintaining organization, and avoiding interruptions to instruction. Such procedures indicate when and how to access and use materials, supplies, and technology in a respectful and orderly manner. The teacher should clearly communicate expectations for access and use, as well as utilize a specific signal to indicate when students are permitted to move. These procedures should also include methods for proper cleanup at the end of the activity.
- **Finishing work early:** A procedure for finishing work early minimizes idle time and limits student disruption. Students that finish early may be permitted to work on other assignments or read quietly, or the teacher can dedicate an area of the room for extra practice and review activities for students to work on if they finish early. The teacher may also permit early finishers to assist other students in applicable learning situations.
- **Emergency drills:** Procedures for emergency drills ensure that students know how to complete them in a safe, orderly manner. When the drill begins, students should immediately stop what they are doing, leave all materials on their desks, and line up by the door in an organized fashion. Students should exit the room with the teacher and move quickly and quietly through the hallways to the designated drill location. For emergency drills that occur inside the classroom, students should move quickly and quietly to a previously designated location within the room and remain there until the drill is over.
- **Attention signal:** A dedicated signal to capture students' attention indicates that they need to stop what they are doing, focus, and listen quietly to the teacher for further information or instructions. This signal could be in the form of a hand signal, call and response, phrase, or sound and should be used consistently.
- **Direct instruction:** A procedure for direct instruction is beneficial in maintaining students' focus on learning. This should include steps for active listening, including sitting up straight, facing the teacher, maintaining eye contact, and refraining from distracting neighboring classmates. Students should have clear steps regarding how to ask questions, such as raising their hand or utilizing color-coded cards to indicate levels of understanding, and how to take notes, when applicable.
- **Independent work:** An independent work procedure limits distractions and promotes students' ability to focus. This should include communicating expectations for quiet time during this period, including refraining from talking to neighboring peers, working at and remaining in assigned seats, and engaging in the proper procedure if a student finishes early. If a student needs assistance, he or she can indicate it by raising a hand, or utilizing a dedicated signal to request help, such as color-coded cards.

- **Collaborative work:** A procedure for collaborative work indicates to students how to move from independent to group activities. This includes moving to a group setting without disruption, maintaining a normal volume, communicating respectfully, and cleaning up materials when finished before moving back to assigned seats in an orderly manner.

Developmental Characteristics of Young Children in Relation to Interactions with Others

Designing group activities that align with young children's ability to collaborate while supporting social development requires a realistic understanding of their capacity to do so. This entails understanding the **developmental characteristics** of young children at varying stages, including how the nature of their interactions with others evolves. Young children learn by exploring and interacting with their environment, so they need ample opportunities for play and active movement to do so. However, the teacher must recognize that the way young children play and collaborate develops over time. Young children typically exhibit little interest in actively playing with others until approximately age four. Until then, they progress through stages of solitary play, observing their peers, playing independently alongside others, and eventually, loosely interacting, perhaps with the same toys, while still primarily engaging in independent play. During these stages, it is important that the teacher foster **collaboration** by providing multiple opportunities for play as well as learning materials that encourage **cooperation** and **sharing**. The teacher must, however, maintain the understanding that these children have yet to develop the capacity to intentionally work with others. Once this ability is developed, the teacher can integrate coordinated group activities that encourage collaboration toward a common goal.

Considerations When Designing Group Activities for Young Children

For young children, thoughtfully designed group activities are integral in promoting development across domains. These opportunities facilitate social and emotional development by encouraging collaboration and positive communication, as well as physical and cognitive growth as children play, explore, and interact with others in the learning environment. It is therefore important that the teacher carefully consider the particulars of group activities when planning to ensure maximized learning and development. The teacher must consider the **developmental characteristics** of their students' age group, including their capacity to collaborate with others. This enables the teacher to plan group activities that align with students' abilities while promoting collaboration and development. All **learning materials** must be carefully selected to encourage collaboration, sharing, and the development of positive social skills at a developmentally appropriate level. The teacher must also consider **desired learning outcomes** and the nature of the learning taking place to determine whether group activities should be structured or unstructured. Unstructured play is valuable in allowing students to develop their social and emotional skills in a natural setting, whereas structured, teacher-led group activities allow for more focused learning. Desired outcomes also determine the size of groups for the activity to best promote collaboration and learning.

Group Activities that Reflect and Develop Young Children's Ability to Collaborate

Young children benefit from a variety of **whole-class** and **small-group** activities designed to reflect and develop their collaborative skills. When the teacher incorporates group activities to encourage cooperation, sharing, and positive interactions, young children gain important social and emotional skills necessary for development across domains. Whole-group activities such as **circle time** provide young children with the opportunity to interact with others, express ideas, and ask questions in a developmentally appropriate setting. This activity develops important collaborative skills, such as taking turns, active listening, and respectful communication. Other **whole-group activities**, such as reading aloud, group songs, dances, games, or class nature walks, are effective in teaching young children how to productively contribute to and function in a group setting. **Small-group activities** can be incorporated throughout all aspects of structured and unstructured learning to develop young children's collaborative skills. Learning centers, such as a science area, pretend play area, or building block center, provide materials that encourage collaboration while allowing students to interact with others according to their abilities in a student-led setting. Problem-solving activities, such as puzzles, games, age-appropriate science experiments, or scavenger hunts, are effective in teaching young children how to work together toward a common goal.

Organizing and Managing Group Activities to Promote Collaborative Skills and Individual Accountability

Well-planned group activities are beneficial in developing students' collaborative skills and sense of individual accountability. Such group activities are well-organized, effectively managed, and intentionally structured with a **clear goal** or problem that must be solved while allowing room for creativity to enhance the collaborative process. When designing these activities, the teacher must incorporate enough **significant components** to ensure all students within the group can productively contribute. If the assignment is too simple, students can easily complete it on their own, whereas a multifaceted activity instills a sense of interdependence within the group that fosters the development of collaborative skills. To promote individual accountability, **meaningful roles** and responsibilities should be assigned to each group member because when students feel others are relying on their contributions to complete a task, they develop a sense of ownership that motivates active participation. To further develop collaborative skills and individual accountability, students should be graded both as a **whole-group** and **individually**. This encourages group cooperation while ensuring that students' individual contributions are recognized. Including **self-assessments** at the end of group activities is beneficial in allowing students to reflect on the quality of their contributions to the group and ways they could improve their collaborative skills.

Thoughtful consideration of how to best organize and manage collaborative activities helps establish an environment that supports students in learning to work together productively and assume responsible roles within a group. When planning group activities, the teacher must consider the **desired learning outcomes** and the **nature of the task** to determine whether there are enough significant components that would benefit from collaboration. **Group size** must also be considered to most effectively foster collaboration and individual accountability when assuming responsible roles. Groups with too few students may be inadequate for addressing all the components of a complex task, whereas grouping too many students together limits productive collaboration and makes it difficult for each member to assume a significant, responsible role. The teacher must be selective regarding which students are grouped together to best facilitate productive collaboration. This includes determining which students will work well together, as well as grouping students that may need support with others that can provide scaffolding. It is also important to consider how **responsibilities** will be divided to ensure each member is given a significant role that allows them to contribute productively to the group, as well how their contributions will be monitored and **assessed**.

Ideal Schedule for Young Children

An ideal schedule for young children reflects their developmental characteristics and capabilities to maximize their learning. A **predictable** routine is necessary for young children to feel secure in their learning environment, and therefore, each day should follow a similar schedule while allowing room for **flexibility** if an activity takes longer than expected. Each day should begin with a clear routine, such as unpacking, a "warm-up" activity, and a class meeting to allow students to share thoughts, ask questions, and allow the teacher to discuss what will occur that day. This establishes a positive tone for the day while focusing the attention on learning. Similarly, the end of the day should have a specific routine, such as cleaning up materials and packing up for dismissal. Young children learn best by physically interacting with and exploring their environment. As such, each day should include large blocks of time for **active movement** throughout the day in the form of play, projects, and learning centers. Periods of **rest** must follow such activities, as this enables young children to process and internalize what they learned. **Direct instruction** should occur before active movement periods and last approximately 15-20 minutes to sustain engagement and attention on learning.

Example Daily Schedule for the Early Childhood Education Classroom	
8:00-8:30	Welcome, unpack, morning work
8:30-8:45	Circle time, review class calendar

8:45-9:30	Literacy/Language Arts
9:30-10:15	Learning Stations
10:15-11:00	Math
11:00-11:30	Music/Dance/Movement
11:30-12:15	Lunch
12:15-1:00	Recess/Unstructured play
1:00-1:20	Rest/Quiet time
1:20-2:00	Science
2:00-2:45	Creative Arts
2:45-3:15	Daily reflection, pack up, dismissal

Some examples of restful and active movement activities for young children are discussed below:

- **Restful:** Incorporating restful activities into the early childhood classroom are beneficial in helping young children process and retain new concepts and providing them the opportunity to unwind after active movement activities. Examples of such activities include nap time, class meditation, self-reflection activities, independent art projects, or self-selected reading time. Teachers can also read aloud to students or play an audiobook during these periods.
- **Active:** Providing young children with multiple opportunities for active movement throughout the day is beneficial in promoting the development of gross motor skills, connections to learning, and the ability to function in a group setting. Active movement opportunities should include whole-class, small group, and independent activities. Examples include class dances, songs, or games, nature walks, or total participation activities such as gallery walks or four corners. Physical education activities, such as jump rope, tag, sports, or using playground equipment are also beneficial. Young children should also be provided with ample time for both structured and unstructured play throughout the day.

Balancing Restful and Active Movement Activities

A schedule that balances **rest** and **active movement** is necessary for positive cognitive, physical, emotional, and social development in young children. Connecting learning to active movement strengthens students' understanding of new concepts, as it allows them to physically explore and interact with their environment, experiment with new ideas, and gain new experiences for healthy **cognitive development**. In addition, incorporating active movement encourages the use of **gross motor skills** and provides students with the space to physically express themselves in an appropriate setting, thus promoting physical and emotional development. Active movement also encourages the development of positive **interpersonal skills** as young children interact and explore with one another. Restful periods are equally as important to young children's development. Incorporating rest after a period of active movement further strengthens young children's connection to learning by providing them the opportunity to reflect, process, and internalize new information.

Providing Large Blocks of Time for Play, Projects, and Learning Centers

Providing young children with ample time for play, projects, and learning centers throughout the school day is integral to fostering their development across domains. Young children learn most effectively through active movement as they physically interact with their environment, and incorporating large blocks of time for such activities allows them to do so. Significant time dedicated to active play, projects, and learning centers on a variety of topics allows young children to explore and experiment with the world around them, test new ideas, draw conclusions, and acquire new knowledge. This supports healthy **physical** and **cognitive development**, as it provides young children the opportunity to engage in learning across subject areas while connecting it to active movement for strengthened understanding. In addition, allowing large blocks of time for these activities is necessary for **social** and **emotional development**, as it provides young children the space to interact with one another and develop important skills such as cooperation, sharing, conflict resolution, and emotional self-regulation. Dedicating large blocks of time to play, projects, and learning centers establishes a student-led, hands-on learning environment that is reflective of the developmental characteristics and needs of young children.

Noninstructional Duties and Instructional Activities Maximizing Efficiency

Many non-instructional duties, such as taking attendance, grading papers, and facilitating communication, can be coordinated with instructional activities when effective **routines** and **procedures** are instilled to accomplish them. This enhances overall efficiency in the classroom, as time is not lost on completing administrative tasks, allowing more dedicated time to instruction for maximized student learning. Taking attendance, for example, can be incorporated into students' morning work routine, as they can mark their own presence as part of the procedure for entering the classroom and beginning the day. Grading and communication with colleagues or families can take place during independent work, assessments, or recreational time. The teacher can also observe, monitor, and assess students' progress as they engage in learning. Student **self-correction** in lieu of formal grading can be beneficial in allowing students to reflect on their performance, seek areas for improvement, and strengthen their understanding, while integrating grading as an instructional activity. In addition, a variety of **digital resources** are available that allow for immediate student feedback and communication with families throughout instruction. In utilizing such resources, the teacher can efficiently coordinate administrative duties with instructional activities to maximize time for student learning.

Effective Time Management

Practicing effective time management is beneficial in establishing an efficient, orderly classroom environment focused on productivity and maximizing student learning. By instilling specific **procedures** for managing daily routines such as transitioning, accessing materials and supplies, and using technology, the teacher can ensure that these tasks are completed in a timely manner while minimizing time lost on non-instructional activities and student distraction. This allows more time to be focused on instruction and student learning. To achieve this, procedures for such tasks must be **explicit** and consistently reinforced. Prior to transitioning between activities, accessing materials, or using technology, the teacher must provide a clear, detailed explanation of each step of the procedure, as well as expectations for how students will complete it. Modeling the procedure is beneficial in providing a visual example to ensure student understanding. In order to be effective, each procedure must include a specific **signal** to indicate when students can begin, and the teacher must consistently monitor to ensure students are completing the task correctly. When students have a clear understanding on how to accomplish daily activities, they can do so quickly, effectively, and without disruption. This increases overall efficiency in the classroom and maximizes time dedicated to student learning.

Using Technology to Perform Administrative Tasks

Technology resources are widely available to assist teachers in accomplishing a variety of administrative tasks, and therefore, are highly beneficial in establishing a **well-managed**, **organized**, and **productive** learning environment. Completing such tasks as taking attendance, maintaining gradebooks, or facilitating communication through technology allows the teacher to do so more **efficiently**. This allows for more time dedicated to productive teaching and learning, as well as smoother transitions between activities, as time is not lost on completing such duties. Increased efficiency in completing administrative duties is beneficial in sustaining students' attention, engagement, and productivity in learning, as it minimizes idle time that could lead to distraction or disruption. In addition, utilizing technology to perform administrative duties enhances overall organization, as all tasks performed digitally can be stored in a single area on the device used for easy access and recall of information. Through email, digital apps, or class websites, the teacher can efficiently communicate with colleagues and students' families to update them regarding important events, assignments, and individual progress. This creates a sense of connectedness between the teacher and community that contributes to a positive, productive classroom climate.

Volunteers and Paraprofessionals

Enhancing and Enriching Instruction

Paraprofessionals and **volunteers** are highly valuable in enhancing and enriching the overall learning experience, as their efforts contribute to an organized, positive, and productive classroom environment. These aides collaborate with the teacher throughout planning and instruction to implement best practices in meeting students' learning needs. Paraprofessionals and volunteers can lead small groups of students as they engage in instruction for a more focused, **student-centered** learning experience. They can also provide additional support to struggling students while the teacher engages in whole-class instruction. Specifically, paraprofessionals are typically licensed in the educational field and are qualified to provide **individual accommodations** to students with individual learning needs to create an inclusive learning environment. In addition, working with paraprofessionals and volunteers is beneficial in creating an efficient, organized classroom that enhances student learning, as they can assist with **non-instructional duties** that allow for smooth transitions during instruction, such as preparing learning materials, handing back papers, or grading assignments. **Classroom management** is also enhanced when paraprofessionals and volunteers are present, as they can assist in reinforcing expectations and monitoring behavior to ensure all students are positively and productively engaging in learning.

Monitoring Their Performance in the Classroom

Paraprofessionals and volunteers are invaluable resources for creating a positive, productive classroom environment. However, to ensure the contributions of these aides are consistently beneficial in meeting students' needs and maximizing learning, it is important to continuously monitor their performance in the classroom. Paraprofessionals and volunteers are typically interviewed by administration prior to entering the classroom to determine whether their qualifications are aligned with meeting students' needs to enhance instruction. The administration is also often responsible for monitoring their performance throughout the school year. Specifically, paraprofessionals are licensed in the field of education, and therefore, are often formally evaluated against specific **performance measurement tools**. **Observations** by administration can either be scheduled or conducted as an informal "walk-through" to assess how the paraprofessional or volunteer interacts with the teacher and students and their effectiveness in contributing to a productive learning environment. The teacher can also monitor the performance of volunteers and paraprofessionals in their classroom. By analyzing **students' progress** when working with these aides and eliciting **feedback** from students, the teacher can determine their effectiveness in enhancing the learning experience. Frequently communicating with paraprofessionals and volunteers provides valuable insight regarding whether they contribute to a positive classroom climate focused on student learning.

Instructional Techniques

Implementing Multiple Instructional Techniques to Maximize Student Learning

Incorporating multiple instructional techniques into the classroom maximizes student learning by enhancing intellectual involvement and overall engagement. When instructional material is presented through a variety of means, it facilitates an **active learning** environment in which students' interest is captured and they are motivated to participate in learning. Varying teaching strategies stimulates engagement and fosters achievement by encouraging students to actively participate in their own learning and implement critical thinking skills to consider information more deeply. Students' understanding is strengthened when content is presented in different ways through various instructional techniques by providing them with multiple frames of reference for making connections and internalizing new concepts. In addition, utilizing multiple instructional techniques allows the teacher to effectively **differentiate instruction** to access multiple learning styles and address individual student needs to ensure understanding and enhance the overall learning process.

Instructional Strategies to Differentiate Instruction

Implementing a variety of strategies for differentiation helps to ensure that instruction appeals to students' varying learning styles and needs. By incorporating **multiple modalities** into direct instruction, such as visual representations, written directions, video or audio clips, songs, graphs, or mnemonic devices, teachers can differentiate the presentation of new concepts and information. Using strategies to differentiate instructional activities is also beneficial in diversifying the learning experience. By providing opportunities for **independent, collaborative**, and **hands-on** learning, teachers can ensure that learning is accessible and engaging to all students. In addition, learning activities should allow for a degree of flexibility in order to appeal to students' varying needs and preferences. Activities such as task cards, educational technology resources, and learning stations provide this **flexibility** and allow for a student-directed experience in which they can choose to learn in the way that best suits their needs. Similarly, assigning open-ended projects as summative assessments allows for a degree of **student-choice**, thus differentiating the method in which students demonstrate their understanding.

Varying the Teacher and Student Roles in the Instructional Process

Varying the roles of the teacher and students as an instructional technique is beneficial in creating an engaging, dynamic classroom environment that maximizes learning. When different roles are implemented, instruction is diversified, thus stimulating student interest and engagement. In addition, certain teacher and student roles are most applicable and effective in specific learning situations. When teachers acknowledge this and understand when to adopt and assign particular roles, they can effectively deliver instruction in a way that deepens student understanding and fosters success in learning. In presenting new content, directions, or modeling new skills for example, the roles of **lecturer** and student **observer** are effective. In hands-on learning situations, students can take on the role of **active participant** while the teacher acts as a **facilitator** to create a student-centered and engaging learning environment in which students are given ownership over their own learning. Such variation enhances intellectual involvement by promoting critical thinking and problem-solving skills through self-directed learning. Skillfully assigning different roles throughout the learning process also allows the teacher to effectively address students' individual learning needs and preferences to promote engagement and enhance the learning experience.

Fostering Intellectual Involvement and Engagement

Effective instruction includes a variety of strategies for fostering intellectual involvement and engagement to promote academic success. Presenting instruction using various approaches provides multiple avenues for learning new content, thus ensuring and strengthening student understanding to facilitate achievement. In addition, diversifying instructional strategies creates variety in the classroom that effectively stimulates students' interest and motivation to engage in learning. Such strategies as **cooperative learning, discussion**, and **self-directed opportunities** encourage active student participation that enhances intellectual involvement by allowing students to build on background knowledge, deepen understanding by exploring others' perspectives, and take ownership over their own learning. This ultimately increases student engagement and motivation for success in learning. Similarly, incorporating **inquiry**, **problem-solving**, and **project-based** strategies promote curiosity in learning, creativity, and the development of critical thinking skills that stimulate intellectual participation and engagement to create a productive learning environment. Implementing **digital resources** and media throughout instruction is integral in enhancing academic success by making learning relevant, interesting, and differentiated to accommodate various learning needs. At the end of a lesson or activity, allowing students the opportunity to reflect is a valuable strategy in increasing intellectual involvement, retainment, and academic success by facilitating personal connections with learning to build understanding.

Actively Engaging Students by Incorporating Discussion into Instruction

Classroom discussion is a valuable instructional technique in engaging students throughout the learning process. When the teacher skillfully poses higher-level questions in discussions, they establish an active learning environment in which students are encouraged and motivated to participate, thus enhancing overall engagement. Effective discussions prompt students to become **intellectually invested** in instruction by promoting the use of **critical** and **higher-order thinking** skills to consider information more deeply and devise creative solutions to problems. In addition, discussions stimulate engagement by providing students the opportunity to express their own thoughts and reasoning regarding a given topic to establish a sense of ownership over their learning. Furthermore, discussions foster a collaborative learning environment that actively engages students by prompting them to understand others' perspectives, consider alternative approaches, and build on one another's experiences to make deeper connections to learning.

Promoting Student Inquiry

The promotion of inquiry is a valuable instructional technique in enhancing student engagement and intellectual involvement. In an **inquiry-based** learning environment, students are encouraged to explore instructional material and devise their own conclusions or solutions to problems. This increases the effectiveness of the learning process by providing students with a sense of agency over their own learning. In addition, implementing this strategy fosters curiosity, self-motivation, and active participation, as it allows for hands-on, **student-led** learning that increases overall engagement. Incorporating inquiry into the classroom stimulates critical and higher-order thinking skills as students construct their own understanding by interacting with learning materials, analyzing their findings, and synthesizing their learning to create new conclusions, results, and responses. To effectively incorporate inquiry int the learning process, the teacher must provide several opportunities for self-directed and project-based learning, as well as student choice, to stimulate curiosity. Questions must be open-ended, and students must be encouraged to hypothesize, predict, and experiment in their learning. The teacher must be flexible in instruction to allow space and opportunity for exploration and allow time for reflection and extended learning opportunities to facilitate further inquiry.

Incorporating Problem-Solving into Instruction

Providing opportunities for creative problem solving within instruction effectively creates an engaging and successful learning experience. Students become more **intellectually involved** when encouraged to actively participate in learning and utilize **critical thinking skills** to test hypotheses, analyze results, and devise creative solutions to problems. This hands-on, **student-directed** approach promotes success in learning by allowing students to interact with learning materials as they seek answers to complex ideas and problems in an engaging environment. Problem-solving enables students to make deeper connections to their learning to enhance understanding, as this strategy prompts them to employ and develop background knowledge. In addition, problem-solving activities allow for collaborative learning in which students can actively engage with peers to build on one another's knowledge and experience, thus enhancing successful learning.

Relationship Between Intellectual Involvement, Active Student Engagement, and Success in Learning

A productive learning environment is comprised of intellectually involved students that are actively engaged in successful learning. A strong correlation exists between **intellectual involvement, active student**

engagement, and **success in learning**, and each component is necessary for effective instruction. Effective instruction consists of challenging students based on their abilities and teaching them to think deeply about new ideas and concepts. This ultimately encourages students' intellectual involvement, as it prompts them to utilize their critical thinking skills to build on their background knowledge, consider alternative perspectives, and synthesize their learning to devise creative solutions. When students are intellectually involved in instruction, they become more personally invested and engaged, as learning becomes relevant, interesting, and challenging. Engaged students are active participants in their learning, thus enhancing their overall productivity and academic success.

Effectively Structuring Lessons

When developing instruction, it is imperative that the teacher is knowledgeable on how to effectively structure lessons to maximize student engagement and success. Each lesson must include a clear **objective** and explicitly state the process for achieving it. To initiate engagement, effective lessons begin with an **opening**, or "warm-up," activity to introduce a new topic, diagnose student understanding, and activate prior knowledge. Instruction of new material must be delivered through a variety of teaching strategies that are consciously tailored to students' individual learning needs to enhance participation and ensure comprehension. Direct instruction should be followed by **active learning** activities with clear directions and procedures to allow students to practice new concepts and skills. Throughout a successful lesson, the teacher checks frequently for understanding and comprehension by conducting a variety of **formative assessments** and adjusts instruction as necessary. Including **closure** activities is essential to successful learning, as it gives students the opportunity to reflect, process information, make connections, and demonstrate comprehension. In structuring lessons effectively according to students' learning needs, the teacher establishes a focused and engaging learning environment that promotes academic success.

Example of a Daily Lesson Plan Structure

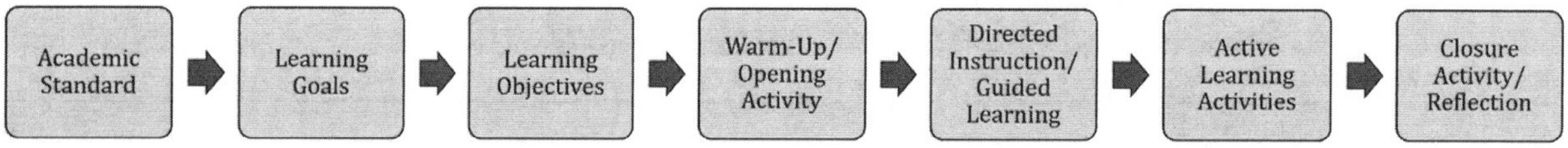

Flexible Instructional Groupings

Flexible instructional groupings provide the teacher and students with a versatile, engaging environment for successful learning. Skillfully grouping students allows for productive, cooperative learning opportunities in which individual strengths are enhanced and necessary support is provided, thus enhancing motivation and engagement. When working in groups, students' understanding of instruction is strengthened, as they are able to learn and build upon one another's background knowledge, perspectives, and abilities. Instructional groups can include students of the **same** or **varied abilities** depending on the learning objective and task to increase productivity and provide scaffolding as necessary for support. This strategy is effective in enabling the teacher to **differentiate** instruction and adjust groups as needed to accommodate varying learning styles, abilities, and interests to maximize engagement and success in learning.

Effective Pacing of Lessons and Importance of Flexibility to Students' Needs

Effective pacing is imperative to focused and engaging instruction. The teacher must be conscientious of the pace of their instruction and ensure that it is reflective of their student's learning needs and sustains their attention. Instruction that is delivered too quickly results in confusion and discouragement, whereas if instruction is too slow, students will lose interest and become disengaged. A well-paced lesson states clear learning goals and objectives while clearly outlining the means to achieve them to elicit student motivation. The teacher must consider the most **efficient** and **engaging** instructional strategies for presenting new material to establish a steady pace and maintain it by incorporating smooth **transitions** from one activity to the next. It is important that the teacher is conscious of the rate of instruction throughout all stages of learning while maintaining **flexibility** in pacing in order to be responsive to their students. As individual students have different learning needs and processing times, they may require a faster or slower rate of instruction to understand new concepts and remain engaged in learning. Frequent checks for understanding and reflection activities are essential strategies in determining if the pace of instruction must be adjusted to accommodate students' needs.

Connecting Content to Students' Prior Knowledge and Experiences

When the teacher implements effective instructional strategies for connecting content to students' prior knowledge and experiences, it enhances the relevancy of learning and fosters deeper connections that strengthen understanding. To achieve this, the teacher must educate themselves on students' backgrounds, experiences, communities, and interests to determine what is important and interesting to them. With this knowledge in mind, the teacher can successfully locate and implement **authentic materials** into instruction to enhance relevancy. Additionally, encouraging students to bring materials to class that reflect their backgrounds and including these materials in instruction makes learning relevant by allowing students to make **personal connections** to content. Instructional strategies such as brainstorming, KWL charts, prereading, and anticipation guides allow the teacher to determine what students know prior to learning a new concept, thus enabling them to connect content to students' background knowledge in a relevant way. Incorporating digital resources further enhances relevancy in learning in that the teacher can locate videos or audio clips that relate to instruction and reflect students' background experiences and interests. Using digital resources to introduce a new concept is a valuable strategy in developing students' **schema** on a topic to build prior knowledge and make learning meaningful by fostering connections.

Making Learning Relevant and Meaningful

For learning to be relevant and meaningful, it is essential that the teacher present content in a way that connects with students' **prior knowledge** and experiences. When students are able to apply new ideas and information to what they already know through effective instructional techniques, it facilitates strong **personal connections** that make learning relevant and meaningful. In addition, personal connections and **relevancy** are strengthened when the teacher consciously incorporates materials to reflect students' individual backgrounds and experiences in instruction. Linking content to students' background experiences enables them to relate instruction to real-world situations, thus establishing a sense of purpose for learning by making it applicable to their lives. Intentionally connecting content with students' prior knowledge and experiences enhances the effectiveness of the instructional process and fosters positive attitudes toward learning.

Enhancing Student Engagement and Success in Learning

Engaging instruction employs a variety of instructional strategies and materials to create a relevant, meaningful, and successful learning experience. Effective content establishes a clear and applicable purpose for instruction that increases student participation in the learning process. Presenting relevant and meaningful content enhances understanding and engagement by enabling students to create real-world, **personal connections** to learning based upon their own backgrounds and experiences. In addition, when instruction is tailored to reflect students' unique interests and preferences, content becomes more appealing and students' willingness to learn is enhanced. When students can perceive content through their own frames of reference with instructional materials that reflect their unique differences, they are able to effectively internalize and relate information to their lives, thus increasing engagement. Engaged learning ultimately facilitates academic success in that when students are motivated to learn, they demonstrate positive attitudes toward learning and are more likely to actively participate.

Evaluating Activities and Materials to Meet Individual Characteristics and Learning Needs

The careful selection of instructional activities and materials is integral to accommodating students' varying characteristics and needs to foster success in learning. When evaluating the appropriateness of activities and materials, several considerations must be made. The teacher must consider whether activities and materials align with state and district **academic standards**, as well as their quality and effectiveness in supporting students' unique differences as they achieve learning goals and objectives. All materials and activities must be

developmentally appropriate across domains, yet adaptable to individual students' learning needs. In addition, they must be challenging, yet feasible for student achievement relative to students' grade level and abilities to promote engagement and the development of critical and **higher-order thinking** skills. The teacher must evaluate activities and materials for versatility to allow for student choice and differentiation in order to address varying characteristics and needs. The teacher must also ensure that activities and materials are accurate, **culturally sensitive**, and reflective of students' diversities to foster an inclusive learning environment that promotes engagement.

Instructional Resources and Technologies

The implementation of varied instructional resources and technologies is highly valuable in supporting student engagement and achievement. Effective use of resources and technologies requires the teacher to evaluate their appropriateness in addressing students' individual characteristics and learning needs for academic success. The teacher must be attuned to students' unique differences in order to seek high quality technologies and resources that address their students' needs to support and enhance the achievement of learning goals and objectives. Technologies and resources must be **accurate**, **comprehensible**, and easily **accessible** to students, as well as **relevant** to the curriculum and the development of particular skills. The teacher must also consider the grade-level and **developmental appropriateness** of technologies and resources, as well as their adaptability to allow for differentiation. Effective technologies and resources are interactive, engaging, and multifaceted to allow for varying levels of complexity based on students' abilities. This allows the teacher to provide appropriate challenges while diversifying instruction to appeal to varied characteristics and learning needs, thus fostering an engaging environment that supports success in learning for all students.

Adapting Activities and Materials to Meet Individual Characteristics and Needs

In effective instruction, activities and materials are adapted to accommodate students' individual characteristics and needs. The teacher must be attuned to students' unique differences and understand how to adjust activities and materials accordingly to facilitate academic success and growth. To achieve this, the teacher must incorporate a **variety** of activities and materials that appeal to all styles of learners. Activities and materials should provide **student choice** for engagement in learning and demonstration of understanding. By differentiating instruction, the teacher can effectively scaffold activities and materials to provide supports as necessary, as well as include extensions or alternate activities for enrichment. **Chunking** instruction, allowing extra time as necessary, and accompanying activities and materials with aids such as graphic organizers, visual representations, and anticipation guides further differentiates learning to accommodate students' learning characteristics and needs. Conducting **formative assessments** provides the teacher with valuable feedback regarding student understanding and engagement, thus allowing them to modify and adjust the complexity of activities and materials as necessary to adapt to varied characteristics and learning differences.

Instructional Resources and Technologies

When the teacher understands students' individual characteristics and needs, they can adapt instructional resources and technologies accordingly to maximize learning. To do so effectively, the teacher must incorporate a diverse array of **multifaceted** resources and technologies that support and enhance learning through a variety of methods. This ensures that varying learning needs are met, as students of all learning styles are provided with several avenues for building and strengthening understanding. Additionally, the teacher can adapt resources and technologies to accommodate individual students by **varying the complexity** to provide challenges, support, and opportunities for enrichment based on ability level. Supplementing technologies and resources with **scaffolds**, such as extra time, visual representations, or opportunities for collaborative learning, further enables the teacher to adapt to individual learning needs. When effectively implemented and adapted to students' characteristics and needs, instructional technologies and resources serve as valuable tools for differentiating curriculum to enhance the learning experience.

Significance of Evaluation of Instruction in Facilitating Success in Learning

Evaluating the appropriateness of instructional materials, activities, resources, and technologies is integral to establishing a successful learning environment. Doing so provides students with high-quality and inclusive instruction by ensuring **clarity**, **accuracy**, **relevancy**, and **reflection** of student diversities. By determining whether these components of instruction meet varying characteristics and learning needs, the teacher can deliver **student-centered** instruction, that is challenging based on individual ability, to promote development and academic success. This process also allows the teacher to effectively **differentiate** instruction to provide necessary personalized support for success in achieving learning targets, as well as create engaging learning opportunities tailored to students' unique differences and interests. Effectively determining the appropriateness of activities, materials, resources, and technologies in meeting students' learning needs ultimately maximizes academic achievement and fosters positive attitudes toward learning that establish a foundation for future success.

Continuous Monitoring of Instructional Effectiveness

Successful instruction must be flexible and adaptable to meet students' dynamic learning needs. To achieve this, teachers must continuously monitor the effectiveness of their instruction to determine if their teaching strategies, activities, and communication are effective. Frequent evaluation of instructional effectiveness is necessary to ensure that students understand **foundational concepts** before moving on to more advanced concepts. **Adaptations** to instruction, communication, or assessment may be necessary to ensure students are able to comprehend and retain concepts before moving on to more advanced topics. **Remediation** of missed concepts is often much more challenging and less successful than checking for comprehension within context and providing more detailed instruction. This ultimately fosters long-term achievement, as the teacher can identify and address student needs as they arise and prevent compounding issues. Continuous monitoring enables the teacher to ensure that learning opportunities are engaging, relevant, and challenging based on students' ability levels, as it provides immediate feedback on the effectiveness of instruction, which allows the teacher to make necessary changes. This ultimately enhances instruction by establishing a student-centered learning environment that is tailored to individual needs, interests, and abilities.

Pre-Instructional, Peri-Instructional, and Post-Instructional Strategies

Instructional effectiveness must be monitored on a whole-class and individual level throughout all stages of teaching. Prior to instruction, administering **pre-tests** provides the teacher with insight regarding whole-class and individual understanding. This enables them to select effective and appropriate instructional strategies that can be differentiated to meet individual needs. Pre-tests allow the teacher to identify and clarify misunderstandings before instruction to ensure effectiveness. During instruction, **observation** of students' participation in instruction during independent and group activities enables the teacher to evaluate overall and individual understanding and engagement. Frequent checks for understanding and **formative assessments** throughout instruction provide feedback on whole-group and individual learning, as the teacher can assess understanding and participation to adapt teaching strategies or individualize instruction. Leading student discussions allows the teacher to identify areas of misunderstanding among the class or individuals that may need reteaching through a different approach. Closure and reflection activities after instruction are valuable in monitoring effectiveness, as they indicate both whole-class and individual comprehension and retainment of new concepts. Likewise, incorporating **summative assessments** and analyzing the results provides the teacher with information regarding the overall effectiveness of their teaching process, as well as students' individual strengths and weaknesses to consider for future instruction.

Applying Feedback to Make Necessary Changes to Instruction

Continuous monitoring of instruction indicates the instruction's effectiveness on a **whole-class** and **individual** level, as it provides the teacher with immediate insight on student understanding, progress, and areas for improvement. Monitoring instructional effectiveness enables the teacher to evaluate students' **pace** in achieving learning goals and adjust the rate of instruction as necessary. Additionally, it allows the teacher to identify whole-class and individual **misconceptions** that require correction to ensure students do not fall behind schedule in meeting academic benchmarks. If monitoring reveals misunderstanding among the whole class, the teacher must alter their overall instructional approach and teaching strategies to clarify and regain understanding. Individual misconceptions indicate the need to differentiate instruction, adjust groupings, and provide supports and remediation as necessary to ensure the student progresses at the same rate as the rest of the class. By identifying student strengths and weaknesses through consistent monitoring of instructional effectiveness, the teacher can effectively make instructional decisions that are attuned to whole-class and individual student needs to maximize learning.

Assessment Methodology

Assessment Methods

Effective teaching requires multiple methods of assessment to evaluate student comprehension and instructional effectiveness. Assessments are typically categorized as diagnostic, formative, summative, and benchmark, and are applicable at varying stages of instruction. **Diagnostic** assessments are administered before instruction and indicate students' prior knowledge and areas of misunderstanding to determine the path of instruction. **Formative** assessments occur continuously to measure student engagement, comprehension, and instructional effectiveness. These assessments indicate instructional strategies that require adjustment to meet students' needs in facilitating successful learning, and include such strategies as checking for understanding, observations, total participation activities, and exit tickets. **Summative** assessments are given at the end of a lesson or unit to evaluate student progress in reaching learning targets and identify areas of misconception for reteaching. Such assessments can be given in the form of exams and quizzes, or project-based activities in which students demonstrate their learning through hands-on, personalized methods. Additionally, portfolios serve as valuable summative assessments in allowing students to demonstrate their progress over time and provide insight regarding individual achievement. **Benchmark** assessments occur less frequently and encompass large portions of curriculum. These assessments are intended to evaluate the progress of groups of students in achieving state and district academic standards.

Assessment Types

- **Diagnostic:** These assessments can either be formal or informal and are intended to provide teachers with information regarding students' level of understanding prior to beginning a unit of instruction. Examples include pretests, KWL charts, anticipation guides, and brainstorming activities. Digital resources, such as online polls, surveys, and quizzes are also valuable resources for gathering diagnostic feedback.
- **Formative:** These assessments occur throughout instruction to provide the teacher with feedback regarding student understanding. Examples include warm-up and closure activities, checking frequently for understanding, student reflection activities, and providing students with color-coded cards to indicate their level of understanding. Short quizzes and total participation activities, such as four corners, are also valuable formative assessments. Numerous digital resources, including polls, surveys, and review games, are also beneficial in providing teachers with formative feedback to indicate instructional effectiveness.
- **Summative:** Summative assessments are intended to indicate students' level of mastery and progress toward reaching academic learning standards. These assessments may take the form of written or digital exams and include multiple choice, short answer, or long answer questions. Examples also include projects, final essays, presentations, or portfolios to demonstrate student progress over time.
- **Benchmark:** Benchmark assessments measure students' progress in achieving academic standards. These assessments are typically standardized to ensure uniformity, objectivity, and accuracy. Benchmark assessments are typically given as a written multiple choice or short answer exam, or as a digital exam in which students answer questions on the computer.

Review Video: Formative and Summative Assessments
Visit mometrix.com/academy and enter code: 804991

Determining Appropriate Assessment Strategies

As varying assessment methods provide different information regarding student performance and achievement, the teacher must consider the most applicable and effective assessment strategy in each stage of instruction. This includes determining the **desired outcomes** of assessment, as well as the information the teacher intends to ascertain and how they will apply the results to further instruction. **Age** and **grade level** appropriateness must be considered when selecting which assessment strategies will enable students to successfully demonstrate their learning. Additionally, the teacher must be cognizant of students' individual differences and learning needs to determine which assessment model is most **accommodating** and reflective of their progress. It is also important that the teacher consider the practicality of assessment strategies, as well as methods they will use to implement the assessment for maximized feedback regarding individual and whole-class progress in achieving learning goals.

TECHNOLOGY-BASED ASSESSMENTS

Technology-based assessments provide teachers with multiple resources for evaluating student progress to guide instruction. They are applicable in most formal and informal instructional settings and can be utilized for formative and summative assessments. Technology-based assessments simplify and enhance the efficiency of determining comprehension and instructional effectiveness, as they quickly present the teacher with information regarding student progress. This data enables the teacher to make necessary adjustments to facilitate student learning and growth. Implementing this assessment format simplifies the process of aligning them to school and district academic standards. This establishes objectivity and uniformity for comparing results and progress among students, as well as ensures that all students are held to the same academic expectations. While technology-based assessments are beneficial, there are some shortcomings to consider. This format may not be entirely effective for all learning styles in demonstrating understanding, as individualization in technology-based assessment can be limited. These assessments may not illustrate individual students' growth over time, but rather their mastery of an academic standard, thus hindering the ability to evaluate overall achievement. As technology-based evaluation limits hands-on opportunities, the real-world application and relevancy of the assessment may be unapparent to students.

ASSESSMENTS THAT REFLECT REAL-WORLD APPLICATIONS

Assessments that reflect **real-world applications** enhance relevancy and students' ability to establish personal connections to learning that deepen understanding. Implementing such assessments provides authenticity and enhances engagement by defining a clear and practical purpose for learning. These assessments often allow for hands-on opportunities for demonstrating learning and can be adjusted to accommodate students' varying learning styles and needs while measuring individual progress. However, assessments that focus on real-world applications can be subjective, thus making it difficult to extract concrete data and quantify student progress to guide future instructional decisions. In addition, teachers may have difficulty analyzing assessment results on a large scale and comparing student performance with other schools and districts, as individual assessments may vary.

FORMATIVE ASSESSMENT

Formative assessment refers to any evaluation of a student's knowledge while they are still in the process of learning the content. The general purpose of formative assessment is to provide both the teacher and the student with an idea of comprehension throughout a unit. This allows for the teacher to make adjustments to instruction to meet the needs of the student or whole class, and it may help the student recognize deficiencies in understanding that they can improve on. Formative assessments can be formal or informal, including classroom discussion, checks for comprehension, homework, quizzes, or portfolio assessments, as these all demonstrate the students' understanding during the course of the unit. Formative assessments can be focused on students as individuals or on the whole-class, as both help to shape future instruction. In addition, **total participation activities** such as response cards, surveys, games, or digital response activities enable the entire class to indicate their level of engagement and understanding. Formative assessment allows for more successful teaching and learning, as it enables the teacher to make informed present and future educational decisions that meet the needs of all students.

SUMMATIVE ASSESSMENTS

Summative assessment refers to an evaluation at the end of a discrete unit of instruction, such as the end of a course, end of a unit, or end of a semester. Classic examples of summative assessments include end of course assessments, final exams, or even qualifying standardized tests such as the SAT or ACT. Most summative assessments are created to measure student mastery of particular **academic standards**. Whereas formative assessment generally informs current instruction, summative assessments are used to objectively demonstrate that each individual has achieved adequate mastery of the standards in question. If a student has not met the benchmark, they may need extra instruction or to repeat the course. These assessments usually take the form of **tests** or formal portfolios with rubrics and clearly defined goals. **Project-based** assessments are beneficial in evaluating achievement, as they incorporate several elements of instruction and highlight real-world applications of learning. This allows students to demonstrate understanding through a hands-on, individualized approach that reinforces connections to learning and increases retainment. **Portfolios** of student work over time serve as a valuable method for assessing individual progress toward reaching learning targets. Summative assessments provide insight regarding overall instructional effectiveness and are necessary for guiding future instruction in subsequent years but are not usually used to modify current instruction.

Diagnostic Tests

Diagnostic tests are integral to planning and delivering effective instruction. These tests are typically administered prior to beginning a unit or lesson and provide valuable feedback for guiding and planning instruction. Diagnostic tests provide **preliminary information** regarding students' level of understanding and prior knowledge. This serves as a baseline for instructional planning that connects and builds upon students' background knowledge and experiences to enhance success in learning. Diagnostic tests allow the teacher to identify and clarify areas of student misconception prior to engaging in instruction to ensure continued comprehension and avoid the need for remediation. They indicate areas of student strength and need, as well as individual instructional aids that may need to be incorporated into lessons to support student achievement. In addition, these tests enable the teacher to determine which instructional strategies, activities, groupings, and materials will be most valuable in maximizing engagement and learning. Diagnostic tests can be **formal** or **informal**, and include such formats as pre-tests, pre-reading activities, surveys, vocabulary inventories, and graphic organizers such as KWL charts to assess student understanding prior to engaging in learning. Diagnostic tests are generally not graded as there is little expectation that all students in a class possess the same baseline of proficiency at the start of a unit.

Benchmark Assessments

Benchmark assessments are intended to quantify, evaluate, and compare individual and groups of students' achievement of school-wide, district, and state **academic standards.** They are typically administered in specific intervals throughout the school year and encompass entire or large units of curriculum to determine student mastery and readiness for academic advancement. Benchmark assessments provide data that enable the teacher to determine students' progress toward reaching academic goals to guide current and continued instruction. This data can be utilized by the school and individual teachers to create learning goals and objectives aligned with academic standards, as well as plan instructional strategies, activities, and assessments to support students in achieving them. In addition, benchmark assessments provide feedback regarding understanding and the potential need for remediation to allow the teacher to instill necessary supports in future instruction that prepare students for success in achieving learning targets.

Alignment of Assessments with Instructional Goals and Objectives

To effectively monitor student progress, assessments must align with **instructional goals** and **objectives.** This allows the teacher to determine whether students are advancing at an appropriate pace to achieve state and district academic standards. When assessments are aligned with specific learning targets, the teacher ensures that students are learning relevant material to establish a foundation of knowledge necessary for growth and academic achievement. To achieve this, the teacher must determine which instructional goals and objectives their students must achieve and derive instruction, content, and activities from these specifications. Instruction must reflect and reinforce learning targets, and the teacher must select the most effective strategies for addressing students' needs as they work to achieve them. Assessments must be reflective of content instruction to ensure they are aligned with learning goals and objectives, as well as to enable the teacher to evaluate student progress in mastering them. The teacher must clearly communicate learning goals and objectives throughout all stages of instruction to provide students with clarity on expectations. This establishes a clear purpose and focus for learning that enhances relevancy and strengthens connections to support student achievement.

Clearly Communicating Assessment Criteria and Standards

Students must be clear on the purpose of learning throughout all stages of instruction to enhance understanding and facilitate success. When assessment **criteria** and **standards** are clearly communicated, the purpose of learning is established, and students are able to effectively connect instructional activities to learning goals and criteria for assessment. Communicating assessment criteria and standards provides students with clarity on tasks and learning goals they are expected to accomplish as they prepare themselves for assessment. This allows for more **focused instruction** and engagement in learning, as it enhances relevancy and student motivation. Utilizing appropriate forms of **rubrics** is an effective strategy in specifying assessment criteria and standards, as it informs students about learning goals they are working toward, the quality of work they are expected to achieve, and skills they must master to succeed on the assessment. Rubrics indicate to students exactly how they will be evaluated, thus supporting their understanding and focus as they engage in learning to promote academic success.

The following are varying styles of rubrics that can be used to communicate criteria and standards:

- **Analytic:** Analytic rubrics break down criteria for an assignment into several categories and provide an explanation of the varying levels of performance in each one. This style of rubric is beneficial for detailing the characteristics of quality work, as well as providing students with feedback regarding specific components of their performance. Analytic rubrics are most effective when used for summative assessments, such as long-term projects or essays.
- **Holistic:** Holistic rubrics evaluate the quality of the student's assignment as a whole, rather than scoring individual components. Students' score is determined based upon their performance across multiple performance indicators. This style of rubric is beneficial for providing a comprehensive evaluation but limits the amount of feedback that students receive regarding their performance in specific areas.
- **Single-Point:** Single point rubrics outline criteria for assignments into several categories. Rather than providing a numeric score to each category, however, the teacher provides written feedback regarding the students' strengths and ways in which they can improve their performance. This style of rubric is beneficial in providing student-centered feedback that focuses on their overall progress.
- **Checklist:** Checklists typically outline a set of criteria that is scored using a binary approach based upon completion of each component. This style increases the efficiency of grading assignments and is often easy for students to comprehend but does not provide detailed feedback. This method of grading should generally be reserved for shorter assignments.

Communication of High Academic Expectations

Assessment Criteria And Standards

The attitudes and behaviors exhibited by the teacher are highly influential on students' attitudes toward learning. Teachers demonstrate belief in students' abilities to be successful in learning when they communicate **high academic expectations**. This promotes students' **self-concept** and establishes a **growth mindset** to create confident, empowered learners that are motivated to achieve. High expectations for assessments and reaching academic standards communicates to students the quality of work that is expected of them and encourages them to overcome obstacles as they engage in learning. When communicating expectations for student achievement, it is important that the teacher is aware of students' individual learning needs to provide the necessary support that establishes equitable opportunities for success in meeting assessment criteria and standards. Setting high expectations through assessment criteria and standards while supporting students in their learning enhances overall achievement and establishes a foundation for continuous academic success.

Effective Communication and Impact on Student Learning

Communicating high academic expectations enhances students' self-concept and increases personal motivation for success in learning. To maximize student achievement, it is important that the teacher set high academic expectations that are **clearly** communicated through **age-appropriate** terms and consistently reinforced. Expectations must be reflected through learning goals and objectives, and **visible** at all times to ensure student awareness. The teacher must be **specific** in communicating what they want students to accomplish and clearly detail necessary steps for achievement while assuming the role of facilitator to guide learning and provide support. Providing constructive **feedback** throughout instruction is integral in reminding students of academic expectations and ensuring they are making adequate progress toward reaching learning goals. When high academic expectations are communicated and reinforced, students are empowered with a sense of confidence and self-responsibility for their own learning that promotes their desire to learn. This ultimately enhances achievement and equips them with the tools necessary for future academic success.

Ensuring Assessments Are Congruent with Instructional Goals and Objectives

Assessments that are congruent to instructional goals and objectives provide a **clear purpose** for learning that enhances student understanding and motivation. When learning targets are reflected in assessments, instructional activities and materials become more **relevant**, as they are derived from these specifications. Such clarity in purpose allows for more focus and productivity as students engage in instruction and fosters connections that strengthen overall understanding for maximized success in learning. Aligning assessments with instructional goals and objectives ensures that students are learning material that is relevant to the curriculum and academic standards to ensure **preparedness** as they advance in their academic careers. In addition, it enables the teacher to evaluate and monitor student progress to determine whether they are progressing at an ideal pace for achieving academic standards. With this information, the teacher can effectively modify instruction as necessary to support students' needs in reaching desired learning outcomes.

Assessment Reliability

Assessment reliability refers to how well an assessment is constructed and is made up of a variety of measures. A test should perform similarly with different test administrators, graders, and test-takers and perform consistently over multiple iterations.

- **Test-retest reliability** refers to an assessment's consistency of results with the same test-taker over multiple retests. If one student shows inconsistent results over time, the test is not considered to have test-retest reliability.
- **Intertester reliability** refers to an assessment's consistency of results between multiple test-takers at the same level. Students at similar levels of proficiency should show similar results.
- **Interrater reliability** refers to an assessment's consistency of results between different administrators of the test. This plays an especially critical role in tests with interactive or subjective responses, such as Likert-scales, cloze tests, and short answer tests. Different raters of the same test need to have a consistent means of evaluating the test-takers' performance. Clear rubrics can help keep two or more raters consistent in scoring.
- **Intra-rater reliability** refers to an assessment's consistency of results with one rater over time. One test rater should be able to score different students objectively to rate subjective test formats fairly.
- **Parallel-forms reliability** refers to an assessment's consistency between multiple different forms. For instance, end-of-course assessments may have many distinctive test forms, with different questions or question orders. If the different forms of a test do not provide the same results, it is said to be lacking in parallel-forms reliability.
- **Internal consistency reliability** refers to the consistency of results of similar questions on a particular assessment. If there are two or more questions targeted at the same standard and at the same level, they should show the same results across each question.

Assessment Validity

Assessment validity is a measure of the relevancy that an assessment has to the skill or ability being evaluated, and the degree to which students' performance is representative of their mastery of the topic of assessment. In other words, how well does an assessment correlate to what it is looking to assess. Assessments should be evaluated for validity on both the individual question level and as a test overall. This can be especially helpful in refining tests for future classes. The overall validity of an assessment is determined by several types of validity measures.

- **Face validity** refers to the initial impression of whether an assessment seems to be fit for the task. As this method is subjective to interpretation and unquantifiable, it should not be used singularly as a measurement of validity.
- **Construct validity** asks if an assessment actually assesses what it is intended to assess. Some topics are more straightforward, such as assessing if a student can perform two-digit multiplication. This can be directly tested, which gives the assessment a strong content validity. Other measures, such as a person's overall happiness, must be measured indirectly. If an assessment asserted that a person is generally happy if they smile frequently, it would be fair to question the construct validity of that assessment because smiling is unlikely to be a consistent measure of all peoples' general happiness.
- **Content validity** indicates whether the assessment is comprehensive of all aspects of the content being assessed. If a test leaves out an important topic, then the teacher will not have a full picture as a result of the assessment.
- **Criterion validity** refers to whether the results of an assessment can be used to **predict** a related value, known as **criterion**. An example of this is the hypothesis that IQ tests would predict a person's success later in life, but many critics believe that IQ tests are not valid predictors of success because intelligence is not the only predictor of success in life. IQ tests have shown validity toward predicting academic success, however. The measure of an assessment's criterion validity depends on how closely related the criterion is.
- **Discriminant validity** refers to how well an assessment tests only that which it is intended to test and successfully discriminates one piece of information from another. For instance, a student who is exceptional in mathematics should not be able to put that information into use on a science test and gain an unfair advantage. If they are able to score well due to their mathematics knowledge, the science test did not adequately discriminate science knowledge from mathematics knowledge.
- **Convergent validity** is related to discriminant validity, but takes into account that two measures may be distinct, but can be correlated. For instance, a personality test should distinguish self-esteem from extraversion so that they can be measured independently, but if an assessment has convergent validity, it should show a correlation between related measures.

Family Involvement and Collaboration

Effectively Working and Communicating with Families

Utilizing multiple means of communication when working with students' families ensures information is **accessible** to and **inclusive** of all involved family members. As students' home lives are dynamic, conveying information through several avenues allows families in various situations to participate in their child's education. This is invaluable in establishing and maintaining the positive relationships necessary between students' families and schools for effective teaching and learning. General classroom information, including concepts being taught, important dates, assignments, or suggestions for activities to do at home that reinforce learning in the classroom, can be communicated both digitally and in written form. Newsletters, calendars, or handouts can be both printed and included on a class website to ensure accessibility for all families. Updates regarding individual students can be communicated electronically, through writing, or in person. Email, digital communication apps, and the telephone allow for frequent communication to address students' progress, express concerns, or offer praise. Teachers and families can also communicate through handwritten notes, progress reports, or students' daily agendas. In-person communication, such as during a scheduled conference, is beneficial for discussing individual students' progress and goals related to the education program in depth, as well as ways to support their success in learning.

Building Positive Relationships That Enhance Overall Learning

Students are more supported and learn more effectively when the relationships between their teachers and families are founded on **mutual respect**, **understanding**, and **cooperation**. Establishing this positive rapport requires the teacher to work and communicate frequently with students' families. Doing so creates an inviting learning atmosphere in which family members feel welcomed and included as **equal contributors** to the educational program. This sentiment empowers and encourages family members to take an active role in their children's education, thus strengthening students' support system and enhancing the overall learning experience. In addition, family members that feel a strong connection to their children's school are more likely to model positive attitudes toward education and reinforce learning at home. When teachers and family members communicate frequently, they develop a mutual sense of trust for one another. This allows for **productive collaboration** and the exchange of valuable insight regarding how to best support students' learning needs both within and outside of the classroom.

Appropriate Collaboration and Communication with Families

To effectively collaborate and communicate with students' families, the teacher must carefully consider appropriate methods for doing so. Communication and collaboration must always be **positive**, **respectful**, and **inclusive** to all families to ensure they feel welcomed as equal participants in their children's education. As such, the teacher must be mindful and responsive to the fact that students come from a variety of backgrounds, family dynamics and living situations. This includes demonstrating **cultural competency** when interacting with families from different backgrounds, providing multiple and varied opportunities for family involvement, and communicating through a variety of means. Doing so ensures that families of varying situations have access to pertinent information and feel equally included in the educational program. The teacher must also be mindful of the nature and purpose of communication in order to ensure that sensitive details about individual students are shared only with appropriate family members. General classroom information, such as important dates, events, or assignments, may be shared publicly among the classroom community, whereas such matters as individual student progress or behavior records must be reserved for private communication with the appropriate family members.

Involvement of Families, Parents, Guardians, and Legal Caregivers

Strategies to Encourage Engagement

As students' family dynamics are diverse, it is important that the teacher implement a variety of methods to engage parents, guardians, and legal caregivers into the educational program. Doing so creates an inviting atmosphere in which family members of all situations feel encouraged to participate in their children's education. Efforts to engage families must always be **positive, inclusive**, and **accommodating** to a variety of needs, schedules, and situations. This includes ensuring that all opportunities for involvement are culturally sensitive, meaningful, and accepting of all families. Utilizing a variety of **communication methods**, such as weekly newsletters, calendars, phone calls, and electronic communication, ensures that opportunities to engage in the educational program are accessible to all families. Providing **multiple** and **varied** opportunities for involvement, such as family nights, field trips, award ceremonies, or inviting families to participate in classroom activities, further encourages family engagement in the educational program. This enables families in various situations to become involved in their children's education in the way that best suits their needs and abilities.

Forms of Active Involvement

Active involvement in the educational program can take a variety of forms both within and outside of the classroom to accommodate differences in families' schedules, dynamics, and abilities. Providing multiple avenues for involvement engages families of various situations to actively participate in their children's education. Within the classroom, family members can **volunteer** their time to assist as teacher's aides, tutors, or chaperones. In addition, if a family member is skilled in an area related to instruction, the teacher can ask them to come in to speak or teach a lesson. Inviting family members to **visit the classroom** or participate in special class activities allows them to actively engage in the learning process and gain insight into the educational program. Outside of daily classroom activities, family members can be encouraged to participate by attending **family nights, school social events, fundraisers**, or **parent-teacher association meetings**. Active involvement in the educational program can also occur at home. By frequently communicating with teachers, assisting with projects or homework, and emphasizing the importance of learning at home, family members can be informed and actively involved in their children's education.

Importance in Children's Education

As students spend a great deal of time between school and home, the degree to which their family is involved in the educational program significantly influences the quality of the learning experience. When teachers take measures to engage families in their children's education, they establish a welcoming tone that facilitates relationships founded on mutual respect, understanding, and acceptance. These positive relationships are necessary for encouraging and empowering families to actively participate in the learning process. Such involvement contributes to establishing a **positive learning community** in which teachers and families can collaborate productively to enhance students' learning. When students' families are actively involved in their education, it strengthens the **support system** in both influential areas of their lives, thus establishing a sense of security that allows them to confidently engage in learning. Families that participate in the educational program are more likely to emphasize its value at home by extending and reinforcing learning outside of the classroom. This is highly beneficial in promoting positive attitudes toward learning, academic achievement, and social and emotional development.

Influence on Student Learning and Development

The degree of family involvement in the educational program significantly influences the quality of students' learning and development. Learning is more effective when parents, guardians, or legal caregivers are actively engaged in their child's education, as this promotes positive relationships between students' school and home lives that strengthen their **support system** and encourage the extension of learning beyond the classroom. Families that participate in the educational program are likely to emphasize and model its importance at home, thus influencing students to adopt the same positive attitudes toward learning. This facilitates **academic achievement, decreased absences** from school, and **positive learning habits**. In addition, when families are actively involved in the educational process, they are more effectively able to support students with resources at home that reinforce concepts learned in the classroom to strengthen connections and understanding. Students develop healthy **social and emotional skills** as well when their families are actively involved in the educational program. This facilitates positive self-esteem and interpersonal skills that contribute to academic success and fewer behavioral issues in the classroom.

Benefits for Parents, Families, Guardians, and Legal Caregivers

Families, parents, guardians, and legal caregivers that are actively involved in the educational program gain greater **insight**, **understanding**, and **resources** that enable them to support their children's learning more effectively both within and outside of the classroom. Active engagement in the educational program fosters a positive rapport founded on mutual respect and support among family members, teachers, and school. This provides family members with a sense of **confidence** in the merits of the educational program while contributing to the sense that they are **equal participants** in the learning process. These family members are more informed regarding what is being taught in the classroom, as well as beneficial resources to reinforce learning at home. This leaves family members feeling more **empowered** and willing to reinforce their students' learning. In addition, participating in the learning process provides family members with a greater understanding of the characteristics and capabilities of their children's developmental level, thus equipping them with the knowledge to effectively support learning and growth.

Benefits for Effective Teaching

The involvement of families, parents, guardians, and legal caregivers in the educational program is highly beneficial for effective teaching. Family members that actively participate in the learning process are likely to develop a greater sense of **understanding** and **appreciation** of the teacher's role within it. Such involvement also facilitates positive and frequent communication with families that fosters relationships founded on mutual respect and increases the teacher's **morale**, and therefore effectiveness, in the classroom. Active engagement from family members also allows the teacher to gain a better understanding of how to support individual students' needs. Family members provide valuable insight regarding students' cultures, values, beliefs, educational goals, and learning needs to allow for more effective teaching. In addition, family members that are involved in their children's education are more likely to reinforce and extend learning at home, thus allowing for more effective teaching in the classroom.

Positive Rapport

A positive rapport between teachers and families enhances the quality of the learning experience. Establishing these positive relationships requires that teachers frequently take measures to engage families in the educational program in ways that are **meaningful**, **relevant**, and **responsive** to varying situations, backgrounds, and needs. In doing so, teachers communicate the sentiment that all families are welcomed, valued, and considered equal participants in the learning process. This serves to create an open, inviting learning atmosphere in which family involvement is encouraged, thus fostering the **participation** and **communication** necessary for developing a mutual positive rapport. Working to build positive relationships strengthens the connection between schools and families that facilitates productive **collaboration** to best support and enhance students' learning.

Interacting with Families of Various Backgrounds

Diversities That May Be Encountered

Appropriate interaction when working and communicating with students' families requires the teacher to recognize the wide range of diversities in characteristics, backgrounds, and needs that they will inevitably encounter. With **culturally diverse** families, the teacher will likely experience variances in language, values, traditions, and customs, including differences in beliefs regarding best practices for raising and educating children. **Socioeconomic** differences may influence the degree to which families have the ability and access to resources to support their children in learning. In some instances, socioeconomic differences may also impact the level of education that family members have attained and potentially the value they place on the importance of education. The teacher must also be mindful of the diversities that exist among **family dynamics**. Some families may have a single caregiver, whereas others may have many. Students may be only children, have several siblings, or come from a blended family. Differences in dynamics also include varying work schedules, lifestyle demands, and living situations that the teacher must consider when working and communicating with families. By acknowledging the diverse characteristics, backgrounds, and needs of students' families, the teacher can take measures to ensure appropriate and inclusive interactions that enhance the learning experience.

Appropriate and Productive Interactions

Recognizing the diverse nature of students' cultures, backgrounds, and experiences provides teachers with insight regarding how to interact with their families appropriately and productively. By self-educating to become **culturally competent** and building relationships with students, teachers develop an understanding of the unique characteristics, values, beliefs, and needs of each family. This enables teachers to tailor their communication with individual families in a way that is respectful, **culturally sensitive**, and responsive to their concerns and needs. Doing so ensures that all families feel welcomed and supported in the school environment, thus establishing positive relationships that encourage families to actively engage in the educational program and collaborate productively with teachers to enhance students' learning.

Possible Obstacles

As teachers work and interact with families of diverse backgrounds and experiences, they likely will encounter obstacles that must be addressed to facilitate effective communication. **Cultural differences** in values, beliefs, language, and nonverbal communication may cause misinterpretations between teachers and families that make it difficult to understand one another. It is, therefore, important that the teacher educate themselves regarding students' backgrounds to learn how to communicate in a culturally sensitive manner. When language barriers are present, learning common words and phrases in the language or utilizing an interpreter is beneficial in facilitating communication. Family members may have experienced **negative interactions** with teachers in the past that affect their willingness to engage in communication. Taking measures to establish an inviting, accepting atmosphere that promotes open communication is beneficial in encouraging these families to become involved. **Lifestyle differences**, including varying work schedules, living situations, and family dynamics, may make it difficult to establish effective communication. In addition, **accessibility issues**, including lack of access to transportation, technology devices, or the internet, may hinder family members' abilities to maintain frequent communication. To address these issues, teachers must utilize several communication methods that accommodate families' varying needs and situations.

Considerations to Ensure Beneficial Interactions

The ultimate goal when working and communicating with families is to benefit students' learning and development. When teachers and families develop a positive rapport between one another, it fosters productive collaboration to support the students' educational and developmental goals. Doing so requires that teachers ensure all interactions with students' families are appropriate, respectful, and considerate. This includes demonstrating awareness of varying **backgrounds, characteristics**, and **needs** of each family and interacting in a way that is responsive and accepting of differences. Teachers must practice **cultural competency** when communicating with families, including recognizing differences in perspectives, values, beliefs, and nonverbal communication. Teachers must also consider families' unique situations, including differing **work schedules, living arrangements**, and **family dynamics** to ensure that all interactions are considerate of their time, accommodating to their needs, and supportive of their role in the educational program. When interacting with families, it is important that teachers practice active listening and respond appropriately, meaningfully, and constructively. This communicates to families that their opinions, goals, and concerns related to the educational program are respected, thus encouraging them to actively participate in supporting their children's progress and development.

Regular Communication with Families

Students' Progress and Important Classroom Information

Frequent communication regarding individual student progress and important classroom information is essential to actively engaging family members as equal contributors to the educational program. Doing so creates an inviting atmosphere focused on open and productive dialogue to enhance students' learning and development. Regular communication with families through a variety of methods establishes a strong connection between students' school and home lives that supports their achievement. When families are consistently updated and informed regarding their children's progress in the educational program, they can more effectively collaborate with the teacher to **proactively** address concerns and **implement necessary supports** for successful learning. Frequently communicating important classroom information, including curriculum, assignments, events, and opportunities for involvement, ensures that families are always informed regarding their children's educational program and ways in which they can actively participate. This equips family members with the knowledge and resources necessary to effectively support and reinforce learning both in the classroom and at home.

Positive Rapport That Enhances Teaching and Learning

Regularly interacting and working with students' families facilitates the **continuous** and **open** line of communication necessary to establishing and sustaining a positive rapport. Building such positive relationships is integral to quality teaching and learning, as frequent communication allows families and teachers to develop a sense of mutual respect, trust, and understanding over time. By frequently communicating with families, teachers create a welcoming, inclusive learning environment in which family members feel encouraged and empowered to contribute as **equal participants** in their child's educational program. This facilitates productive collaboration between teachers and families that supports and enhances students' learning. Developing a positive rapport with family members is also valuable in providing teachers with insight regarding strategies to best support and accommodate students' learning styles, needs, and individual differences. When teachers and families have a positive relationship with one another, students feel more supported in their learning both within and outside of the classroom, thus promoting positive attitudes toward learning and academic achievement.

Listening and Responding to Families' Concerns

Actively **listening** and **responding** to students' families when interacting with them is an important part of building positive relationships that enhance teaching and learning. By listening attentively to families' concerns, ideas, and information regarding their child and the educational program, teachers gain a greater awareness of their unique backgrounds, characteristics, and experiences. With this understanding in mind, teachers can ensure that they respond to family members in a **sensitive**, **accepting**, and **empathetic** manner to promote the development of a mutual positive rapport. Doing so conveys the sentiment that family members are valued and respected as equal participants in the educational program, thus encouraging them to engage in positive communication to support their children's learning. Families can provide valuable insight regarding their children's learning styles, needs, and behaviors. When teachers listen and respond constructively to this information, they foster positive relationships with families by validating and including them in the learning process. In addition, listening and responding appropriately to students' families indicates acknowledgement and appreciation for their participation in the educational program that contributes to building positive relationships and encourages continued communication.

Conferences

Building Positive Relationships Between Schools and Families

Frequently conducting conferences with parents, guardians, and legal caregivers facilitates the consistent **in-person communication** necessary for building positive relationships founded on mutual understanding and respect. The conference setting provides a space in which teachers, school staff, and families can discuss the educational program and the student's individual progress, as well as address concerns and collaborate in developing goals. By conducting conferences regularly, teachers, school staff, and families can maintain a continuous, **open dialogue** that provides insight regarding one another's perspectives, intentions, and roles in the educational program. This allows for increased understanding and appreciation for one another that contributes to building positive relationships. Families that attend conferences regularly feel more included in the educational program as equal contributors to their children's learning, thus encouraging them to establish positive strong connections with the school.

SUPPORT OF STUDENTS' SUCCESS IN LEARNING

Effective conferences between teachers and families are focused on open communication, productive collaboration, and strengthening the connection between students' home and school lives. When families and teachers work together in conferences to benefit the student, it strengthens their **support system** in both influential areas of their lives. This is beneficial in enhancing students' **academic achievement**, promoting **healthy development**, and encouraging **positive attitudes toward learning**. Conducting conferences frequently ensures that family members are consistently **informed** and **involved** as equal participants in their child's progress and the educational program. This equips families with the information, understanding, and resources to more effectively support their child's learning both within and outside of the classroom. In addition, effective conferences provide teachers with insight from families regarding students' learning needs, behaviors, and individual situations. With this knowledge in mind, teachers can work with families to develop a plan and implement strategies that best support students' learning and development.

GUIDELINES FOR EFFECTIVENESS

Family conferences are a valuable opportunity to discuss students' individual progress, collaborate to develop educational goals, and address concerns. To ensure conferences are productive, teachers must take measures to make families feel welcomed, respected, and included in the process. Conferences must be scheduled at a **convenient time** for all attending family members in order to accommodate varying needs and situations. It is also important that conferences take place in a comfortable, **inviting atmosphere**, as this establishes a positive tone and facilitates discussion. Teachers must arrive **on time** and **prepared** with specific information to discuss regarding the student, including positive remarks that highlight their strengths. This demonstrates that teachers know the student well and want them to succeed, thus making family members feel comfortable in discussing their child. Asking **open-ended questions**, encouraging families to talk, and practicing active listening is important in facilitating productive discussion, as well as ensuring families feel heard and respected in their concerns. **Direct criticism** of the student must always be avoided; rather, teachers should focus on discussing ways that student can apply their strengths to improve in other areas.

FAMILY SUPPORT RESOURCES THAT ENHANCE FAMILY INVOLVEMENT

Families that are supported through school, community, and interagency resources are equipped to effectively support their child's learning and development. Often, families may be hesitant to become actively involved in their children's education because they lack the skills and understanding of how to do so. These support systems are beneficial in providing family members with the **tools, knowledge**, and **resources** that prepare them to effectively participate in the educational program and extend learning outside of the classroom. Such resources are valuable in educating families on the characteristics, needs, and abilities of their children's developmental level, as well as strategies for developing and engaging in age-appropriate activities that support learning at home. This instills a sense of confidence within families regarding their ability to successfully support their children's learning that empowers and encourages them to become actively involved.

When families are supported through **school**, **community**, and **interagency** resources, they are able to more effectively become involved in the educational program. Numerous resources dedicated to educating families on ways they can support their children's learning are available to accommodate varying situations, needs, and abilities. Within the school, **teachers**, **guidance counselors**, and other **staff members** can provide valuable information regarding students' developmental characteristics, needs, and abilities, as well as ways families can become involved to enhance learning within and outside of the classroom. **Support groups** hosted by the school enable families to share experiences and discuss ways to become involved in the learning process. Community support resources are often tailored to address the specific needs of families within the community. These resources offer **family education services** such as classes, meetings, or programs designed to provide families with the training, strategies, and knowledge necessary to become actively involved in their children's education. Several **national family support agencies** are also available to educate families on ways to become involved in their children's learning. Such agencies often have multiple locations, as well as an array of digitally printed information, discussion forums, and training opportunities to enhance family involvement in learning.

Professional Interaction and Collaboration

Vertical Teaming

Communication and collaboration among teachers of varying grade levels is integral to effective instruction that supports students' learning and development. Through **vertical teaming**, content specific teachers **across grade levels** have the opportunity to work together in discussing and planning curriculum, instruction, assessments, and strategies that prepare students for achievement. Teachers of lower grade levels are often unsure of what students in upper grade levels are learning. As a result, these teachers may be uncertain of the skills and abilities their students need to be adequately prepared for success as they transition through grade levels. Likewise, teachers of upper grade levels are often unsure of what students have learned in previous grades, thus hindering their ability to adequately plan instruction and implement necessary learning supports. Vertical teaming facilitates the communication necessary for teachers across grade levels to collaborate in **establishing expectations for preparedness** at each grade level and developing a common curriculum path. This enhances teaching and learning, in that teachers are more effectively able to plan instruction that is aligned with learning targets and prepare students with the necessary knowledge, tools, and supports for continued academic success.

Horizontal Teaming

Horizontal teaming refers to the collaboration of **same-grade level** teachers and staff that work with a common group of students. These teams may comprise teachers within a **single subject area** or **across disciplines** and may also include special education workers, grade-level administrators, paraprofessionals, and guidance counselors. Horizontal teaming is beneficial in facilitating the **coordinated planning** of curriculum, instruction, and assessments, as well as discussion regarding students' progress in the educational program. In addition, this method of teaming provides teachers and staff the opportunity to work together in developing educational goals, addressing areas of need, and implementing strategies to support students' success in learning. Horizontal teaming is also beneficial in encouraging teachers and staff to cooperate with one another in alignment with the goals and mission of the school to create a positive learning community focused on promoting student achievement.

Team Teaching

Team teaching refers to the collaboration of two or more teachers, paraprofessionals, instructional aides, or special education workers in planning and delivering instruction and assessments. There are **several structures** to this approach to accommodate varying teaching styles and student needs. One teacher may provide direct instruction while another engages in lesson activities or monitors student progress. Similarly, one teacher may instruct while another observes and collects information to improve future planning. Students may be grouped with teachers according to their needs to provide differentiation, or teachers may participate simultaneously and equally in all aspects of the learning process. The intention of this approach is to create a **student-centered environment** focused on enhancing and deepening the learning experience. Team teaching is beneficial in allowing increased **individualized instruction** that more effectively meets students' learning needs. Additionally, when multiple teachers are present, students have access to varying **ideas** and **perspectives** that strengthen their understanding. Team teaching also benefits teachers, as it enables them to utilize one another's strengths for improved instruction. There are, however, limitations to this approach. Differences in **classroom management** styles, **teaching practices**, and **personalities**, when not addressed properly through respectful communication and flexibility, hinder the effectiveness of team teaching.

Benefits of Mentors in Enhancing Professional Knowledge and Skills

Mentors within the school community are typically experienced teachers that are available to offer support, guidance, and expertise to new teachers. As these individuals typically have a great deal of experience as educators, they are highly valuable resources in increasing professional knowledge and improving teaching skills. Mentors can provide **strategies, tools**, and **advice** for planning and delivering instruction, classroom management, and meeting students' learning needs to promote achievement. This includes suggesting ideas and resources for lesson activities and assessments, as well as techniques for differentiating instruction, enhancing student engagement, and promoting positive behavior. In addition, mentors can offer insight on how to effectively **navigate the school community**, including how to interact appropriately with colleagues and superiors, complete administrative duties, and communicate effectively with students' families. Regularly working with mentors in the school building ensures that new teachers are supported in developing the knowledge and skills necessary to become effective educators.

Interaction with Professionals in the School Community

In order for an educational community to function effectively, professionals in the building must work together cohesively on a daily basis to support the school's mission and student learning. The nature of these interactions significantly determines the climate and culture of the school environment. Appropriate, professional interactions are important in facilitating the productive collaboration necessary to create a positive school community that promotes student success in learning. All interactions must therefore be **respectful**, **constructive**, and **sensitive** to the varying backgrounds, cultures, and beliefs among professionals in the school community. This includes using **appropriate language**, practicing **active listening**, and ensuring that discussions regarding colleagues, superiors, students, and other individuals in the building remain positive. When interacting in a team setting, it is important to maintain open dialogue and support one another's contributions to the educational program. All professionals in the school building must understand one another's roles and appreciate how these roles function together to support the educational program. Doing so ensures that collaboration is productive, purposeful, and aligned with enhancing students' learning experience.

Supportive and Cooperative Relationships with Professional Colleagues

Supports Learning and Achievement of Campus and District Goals

Effective collaboration among school staff and faculty members is reliant on establishing and maintaining supportive, cooperative professional relationships. Doing so facilitates a sense of **mutual respect** and **open communication** that allows colleagues to work together constructively in developing educational goals, plans to support students in achieving them, and strategies to address areas of need within the educational program. Mutual support and cooperation are also beneficial in fostering the **coordinated planning** of curriculum, learning activities, assessments, and accommodations to meet students' individual needs for academic achievement. Such professional relationships allow for more effective teaching and learning, as students are supported by a school community that works together cohesively to promote learning and the achievement of campus and district academic goals.

Strategies for Establishing and Maintaining Relationships

Building and maintaining professional relationships founded on mutual support and cooperation is integral in creating a positive, productive school community focused on student achievement. **Frequent communication** with colleagues in a variety of settings is an important factor in establishing and sustaining such professional relationships. Maintaining continuous and open communication allows professional colleagues in the school building to develop the respect for and understanding of one another necessary to establish a strong rapport. By participating together in **school activities**, **events**, and **programs**, teachers and staff members can build connections while contributing to enhancing the school community and climate. **Community building** strategies, such as participating in activities or games that require teamwork, are also valuable opportunities for developing supportive and cooperative professional relationships among colleagues. In addition, **collaborating** with one another in regard to curriculum, lesson planning, and promoting student achievement, contributes significantly to developing positive professional relationships. There are multiple avenues for such collaboration, including participating in professional learning communities (PLC's), department meetings, vertical or horizontal teaming, or engaging in team teaching. Doing so provides teachers and staff the opportunity to communicate and develop mutual goals that support the educational program and student learning.

Roles and Responsibilities of Building and District Level Professionals

Department Chairpersons

Department chairpersons are appointed to act as **leaders** within their subject area. These individuals are responsible for a variety of instructional and administrative duties to ensure the **efficacy** of their academic department in supporting the goals and mission of the school. This includes contributing to curriculum development, communicating instructional expectations from administration to their colleagues, and ensuring that daily instruction within the department aligns with campus and district academic standards. Department chairpersons also serve as **resources** for their team, including collaborating with them to design instructional activities and assessments, offering support, and facilitating positive communication with administration. When working with administration, department chairpersons discuss the progress of their department in meeting academic goals, collaborate to develop strategies for assisting faculty in supporting student learning, and ensure their colleagues have the support, materials, and resources necessary for effective instruction. In addition, department chairpersons are often responsible for coordinating department activities and programs that promote student achievement and contribute to creating a positive school community.

School Principal

The primary role of the **principal** is establishing and maintaining a **school culture** that supports students, teachers, staff, and families in the educational program. This role comprises a multifaceted array of responsibilities that extend to nearly every aspect of the school. The principal is responsible for supervising the **daily operations** of the school to ensure a safe, orderly environment in which teachers, staff, and students are working in alignment with the school's mission. To achieve this, the principal must communicate expectations for a positive, productive school community, ensure academic and behavioral policies are followed by staff and students, and assign staff members specific duties to facilitate an organized, efficient learning environment. In addition, it is important that the principal support staff, students, and families by engaging in frequent, open communication, addressing concerns, and providing resources necessary to promote growth and achievement. The principal is also responsible for ensuring that the school's educational program is effective in supporting teachers, staff, and students in the achievement of academic standards. This includes overseeing curriculum, monitoring instructional practices, measuring their school's performance in relation to district academic standards, as well as communicating the progress and needs of the school to the board of education.

Board of Trustees

Each school within a district is overseen by a **board of trustees** responsible for making decisions to ensure that the educational program supports students' learning needs for academic achievement. The board of trustees is comprised of a group of **elected individuals** that are typically members of the community in which they serve. As such, they have an understanding of the educational needs of the students within the community and can apply this knowledge to make effective decisions regarding the learning program. Members within a board of trustees are responsible for creating an educational program in alignment with students' needs, as well as setting goals and developing strategies that support students in achieving them. This includes determining a **budget plan, allocating resources**, and making **administrative decisions** that benefit the school. In addition, board members are responsible for analyzing assessment data to make informed decisions regarding strategies to best support individual schools within the district and ensuring that measures are being implemented to effectively meet students' learning needs.

Curriculum Coordinators

Curriculum coordinators are responsible for the **development** and **implementation** of curriculum that is aligned with campus and district academic goals. These individuals work closely with teachers and administrators to analyze student progress in relation to the educational program, primarily through **assessment scores**, to determine the overall effectiveness of the curriculum in supporting students' achievement. Analyzing student progress enables curriculum coordinators to identify strengths and areas for improvement within the curriculum to make adjustments that best meet students' learning needs as they work to achieve learning targets. Ensuring that curriculum aligns with academic standards and students' learning needs facilitates more effective teaching and learning. Doing so provides teachers with a clear understanding of how to adequately prepare students for success, thus allowing them to design focused instruction and implement necessary supports to promote the achievement of campus and district academic standards.

School Technology Coordinators

Incorporating technology into the classroom is highly valuable in diversifying instructional strategies to promote student learning and engagement. School **technology coordinators** facilitate this integration to enhance teaching and learning, as they are responsible for the **organization, maintenance**, and **allocation** of available technology resources within the school building. This includes ensuring that all technology is functional, updated, properly stored, and accessible to teachers. These individuals are also responsible for **staying current** on developing digital resources that could be implemented to improve the learning experience, as well as communicating with the board of education regarding **acquiring** technology resources for their school. Doing so ensures that teachers have the materials necessary to best support students' learning. In addition, technology coordinators **educate** teachers and staff on the uses of technology resources, as well as strategies to implement them in the classroom for more effective instruction.

Special Education Professionals

Special education professionals work with students of various disabilities, their teachers, and families to provide an equitable, inclusive environment that supports learning and development. These individuals are responsible for creating an educational plan that is tailored to support the unique needs of disabled students and ensuring that this plan is followed in all areas of the school. Special educators develop **individualized education programs** (IEPs) according to students' areas of need, develop academic and behavioral goals, as well as provide supports and modifications to accommodate students in achieving them. Special education professionals work with teachers to educate them on the proper implementation of individualized accommodations to ensure all students have the support necessary to successfully engage in learning. This includes collaborating with teachers to adapt and modify curriculum, instructional activities, and assessments to meet the individual needs of students with disabilities. In addition, special educators may work alongside classroom teachers in a team-teaching setting or provide individualized instruction as necessary. Students' academic and behavioral progress is monitored over time, and special educators communicate this information to families in order to collaborate in developing future goals and strategies to support achievement.

Roles and Responsibilities of Professionals Within the Education Program

The roles and responsibilities of various professionals within the educational program are described as follows:

- **Principal**—The principal is responsible for ensuring that the daily operations of the school function in a safe, orderly manner that aligns with the goals of the educational program. This includes delegating tasks to staff, enforcing academic and behavioral policies, ensuring instructional practices support student achievement, and communicating with students, staff, and families to establish a positive learning environment.
- **Vice Principal**—The vice principal's role is to assist the principal in supervising the daily operations of the school to create a safe, orderly, and productive learning environment. They are responsible for working with teachers, staff, students, and families to support them in the educational program. This includes enforcing academic and behavioral policies, addressing concerns, facilitating communication, and ensuring instructional practices support student achievement of campus and district academic goals.

- **Board of Trustees**—The board of trustees is responsible for developing an educational program that reflects the learning needs of students within the community. This includes developing educational goals, strategies to support students in achieving them, and ensuring that schools within the district are in alignment with the educational program. The board of trustees is also responsible for such administrative decisions as developing a budget plan and allocating resources to schools within the district according to students' needs.
- **Curriculum Coordinator**—Curriculum coordinators are responsible for developing a curriculum that aligns with campus and district academic goals, and ensuring it is implemented properly to support student achievement. This includes working with teachers and administrators to measure student progress within the curriculum and adjusting instructional strategies as necessary to support student success.
- **Assessment Coordinator**—Assessment coordinators schedule, disperse, and collect standardized assessments and testing materials within the school building. They are responsible for educating teachers on proper assessment protocols to ensure that all practices align with district policies, collaborating with them to develop strategies that support student achievement, and ensuring all students are provided with necessary accommodations according to individual need.
- **Technology Coordinator**—Technology coordinators facilitate the integration of digital resources into the curriculum. They are responsible for acquiring, organizing, maintaining, and allocating technology within the school. These individuals also work with teachers and staff to educate them on ways to utilize technology resources to enhance instruction.
- **Department Chair**—Department chairpersons act as leaders among the teachers within their content area. Their responsibilities include contributing to curriculum development, facilitating communication between administration and their colleagues, and ensuring instructional practices align with the educational program. They also collaborate with members of their team to develop instructional practices that best support student achievement of campus and district academic goals.
- **Teacher Assistant**—The teacher assistant's role is to support the classroom teacher in both instructional and non-instructional duties. This includes assisting with the preparation, organization, and cleanup of lesson materials, working with small groups of students, managing student behavior, and ensuring the classroom functions in a safe, orderly manner.
- **Paraprofessional**—Paraprofessionals are licensed within the field of education and are responsible for assisting the teacher with daily classroom operations. This includes working with individual or small groups of students to provide instructional support, assisting with the preparation of lesson plans and materials, managing student behavior, and completing administrative duties.
- **Speech-Language Pathologist**—Speech-Language pathologists are special education professionals that work with students that have varying degrees of language and communication difficulties. They are responsible for evaluating and diagnosing disabilities related to speech and language, as well as developing individualized treatment programs. Speech-language pathologists then work with these students to remedy language and communication disabilities, as well as collaborate with teachers, staff, and families regarding ways to support their progress.
- **ESL Specialist**—ESL (English as a second language) specialists work with students for whom English is not their native language. They are responsible for evaluating students' levels of English language proficiency across the domains of reading, writing, speaking, and listening, determining necessary linguistic supports, and working with teachers to develop strategies that support English language acquisition. ESL specialists also work with individual or small groups of students to monitor progress and develop English language proficiency skills.
- **Guidance Counselor**—The role of guidance counselors is to support students' social, emotional, academic, and behavioral needs. This includes providing counseling services, mediation, and for upper grade level students, advice regarding course selection and career choices. These individuals communicate with teachers, staff, and families to develop and implement plans to support students' personal growth and academic achievement.

- **School Nurse**—The school nurse is responsible for providing a range of healthcare to students and staff in the school building. This includes evaluating the physical, mental, and emotional health of students and staff, as well as delivering general first-aid treatments. School nurses are also responsible for organizing and dispersing prescribed medications to students in accordance with their healthcare plan and educating teachers and staff regarding best practices for ensuring students' health and safety. School nurses may work with special education professionals to assess students' needs in the development of an individualized education program.
- **Building Service Worker**—Building service workers are responsible for the general maintenance of the school building and outside campus. This includes ensuring that all areas, equipment, and furniture are clean, functional, and safe for student and staff use. These individuals are also responsible for transporting heavy equipment and furniture throughout the school building.
- **Secretary**—The school secretary is responsible for assisting the principal, vice principal, and other office personnel in daily administrative duties. This individual assumes a variety of responsibilities to ensure the efficient function of daily operations within the school. Their responsibilities include communicating with students, families, and other office visitors, directing phone calls to the appropriate location, handling financial matters, and coordinating the school calendar.
- **Library/Media Specialist**—Library and media specialists coordinate the organization, maintenance, and allocation of all library and media resources within the school building. They are responsible for educating students regarding the proper use of library and media resources to locate information, including how to navigate the internet safely and appropriately for educational purposes. Library and media specialists also direct students toward reading material aligned with their literacy skills and provide teachers with learning materials to incorporate into instruction.
- **Instructional Leadership Team (ILT)**—An instructional leadership team is comprised of individuals responsible for educating teachers regarding current and relevant instructional philosophies and practices to enhance student learning. These individuals collaborate with teachers to educate them regarding how to implement instructional strategies, activities, and assessments to effectively meet students' learning needs and support their achievement of campus and district academic goals.
- **School Resource Officer**—The role of the school resource officer is to maintain a safe, orderly environment for teachers, staff, and students. They are responsible for ensuring the physical security of the school, handling legal infractions within the school, and addressing conflicts among students. The school resource officer also works with administration and staff to develop emergency drill procedures.
- **Pupil Personnel Worker (PPW)**—Pupil personnel workers are responsible for addressing issues that hinder the academic achievement of at-risk students. These individuals communicate with teachers, administration, staff, and families to ensure these students are supported both within and outside of the school building. This includes addressing issues related to behavior, crisis intervention, attendance, and home lives. Pupil personnel workers direct families toward school and community support resources and collaborate with teachers to implement supports that facilitate success in learning.

PARTICIPATING IN SCHOOL AND DISTRICT ACTIVITIES

IMPACT OF VOLUNTEERING ON POSITIVE EDUCATIONAL COMMUNITY

Participating in school activities, events, and projects positively impacts the nature of the school community and culture. When teachers and staff members volunteer their time to contribute in such a way, it strengthens **connections** to the school community that foster positive attitudes toward it. By actively engaging in activities, events, and projects, teachers and staff have the opportunity to collaborate in making **positive contributions** to the school community. This facilitates the development of relationships among colleagues that enhance their ability to work cooperatively in creating a positive learning atmosphere that benefits students and the educational program. Students are more supported in such an environment, and therefore, develop positive attitudes toward learning and strong relationships with their teachers that enhance the overall school **climate**.

In addition, as students are influenced by the behaviors, actions, and attitudes modeled by adults in the building, contributing positively to the school community encourages them to do the same.

Participation Opportunities

Participating in school activities, events, and projects is valuable in integrating oneself into the school community while making positive contributions. Such participation can occur through a variety of avenues, both within and outside of the school campus. Teachers can assist in school fundraisers, food and clothing drives, or field trips, as well as serve as tutors, lead school clubs or other extracurricular activities. By attending school sporting events, recitals, concerts, or plays, teachers can participate in the school community while supporting students. Events such as open-house and parent teacher nights, as well as public forum meetings, are also valuable opportunities to participate in the school community in a way that positively contributes to students' learning.

Enhancing the Educational Community

As teachers work closely with students, colleagues, and administration, their contributions to the school and district are integral in enhancing the school community. Teachers provide valuable insight regarding the needs of the educational program and ways to improve the school environment. As such, their participation in the school and district is beneficial in helping to ensure the needs of staff and students are adequately met to create a positive educational community. In addition, active participation in the school and district facilitates the collaboration necessary for establishing relationships among colleagues that contribute to a positive school culture and climate. Teachers can contribute to building such an educational community in a variety of ways. By participating in **school activities**, **events**, and **projects**, teachers can work cooperatively to create a positive learning atmosphere. Teachers can also attend **school meetings** and serve on focused **committees** to solve problems and influence decisions that improve the nature of the school environment. At the district level, teachers can communicate with members of the board of education and participate in **public forums** to express ideas, discuss concerns, and offer input regarding ways to enhance the educational community.

Legal and Ethical Roles and Responsibilities

Legal Requirements for Educators

Special Education Services

Establishing an inclusive, equitable learning environment for students with disabilities requires educators to adhere to strict legal guidelines regarding special education services. According to **IDEA (Individuals with Disabilities Education Act)**, educators must provide students with disabilities a **free and appropriate public education (FAPE)** in the **least restrictive environment (LRE)**. To do this effectively, educators are required to fully comply with students' **IEP (Individual Education Plan)** at all times. This includes providing students requiring special education services with the necessary supports, accommodations, and modifications according to their IEP throughout all stages of instruction. Educators must also document the academic and behavioral progress of these students in relation to the goals outlined in their IEP to report to the designated case manager. In addition, the specifics of students' special education services must be kept confidential in order to protect their privacy. Adhering to these legal requirements promotes equity in the classroom by ensuring that the unique needs of students with disabilities are met, thus allowing them to effectively participate and engage in learning.

FERPA

Understanding and observing the legal requirements related to students' and families' rights is integral to maintaining their confidentiality and establishing a safe, secure learning environment. Educators are required to follow the guidelines of **FERPA (Family Educational Rights and Privacy Act)** regarding students' education records and personally identifiable information. According to FERPA, educators may not release students' education records or personally identifiable information except in authorized situations, such as when the student enrolls in another school, or the information is requested by a financial aid institution in which the student has applied. In all other instances, the educator must have written permission to disclose this information. FERPA also provides students' parents or legal guardians the right to access their child's education records and request that the education records be amended. While educators may not disclose personally identifiable information, they are permitted to release directory information regarding the student, including their name, phone number, or student identification number. However, educators must provide an appropriate amount of time to allow for the refusal of such disclosure. It is also important to note that the rights guaranteed under FERPA become applicable only to the student once they have turned 18 or begun postsecondary education.

Discipline Procedures and Student Code of Conduct

Adhering to legal requirements regarding student discipline procedures is necessary to ensure a safe, orderly, and unbiased learning environment. School districts are responsible for developing a **student code of conduct** to distribute among teachers, staff, students, and families. This document outlines expectations for student behavior, as well as specific consequences for varying degrees of infractions that may occur on school grounds. Educators must strictly adhere to the guidelines stated in the student code of conduct when enacting disciplinary measures. This includes ensuring that consequences for student misbehavior align with the nature of the action and do not interfere with the student's right to a free public education. Disciplinary actions must be free of bias, and must not endanger the student's physical, mental, or emotional health. In addition, the educator must document instances of student discipline, and keep these records confidential to protect the student's right to privacy. Extended suspensions and expulsions must be reserved for instances in which all other disciplinary measures have been exhausted. In such cases, the student is entitled to a hearing at the board of education, and teachers must provide adequate instructional materials for the time that the student is out of the classroom.

Guidelines for acceptable student behavior on school property are outlined in a student code of conduct. Providing students with this reference helps to ensure that the school functions in a safe, orderly, and productive manner so as to create and maintain an environment focused on learning. This document typically addresses a number of topics related to **daily school procedures**, including student dress code standards, acceptable use policies for the internet and digital devices, attendance, grading policies, and academic integrity. Student codes of conduct also address **potential behavioral issues**, such as acceptable conduct while riding school buses, the use of illegal substances on school property, and harmful or disruptive behavior, including bullying, harassment, or fighting. The expectations iterated in student codes of conduct are typically accompanied by an ascending matrix of classroom, administrative, and district-level **consequences** that coincide with the severity and frequency of student infractions.

Establishing an Equitable Learning Environment for All Students

An **equitable environment** is one in which students receive the individual support necessary to facilitate their success in learning. Establishing such an environment requires educators to adhere to several legal guidelines to ensure all students are provided with fair access to learning opportunities. Educators must be sure that all students are included in the educational program, and therefore, may not discriminate based upon students' race, religion, gender, background, disability, or any other differentiating characteristics. All students must be provided with equal access to learning materials, resources, technologies, and supports. In addition, educators must fully comply with all accommodations outlined in students' **IEPs**, **504 plans**, and **Behavior Intervention Plans (BIP)**, and implement all required supports to provide them with equitable access to learning.

Review Video: 504 Plans and IEPs
Visit mometrix.com/academy and enter code: 881103

Child Abuse

One of the primary responsibilities of an educator is to ensure the safety of all students. In order to do so, it is important that educators understand and follow all legal requirements related to child abuse. Within the classroom, educators are responsible for establishing a safe, secure learning environment. All interactions with students must be appropriate and refrain from harming students' **physical**, **mental**, or **emotional health**. Educators must also recognize the signs of potential **child abuse** or **neglect** among their students. If any abuse or neglect is suspected, educators are legally required to report it immediately to the proper agency according to their state and local laws, regardless of whether there is concrete evidence, as waiting to report it may place the student in continued danger. Reports of potential child abuse or neglect must be **confidential** so as to protect the students' privacy. Depending on the protocols established by individual school districts, educators may be required to notify their school's administration and resource officer of the report.

Significance of Understanding and Adhering to Legal Requirements

Understanding the legal requirements for educators ensures that teachers know what is expected of them to maintain professionalism and establish a safe, secure learning environment. This avoids misconception regarding the teacher's **roles** and **responsibilities** within the educational program so teachers understand how to adhere to legal guidelines properly. When teachers are aware of the legal requirements they must follow, they are more effectively able to implement the appropriate protocols for addressing specific education-related situations. This includes instances related to establishing an equitable learning environment, providing special education services, interacting appropriately with students, colleagues, and families, as well as protecting students' privacy. In addition, understanding the legal requirements for educators ensures that they are aware of their own professional rights and how to protect themselves in various education-related situations.

Legal and Ethical Requirements for Using Resources and Technologies

The legal and ethical requirements regarding the use of educational resources and technologies serves as an important frame of reference for teachers when selecting learning materials. Understanding these guidelines is beneficial in effectively determining which resources and technologies are **safe**, **secure**, **appropriate**, and **legal** for classroom use. This helps to protect the data and privacy of both teachers and students when interacting with instructional materials. In addition, this ensures that teachers and students are aware of what constitutes acceptable use of technology resources to protect their safety when engaging online. It is also important to be cognizant of legal and ethical standards in relation to the **reproduction** and **redistribution** of learning materials and technologies. Doing so ensures teachers understand how to properly adhere to copyright laws so as not to infringe upon the original creator's ability to profit from their work.

Copyright Act

When selecting educational resources and technologies to implement in the classroom, it is important that teachers consider the guidelines of the **Copyright Act**. The Copyright Act protects creators by prohibiting the unauthorized use, reproduction, or redistribution of their original works. This extends to digital resources as well, including photographs, video clips, website articles, or online learning materials. While the **Fair Use Doctrine** permits teachers to utilize copyrighted materials for educational purposes, they must be mindful of its restrictions and take the proper precautions to avoid **copyright infringement**. When using copyrighted resources or technologies, teachers can obtain permission directly from the creator, purchase the materials or licenses for use themselves, or ask their school, district, or students to purchase them. In addition, when using, reproducing, or distributing lesson materials, teachers should always cite the appropriate source in order to give credit to the original creator.

Fair Use Doctrine

Under the **Fair Use Doctrine**, teachers are permitted to utilize, reproduce, and redistribute copyrighted materials for educational purposes. However, this doctrine includes limitations that teachers must adhere to when selecting educational resources and technologies to implement in the classroom. The **purpose** of utilizing copyrighted materials must be strictly educational and intended to achieve specific objectives. Teachers must also consider the **nature** of all copyrighted resources and technologies to determine whether they meet the requirements of the Fair Use Doctrine. All copyrighted materials must be used for informational purposes, and typically should be limited to published, nonfiction works. The **amount** of copyrighted material that is reproduced or redistributed must be limited to small excerpts rather than the entire work, and teachers must appropriately cite the original source. In addition, teachers must consider the effect of their use of copyrighted resources and technologies on the future **potential market**. Use of copyrighted materials must not interfere with the creator's ability to profit from their work.

Data Security

Teachers, staff, and students engage with numerous digital resources for a variety of administrative and educational purposes. As such, protecting **data security** when interacting with these materials is increasingly important in establishing a safe, secure learning environment. When selecting educational technologies, such as student information systems (SIS) or digital learning tools, it is imperative that teachers ensure they are aligned with legal and ethical standards regarding data security. All resources must adhere to the requirements outlined by the **Family Educational Rights and Privacy Act (FERPA)** regarding the disclosure of students' sensitive or personally identifiable information. Teachers must also observe their **district and school's policies** regarding the implementation of educational technologies to ensure they are approved for use. In addition, many education technology companies collect students' data as they interact with digital resources with the intention of utilizing it to inform future educational decisions. It is therefore important that teachers consider the nature of the technology they are implementing to ensure that the data collected from students is used strictly for educational purposes. Taking measures to protect students' data when interacting with educational technology resources ensures their safety both within and outside of the classroom.

Privacy

Protecting students' privacy when interacting with educational resources and technologies is paramount to ensuring their safety both within and outside of the classroom. Prior to selecting learning materials, teachers must ensure that they follow all legal and ethical requirements regarding student privacy. This includes determining whether the resources and technologies in question follow the standards outlined by the **Family Educational Rights and Privacy Act (FERPA)** and the **Children's Online Privacy Protection Act (COPPA)**. In doing so, teachers ensure that students' sensitive and personally identifiable information, such as academic, behavioral, or medical records, are secure when interacting with instructional materials. This is necessary to protecting students from encountering potentially harmful situations or individuals that could compromise their privacy and cause long-term negative impacts.

Acceptable Use Policies

Acceptable use policies to govern the use of educational technologies are integral to ensuring a safe, secure learning environment. These documents give guidelines for **acceptable behavior** when interacting with digital resources under the school network, as well as outline **consequences** for violating the terms. Acceptable use policies also inform teachers, staff, students, and families of the measures in place to protect **data security** and **privacy** within the school, such as only allowing individuals with the proper credentials to access the network. Acceptable use policies are beneficial in discouraging users from engaging in inappropriate behavior by outlining standards for responsible use to ensure that sensitive information remains secure. This helps to prevent interaction with potentially harmful individuals or situations that could threaten the safety and privacy of students, teachers, staff, or families, as well as the security of the school network.

Ethical Guidelines

Confidentiality

Adhering to ethical guidelines in relation to confidentiality is an important part of demonstrating professionalism as well as protecting the privacy of students, their families, and others in the school building. Teachers are required to follow all standards outlined by **FERPA** regarding student and family privacy. This includes preserving the confidentiality of all **personally identifiable information** about students, such as grades, medical history, discipline records, or special education services, except in authorized situations. By following these guidelines, teachers ensure that they do not release any information that may compromise the safety of students or their families. In addition, when students and families feel their personal information is kept confidential, they are more likely to seek necessary supports from the educational program without the fear of being stigmatized. Similarly, teachers must follow ethical guidelines to protect the privacy of their colleagues. Any knowledge about a colleague's personal information must be kept confidential so as to establish positive, professional relationships founded on mutual trust. Doing so facilitates productive collaboration among colleagues to benefit student success in learning.

Interactions with Students and Others in the School Community

The daily interactions among students, teachers, staff, and administration largely determine the quality of the school environment. A positive, safe, and professional school community is one in which educators adhere to ethical guidelines regarding interactions with one another and students. Communication with colleagues must be respectful of one another's privacy and confidentiality. This includes avoiding gossiping situations and ensuring that all discussions about colleagues are factual, neutral, and professional in nature. In addition, interactions with members of the school community must **avoid discrimination** of any sort. Similarly, all interactions with students must be inclusive, accepting, and respectful of differences. In addition, educators must maintain proper **boundaries** when communicating with students. This includes avoiding communication outside of the school setting except in authorized situations and ensuring that all interactions maintain professionalism. Any interactions with students must avoid compromising their **physical or mental health**, **safety**, or **ability to learn**. By adhering to these ethical guidelines, educators can ensure that all communication with students and members of the school community contribute to establishing and maintaining a safe, appropriate, and professional learning environment.

Literacy

English Language Arts Pedagogy

Classroom Materials That Support Literacy Across the Curriculum

In a classroom that supports literacy, the teacher should provide **labels** combining words and pictures on all objects. This continually stimulates students to associate written language with the objects and concepts it represents. Especially to support disabled students, teachers should use their particular interests and needs as a guide for labeling things. Printed directions, signs, calendars, and schedules are materials that students should use regularly in the classroom. These help students realize how language is used in everyday life. When the class is studying a certain topic, theme, or book, the teacher and students can work together to redesign the classroom using printed and written materials that reflect that topic, theme, or book. This enables students to fully experience and "live" the lesson rather than just observing it. All of the materials must be adapted for any students' special needs. For instance, in a class including blind/visually impaired students, labels, signs and other print materials can incorporate Braille words and textured surfaces.

Addressing Diverse Student Abilities and Needs

Teachers must consider the **diversity** among the skills and needs of their students as they design their classroom learning environments. The teachers should **individualize** the setting and their instruction so that every student is represented. Individualization and instructional differentiation should not only address disabled students' needs; they should also regularly provide suitable opportunities for these students to participate on an ongoing basis in activities that involve literacy and integrate it into all content areas. According to research, a salient need of students with diverse literacy backgrounds is that they often have trouble connecting new information to their existing knowledge. This ability is a critical component of learning. When teachers plan and organize their classrooms to offer literacy activities that are accessible to disabled students—and that immerse them in literacy experiences and give them opportunities to connect new with old information, and spoken with printed language—these students can then access the general education curriculum.

Activities for Students with Disabilities to Develop Literacy Skills and Participate in General Curriculum

To participate in the general curriculum, students with disabilities need to understand the **alphabetic principle**, i.e. that printed language represents spoken language; connect print with speech; and be able to relate new information to their prior knowledge. Teachers can support these developments by designing classrooms as literacy-rich settings, immersing special-needs and other students in **accessible literacy activities** across all content areas. For example, students can interact with alphabet-letter magnets, cookie-cutters, and stamps; concrete manipulatives allow students not developmentally ready for exclusively abstract thought to understand concepts using real objects. Discussing daily schedules requires students to read and comprehend printed language, and then use spoken language to demonstrate and apply their understanding. Playing letter/word games like Bingo, Pictionary, Boggle, and Scrabble gives practice with creating and manipulating language, enhancing recognition and cognitive flexibility. Providing photos of peers, teachers, staff, and classroom activities and having students label them helps students connect written language with familiar, meaningful images. Daily communication notebooks help students further integrate literacy into their school days.

Implications of Cultural and Linguistic Differences Regarding Literacy Development

Educational research shows that the **cultural values** of families and/or communities influence children's literacy development, and also that culture is a significant factor to understanding children's home literacy environments. Researchers have also found that cultural purposes, perspectives, and contexts affect how students with disabilities in particular interact with the literacy environments they encounter. They say children's preparation levels entering formal education reflect their families' and communities' values and beliefs about literacy. Cultural attitudes about literacy then influence how schools deliver instruction and literacy experiences. Teachers must assess culturally diverse students' interactions with the environment, and design literacy-rich classrooms, with students' diverse backgrounds in mind. Students learning English (ELL/ESL) enter school either not knowing English or just learning it, lacking exposure to specific vocabulary and literature. Literacy-rich classrooms help them participate in regular curriculum. Teacher should read aloud often to these students, include print in their native language in classrooms, permit mistakes during student attempts to use English, encourage students to reread books repeatedly. and plan activities entailing language use.

Drawbacks of Whole-Class and Small-Group Reading, and Flexible Grouping Model

A major disadvantage of **whole-class reading** is that students who read above the average class level go unchallenged and can become bored, while students reading below average level are lost. Yet the **small-group method** intended to remedy this also has the drawback that, as traditionally implemented, most time is used for skill instruction, leaving far too little time for students to actually read the text. One solution is a **flexible grouping model**, e.g., Grouping Without Tracking (Paratore, 1990). This model uses a "sandwich" structure: teachers give students shared-reading processes at the beginning and end of the lesson, but provide differentiated instruction to two groups in the middle as they read the text. Teachers give indirect guidance to students who can read more independently, and more direct support to struggling readers. Teachers reunite the groups to lead them in a final discussion. Students with reading difficulties gain reading proficiency and comprehension from direct teacher support, enabling them to contribute better to the whole-class discussion, so all share this experience equally.

Jigsaw Approach to Shared Reading

Students reading below grade level may be able to access and comprehend some texts or portions of them, but have difficulty with harder parts/texts—for example, informational texts with more challenging subject matter and specialized vocabulary. When a text intended for the whole class contains such challenging material, one solution the teacher can use is a **jigsaw approach**. The teacher selects various portions of the text that are less difficult and assigns them to students reading below grade level. Whereas such texts overall might present struggles for these students, they find the easier portions more manageable when they tackle only these parts, as selected and assigned by the teacher, in small groups of students with comparable reading levels. The teacher makes each small student group responsible for comprehension of their assigned portion of text. Then the teacher brings the class back together, having each group report what they read, understood, and learned. The whole class then collaborates to help each other make connections among the learning each group reported.

Using Themes to Connect Texts

Any inclusive classroom will contain students who read at various age/grade levels. As a result, some books used as core texts are going to present difficulties for some of the students, who read below grade level and/or lack background knowledge and vocabulary of the subject. One way a teacher can facilitate all students' comprehension of such texts is to provide **supplementary texts** that allow readers at different levels easier access—texts on the same subject or theme as the more difficult core text. Teachers have students read these more accessible texts independently during small-group reading periods. This makes it easier for students with less reading proficiency to learn the core vocabulary and build their background knowledge. Thus, they are more prepared to tackle the more difficult core text during whole-class shared reading periods. With such preparation, less proficient readers are more likely to become engaged and active participants in the shared reading of a difficult text in the whole-group setting.

Assigning Students to Small Groups for Guided Reading Exercises

Expert educators and researchers recommend that when teachers divide classes into small student groups for **guided reading**, they should not be overly concerned with assigning students to exact reading levels. Rather, though they will want to group students whose literacy development is similar and who read around a similar level, they should give more attention to organizing groups according to the students' *areas of need*. For example, a teacher might identify students who share in common a need for help with noticing changes in setting, other students who share difficulties with recognizing and differentiating characters, some students who demonstrate problems with following and/or reproducing events they read in a text in the correct chronological sequence, some students who have trouble identifying and/or articulating the main idea in a text portion, etc. The teacher can create a group of students sharing one of these challenges, announce to the class what this group's focus is, and then invite other students to join this group by choice if they experience the same need.

Helping Teachers Provide More Equitable Learning Opportunities Using Word Counts

Books designed for lower reading levels typically contain fewer words, both per page and overall. Yet students who are reading below their grade levels require not fewer reading opportunities, but more, to practice and improve their reading skills. For example, within one class of second-grade students, the teacher might have one group using a text with over 80 words on just the first page, while another group uses a text with a total of 80 words in the entire book. This difference shows that the teacher will need to use several texts within certain groups to give them equal amounts of reading material and practice as readers of denser/longer texts during group reading times. Teachers can look at the backs of the books they assign during guided reading sessions, and maintain simple logs of their **word counts**. Comparing these word counts among groups can help teachers to equalize the numbers of words that each student group actually works with during small-group guided reading periods.

Connecting Text Sets for Small-Group Guided Reading Across Different Reading Difficulty Levels

When teachers select textbooks to teach a unit/lesson on a certain topic, they often compile **text sets**—groups of books all related to the same topic/theme. Because classes usually include students reading at different levels, teachers also often gather books at different reading levels for text sets. When collecting books representing multiple reading levels, the teacher can also intentionally organize the text set so all books are connected. For example, the books might share similar content; similar language, style, and vocabulary words; or similar layouts. Selecting books sharing such a commonality at different reading levels makes it easier for students to draw useful connections between easier and harder texts. It also facilitates students' flexibility in working across multiple reading levels, which builds their skills and confidence for faster progress. Additionally, to prepare some students to read books that teachers felt would prove too difficult otherwise, they can use easier texts with similar themes/language/formats to establish contexts for the harder ones.

Enhancing Students' Independent Reading Through the Reading Material Provided

In addition to whole-class and small-group reading exercises, students need some time reading **texts of their own choice**, which they can easily read with little or no support, to attain comfort, fluency, and confidence. To ensure more opportunities for practice, with equal time for all students, teachers should provide text sets at multiple reading levels for each content area. Experts suggest 70% of books should be easily accessible, and, in addition to classroom libraries, using rolling carts lets book collections travel among classrooms. Multiple reading levels let more advanced readers peruse a harder text, while less advanced readers read several easier texts; this equalizes the time and words they have for practicing. Because critics find some leveled readers lack variety in gender/race/class/other sociocultural aspects of characters, teachers should build diverse book collections representing all students. Teachers can inform their selections via student interest surveys and familiarity with students' individual identities, personalities, and special interests. Knowing individual students can help match them to texts as effectively as leveled book lists.

Engaging Students in Reading

Experts find excessive attention to **leveling** as a way of matching texts to students can be restrictive, undermining high-quality instruction that balances the needs of the reader with the demands of the text. Teachers must consider that assigning certain texts will cause students to disengage from reading and avoid it rather than engage in it. In the real world, people read many different kinds of materials. Therefore, a teacher has better chances of finding texts that engage students, and that motivate them to read and allow them to perceive themselves as readers, by mindfully selecting **varied text genres** with **varied difficulty**. In classrooms incorporating various student reading levels, this can be the best method to procure classroom acceptability of accessible texts. Teachers can also use **individualized instructional formats**, such as Readers Workshop (Atwell, 1998), which balance issues of difficulty, choice, and engagement; develop reader communities affording more reading experiences with authenticity, meaning, and enjoyment; and form stronger, positive teacher-student relationships via individualized consultations. Teachers should also incorporate **accessible alternative texts** for independent activities.

Alternative Reading and Writing Forms to Help Students Attain Greater Progress in Reading

When students read and write outside of school, they choose many alternative forms of reading and writing. To engage these students while they are in school, teachers should think about adding such **alternative materials** to their own instructional programs. For example, teachers might incorporate such media as graphic novels, magazines, newspapers, plays, anthologies of poetry, e-books and other digital/online content, and texts that students have written themselves. Educational experts advise that just because it can be harder to determine the reading levels of such alternative text formats, teachers should not shy away from using them. Because they represent examples of text that people (including students) read in real life, they provide not only excellent practice for students' present and future reading of real-world materials, but also motivation to read and meaningful experiences in reading. Another boon of using these authentic, alternative texts is that they frequently incorporate multiple reading levels, so that nearly every student can read some portions of them.

Viewing Skills

Viewing skills can be sharpened by having students look at a single image, such as a work of art or a cartoon, and simply asking students what they **see**. The teacher can ask what is happening in the image, and then elicit the details that clue the students in to what is happening. Of course, there may be more than one thing happening. The teacher should also question the students about the message of the image, its purpose, its point of view, and its intended audience. The teacher should ask for first impressions, and then provide some background or additional information to see if it changes the way students look at or interpret the image. The conclusion of the lesson should include questions about what students learned from the exercise about the topic, themselves, and others.

Benefits

Students are exposed to multiple **images** every day. It is important for them to be able to effectively **interpret** these images. They should be able to make sense of images and the spoken and print language that often accompany them. Learning can be enhanced with images because they allow for quicker connections to prior knowledge than verbal information. Visuals in the classroom can also be motivational, can support verbal information, and can express main points, sometimes resulting in instant recognition.

Some of the common types of images that students see every day include: bulletin boards, computer graphics, diagrams, drawings, illustrations, maps, photographs, posters, book covers, advertisements, websites, multimedia presentations, puppet shows, television, videos, print cartoons, models, paintings, animation, drama or dance performances, films, and online newscasts and magazines.

Activities to Strengthen Skills

Activities at school that can be used to strengthen the **viewing skills** of students of varying ages include:

- **Picture book discussions** – Students can develop an appreciation of visual text and the language that goes with it through guided discussions of picture books that focus on the style and color of the images and other details that might capture a child's attention.

- **Gallery walks** – Students can walk around a room or hallway viewing the posted works of other students and hear presentations about the works. They can also view a display prepared by the teacher. Students are expected to take notes as they walk around, have discussions, and perhaps do a follow-up report.
- **Puppet theater and drama presentations** – Students can learn about plots, dialogue, situations, characters, and the craft of performance from viewing puppet or drama presentations, which also stimulate oral communication and strengthen listening skills. Discussions or written responses should follow performances to check for detail acquisition.

Classroom Viewing Center

A **classroom viewing center** should contain magazines, CD-ROMs, books, videos, and individual pictures (photographs or drawings). Students should have a **viewing guide** that explains expectations related to the viewing center (before, during, and after using the center). For younger students, the teacher can ask questions that guide them through the viewing rather than expecting them to read the guidelines and write responses.

- **Before** viewing, students should think about what they already know about the subject and what they want to learn from the viewing.
- **During** the viewing, students should make notes about whatever interests them or is new to them.
- **After** viewing, students could discuss or individually write down what they found to be the most interesting idea or striking image and explain why it caught their attention.

Types of Questions to Ask If Viewing Is a Narrative

A teacher should make students responsible for gaining information or insight from the **viewing**. Setting expectations increases student attention and critical thinking. As with any viewing, the students should consider what they already know about the topic and what they hope to gain by watching the narrative before viewing it. During the viewing, the students should take notes (perhaps to answer questions provided by the teacher).

After the viewing, students should be able to answer the following questions:

- What was the time period and setting of the story?
- Who were the main characters?
- How effective was the acting?
- What was the problem or goal in the story?
- How was the problem solved or the goal achieved?
- How would you summarize the story?
- What did you learn from the story?
- What did you like or dislike about the story or its presentation?
- Would you recommend this viewing to others?
- How would you rate it?

Difficulties Related to Learning by Listening

It is difficult to learn just by listening because the instruction is presented only in spoken form. Therefore, unless students take notes, there is nothing for them to review. However, an active listener will anticipate finding a **message** in an oral presentation and will listen for it, **interpreting** tone and gestures as the presentation progresses. In group discussions, students are often too busy figuring out what they will say when it is their turn to talk to concentrate on what others are saying. Therefore, they don't learn from others, but instead come away knowing only what they already knew. Students should be required to respond directly to the previous speaker before launching into their own comments. This practice will force students to listen to each other and learn that their own responses will be better because of what can be added by listening to others.

Graphic Organizers

The purpose of **graphic organizers** is to help students classify ideas and communicate more efficiently and effectively. Graphic organizers are visual outlines or templates that help students grasp key concepts and master subject matter by simplifying them down to basic points. They also help guide students through processes related to any subject area or task. Examples of processes include brainstorming, problem solving, decision making, research and project planning, and studying. Examples of graphic organizers include:

- **Reading** – These can include beginning, middle, and end graphs or event maps.
- **Science** – These can include charts that show what animals need or how to classify living things.
- **Math** – These can include horizontal bar graphs or time lines.
- **Language arts** – These can include alphabet organizers or charts showing the components of the five-paragraph essay.
- **General** – These can include KWL charts or weekly planners.

Speaking Skills Children in Elementary/Intermediate School Should Have

Children of elementary/intermediate school age should be able to:

- Speak at an appropriate volume, tone, and pace that is understandable and appropriate to the audience
- Pronounce most words accurately
- Use complete sentences
- Make eye contact
- Use appropriate gestures with speech
- Exhibit an awareness of audience and adjust content to fit the audience (adjust word choices and style to be appropriate for peers or adults)
- Ask relevant questions
- Respond appropriately when asked questions about information or an opinion, possibly also being able to provide reasons for opinions
- Speak in turn, not interrupt, and include others in conversations
- Provide a summary or report orally
- Participate in small and large group discussions and debates
- Read orally before an audience
- Conduct short interviews
- Provide directions and explanations orally, including explanations of class lessons

Viewing Skills Elementary/Intermediate School Children Should Have

Children of elementary school age should be developing or have attained the ability to understand the importance of **media** in people's lives. They should understand that television, radio, films, and the Internet have a role in everyday life. They should also be able to use media themselves (printing out material from the Internet or making an audio or video tape, for example). They should also be aware that the purpose of advertising is to sell. Children of intermediate school age should be developing or have attained the ability to **obtain and compare information** from newspapers, television, and the Internet. They should also be able to judge its **reliability and accuracy** to some extent. Children of this age should be able to tell the difference between fictional and non-fictional materials in media. They should also be able to use a variety of media, visuals, and sounds to make a presentation.

Listening Skills Children Should Develop Through Their Elementary/Intermediate School Years

Through the elementary/intermediate school years, children should develop the following listening skills:

- Follow oral instructions consistently
- Actively listen to peers and teachers

- Avoid creating distracting behavior or being distracted by the behavior of others most of the time
- Respond to listening activities and exhibit the ability to discuss, illustrate, or write about the activity and show knowledge of the content and quality of the listening activity
- Respond to listening activities and exhibit the ability to identify themes, similarities, differences, ideas, forms, and styles of activities
- Respond to a persuasive speaker and exhibit the ability to analyze and evaluate the credibility of the speaker and form an opinion describing whether they agree or disagree with the point made
- Demonstrate appropriate social behavior while part of an audience

Stages of Writing

The **three stages of writing** are drawing, dictating, and writing. During the **drawing stage**, young learners use scribbles or pictures to convey their message. When asked to "read" their drawing, children in the drawing stage will use their picture to tell a story, as if they were mimicking a book being read to them. In the **dictation stage**, learners will tell their thoughts to a literate person, who will in turn write the words for the child. During this stage, the student is aware that the written words on the page represent their thoughts and can sometimes recognize the beginning sounds of the words they are saying, including some sight words. In the third and final stage, the **writing stage**, students are able to write their own thoughts in a way that can be recognized by others. Both beginning and ending sounds are represented in the words, along with some vowels. Students in this stage also understand spacing between words and the idea of creating complete sentences.

Norm-Referenced and Criterion-Referenced Assessments

Norm-referenced assessments are used to gauge a student's success by comparing his or her score to a theoretical "average" score achieved by students of the same age or grade level. With a norm-referenced assessment, a student's achievement is decided based on how much better or worse that student scored in comparison to his or her peers. In contrast, **criterion-referenced assessments** are scored based on each student's individual ability to show mastery of specific learning standards. Students are deemed successful if they are able to achieve mastery of concepts that are appropriate for their age or grade level, regardless of how their peers perform.

IRI

The **Informal Reading Inventory (IRI)**, also known as the **Qualitative Reading Inventory (QRI)** is a survey used to assess the instructional needs of individual readers. The IRI is used to determine a reader's grade-level reading, fluency, comprehension, vocabulary, oral reading accuracy, word recognition, word meaning, and reading strategies. The IRI is an ongoing assessment that should be administered several times a year starting from first grade through twelfth grade. Teachers should use the outcomes of these assessments to determine appropriate reading material for individual students and to identify and implement specific needs and strategies for individual learners or groups of learners.

Universal Screening Assessments, Diagnostic Assessments, and Progress Monitoring

Universal screening assessments are brief surveys given to all students at the beginning of each school year, which are used to determine the mastery of critical skills and concepts. These screenings should be repeated approximately three times a year to ensure that students are performing at age-appropriate levels. **Diagnostic assessments** are used to help educators make sense of universal screening assessment scores. Based on diagnostics, teachers can identify the specific educational gaps of individual students and use that information to modify and differentiate instruction. **Progress monitoring** is used to determine if the educational interventions and strategies put in place (based on the diagnostic testing) are actually working. Struggling students are often monitored more closely to ensure that educational gaps are being filled at an appropriate and sufficient rate.

Formal and Informal Assessments

Formal assessments, which include norm-based assessments, criterion-based assessments, intelligence tests, and diagnostic assessments are data driven. These types of assessments are used to determine a student's overall achievement and can be used to compare each student's abilities to his or her peers. Formal assessments are often shared with students and stakeholders to determine whether or not a student is performing at an appropriate level for his or her age or grade level. **Informal assessments**, which include running records, cloze tests, reading inventories, portfolios, and so on are not data driven. Instead, informal assessments use performance-driven tasks to guide instruction and provide informal ratings about each student's individual progress. During these assessments, each student's performance is used to monitor his or her progress and guide future instruction, often in preparation for a formal assessment.

Evaluating Appropriateness of Assessment Instrument or Practice

The two main factors that must be considered when evaluating the appropriateness of assessment instruction and practices are curriculum alignment and cultural bias. **Curriculum alignment** is the act of teaching students the concepts that they will eventually be tested on. To reach proficiency on the standards outlined by state or district mandates, teachers must continuously teach and assess the standards. Avoiding **cultural bias** ensures that all students are given access to all relevant lessons, instruction, and materials. Furthermore, avoiding cultural bias ensures that all students are given a fair opportunity to succeed on any given assessment. This includes accommodating students of certain subgroups with assessment modifications, such as additional testing time, taking the test in his or her native language, and creating types of assessments that are accessible and achievable for students of all backgrounds.

Example Evaluation of Scoring Method

A teacher is assessing a student's ability to identify the main idea of a text. The student correctly identifies the main idea but includes several spelling errors in her written response. The teacher lowers the student's grade, taking points off for misspellings. In this example, the teacher's scoring method is **inappropriate** for the concept being assessed. Although misspellings should be addressed and remedied, the question was designed to assess the student's ability to identify the main idea of the passage. It was not intended to assess the spelling abilities of the student. By lowering the student's score based on misspellings, the teacher is insinuating that the student is unable to correctly identify the main idea of a passage, which is not the case. When assessing a specific skill, it is important that teachers score students based on their ability to complete isolated skills for data to accurately drive future instruction.

Penmanship

Penmanship is a word used to describe a person's *handwriting*. The three main characteristics of penmanship are letter formation, size, and spacing. When teaching penmanship, teachers should start by helping students to correctly form each letter, using arrows to dictate the order and direction in which parts of each letter should be written. Once students have mastered each letter, teachers should focus on letter size or proportion. For example, smaller letters (like c, e, and n) should be half the size of larger letters (such as k, l, or t). Finally, proper spacing should be taught, both between letters and words. Once spacing between words has been mastered, students should begin to work on including punctuation and appropriate spacing between sentences.

Importance of Listening and Speaking Strategies

Both listening and speaking strategies are important skills for students in all areas of education. To achieve the highest success, students should be taught how to effectively **speak** and exchange dialogue in large- and small-group settings. In addition, students should be encouraged to question, retell, or reenact the words of others. Equally important, students must learn to actively **listen** and visualize the words of others so that they are able to understand the purpose of what someone else is saying. To check for listening, students should be encouraged to summarize what they have heard and complete graphic organizers outlining important concepts or facts. When given ample opportunity to both speak and listen, students are more likely to excel across all content areas.

Developing Listening and Speaking Skills with Dramatic Play

Dramatic play is a type of play in which students are assigned specific roles and encouraged to act those roles out. In dramatic play, students are typically assigned a character but not a script. They are encouraged to take on the feelings and actions of the character they have been assigned and act as that character would act. Dramatic play is an excellent strategy for developing speaking skills as students must clearly identify and express the feelings of their characters. They must speak clearly and loudly enough so that the other actors and the audience can hear what they are saying. In addition, students must actively listen to what the other students in the play are saying to appropriately respond to the actions and words of the other characters in an effort to further develop the story line.

Parts of Speech

The Eight Parts of Speech

Nouns

When you talk about a person, place, thing, or idea, you are talking about a **noun**. The two main types of nouns are **common** and **proper** nouns. Also, nouns can be abstract (i.e., general) or concrete (i.e., specific).

Common Nouns

Common nouns are generic names for people, places, and things. Common nouns are not usually capitalized.

Examples of common nouns:

People: boy, girl, worker, manager

Places: school, bank, library, home

Things: dog, cat, truck, car

Review Video: What is a Noun?
Visit mometrix.com/academy and enter code: 344028

Proper Nouns

Proper nouns name specific people, places, or things. All proper nouns are capitalized.

Examples of proper nouns:

People: Abraham Lincoln, George Washington, Martin Luther King, Jr.

Places: Los Angeles, California; New York; Asia

Things: Statue of Liberty, Earth, Lincoln Memorial

Note: When referring to the planet that we live on, capitalize *Earth*. When referring to the dirt, rocks, or land, lowercase *earth*.

General and Specific Nouns

General nouns are the names of conditions or ideas. **Specific nouns** name people, places, and things that are understood by using your senses.

General nouns:

Condition: beauty, strength

Idea: truth, peace

Specific nouns:

People: baby, friend, father

Places: town, park, city hall

Things: rainbow, cough, apple, silk, gasoline

COLLECTIVE NOUNS

Collective nouns are the names for a group of people, places, or things that may act as a whole. The following are examples of collective nouns: *class, company, dozen, group, herd, team,* and *public*. Collective nouns usually require an article, which denotes the noun as being a single unit. For instance, a choir is a group of singers. Even though there are many singers in a choir, the word choir is grammatically treated as a single unit. If we refer to the members of the group, and not the group itself, it is no longer a collective noun.

Incorrect: The *choir are* going to compete nationally this year.

Correct: The *choir is* going to compete nationally this year.

Incorrect: The *members* of the choir *is* competing nationally this year.

Correct: The *members* of the choir *are* competing nationally this year.

PRONOUNS

Pronouns are words that are used to stand in for nouns. A pronoun may be classified as personal, intensive, relative, interrogative, demonstrative, indefinite, and reciprocal.

Personal: *Nominative* is the case for nouns and pronouns that are the subject of a sentence. *Objective* is the case for nouns and pronouns that are an object in a sentence. *Possessive* is the case for nouns and pronouns that show possession or ownership.

Singular

	Nominative	Objective	Possessive
First Person	I	me	my, mine
Second Person	you	you	your, yours
Third Person	he, she, it	him, her, it	his, her, hers, its

Plural

	Nominative	Objective	Possessive
First Person	we	us	our, ours
Second Person	you	you	your, yours
Third Person	they	them	their, theirs

Intensive: I myself, you yourself, he himself, she herself, the (thing) itself, we ourselves, you yourselves, they themselves

Relative: which, who, whom, whose

Interrogative: what, which, who, whom, whose

Demonstrative: this, that, these, those

Indefinite: all, any, each, everyone, either/neither, one, some, several

Reciprocal: each other, one another

Review Video: Nouns and Pronouns
Visit mometrix.com/academy and enter code: 312073

Verbs

If you want to write a sentence, then you need a verb. Without a verb, you have no sentence. The verb of a sentence indicates action or being. In other words, the verb shows something's action or state of being or the action that has been done to something.

Transitive and Intransitive Verbs

A **transitive verb** is a verb whose action (e.g., drive, run, jump) indicates a receiver (e.g., car, dog, kangaroo). **Intransitive verbs** do not indicate a receiver of an action. In other words, the action of the verb does not point to a subject or object.

> **Transitive**: He plays the piano. | The piano was played by him.
>
> **Intransitive**: He plays. | John plays well.

A dictionary will tell you whether a verb is transitive or intransitive. Some verbs can be transitive and intransitive.

Action Verbs and Linking Verbs

Action verbs show what the subject is doing. In other words, an action verb shows action. Unlike most types of words, a single action verb, in the right context, can be an entire sentence. **Linking verbs** link the subject of a sentence to a noun or pronoun, or they link a subject with an adjective. You always need a verb if you want a complete sentence. However, linking verbs on their own cannot be a complete sentence.

Common linking verbs include *appear, be, become, feel, grow, look, seem, smell, sound,* and *taste.* However, any verb that shows a condition and connects to a noun, pronoun, or adjective that describes the subject of a sentence is a linking verb.

Action: He sings. | Run! | Go! | I talk with him every day. | She reads.

Linking:

> Incorrect: I am.
>
> Correct: I am John. | The roses smell lovely. | I feel tired.

Note: Some verbs are followed by words that look like prepositions, but they are a part of the verb and a part of the verb's meaning. These are known as phrasal verbs, and examples include *call off, look up,* and *drop off.*

Review Video: Action Verbs and Linking Verbs
Visit mometrix.com/academy and enter code: 743142

Voice

Transitive verbs come in active or passive **voice**. If something does an action or is acted upon, then you will know whether a verb is active or passive. When the subject of the sentence is doing the action, the verb is in **active voice**. When the subject is acted upon, the verb is in **passive voice**.

> **Active**: Jon drew the picture. (The subject *Jon* is doing the action of *drawing a picture.*)
>
> **Passive**: The picture is drawn by Jon. (The subject *picture* is receiving the action from Jon.)

Verb Tenses

A verb **tense** shows the different form of a verb to point to the time of an action. The present and past tense are indicated by the verb's form. An action in the present, *I talk,* can change form for the past: *I talked.*

However, for the other tenses, an auxiliary (i.e., helping) verb is needed to show the change in form. These helping verbs include *am, are, is* | *have, has, had* | *was, were, will* (or *shall*).

Present: I talk	Present perfect: I have talked
Past: I talked	Past perfect: I had talked
Future: I will talk	Future perfect: I will have talked

Present: The action happens at the current time.

Example: He *walks* to the store every morning.

To show that something is happening right now, use the progressive present tense: I *am walking*.

Past: The action happened in the past.

Example: He *walked* to the store an hour ago.

Future: The action is going to happen later.

Example: I *will walk* to the store tomorrow.

Present perfect: The action started in the past and continues into the present or took place previously at an unspecified time.

Example: I *have walked* to the store three times today.

Past perfect: The second action happened in the past. The first action came before the second.

Example: Before I walked to the store (Action 2), I *had walked* to the library (Action 1).

Future perfect: An action that uses the past and the future. In other words, the action is complete before a future moment.

Example: When she comes for the supplies (future moment), I *will have walked* to the store (action completed before the future moment).

Review Video: Present Perfect, Past Perfect, and Future Perfect Verb Tenses
Visit mometrix.com/academy and enter code: 269472

Conjugating Verbs

When you need to change the form of a verb, you are **conjugating** a verb. The key forms of a verb are singular, present tense (dream); singular, past tense (dreamed); and the past participle (have dreamed). Note: the past participle needs a helping verb to make a verb tense. For example, I *have dreamed* of this day. The following tables demonstrate some of the different ways to conjugate a verb:

Singular

Tense	First Person	Second Person	Third Person
Present	I dream	You dream	He, she, it dreams
Past	I dreamed	You dreamed	He, she, it dreamed
Past Participle	I have dreamed	You have dreamed	He, she, it has dreamed

Plural

Tense	First Person	Second Person	Third Person
Present	We dream	You dream	They dream
Past	We dreamed	You dreamed	They dreamed
Past Participle	We have dreamed	You have dreamed	They have dreamed

MOOD

There are three **moods** in English: the indicative, the imperative, and the subjunctive.

The **indicative mood** is used for facts, opinions, and questions.

Fact: You can do this.

Opinion: I think that you can do this.

Question: Do you know that you can do this?

The **imperative** is used for orders or requests.

Order: You are going to do this!

Request: Will you do this for me?

The **subjunctive mood** is for wishes and statements that go against fact.

Wish: I wish that I were famous.

Statement against fact: If I were you, I would do this. (This goes against fact because I am not you. You have the chance to do this, and I do not have the chance.)

ADJECTIVES

An **adjective** is a word that is used to modify a noun or pronoun. An adjective answers a question: *Which one? What kind?* or *How many?* Usually, adjectives come before the words that they modify, but they may also come after a linking verb.

Which one? The *third* suit is my favorite.

What kind? This suit is *navy blue.*

How many? I am going to buy *four* pairs of socks to match the suit.

Review Video: Descriptive Text
Visit mometrix.com/academy and enter code: 174903

ARTICLES

Articles are adjectives that are used to distinguish nouns as definite or indefinite. **Definite** nouns are preceded by the article *the* and indicate a specific person, place, thing, or idea. **Indefinite** nouns are preceded by *a* or *an* and do not indicate a specific person, place, thing, or idea. *A*, *an*, and *the* are the only articles. Note: *An* comes before words that start with a vowel sound. For example, "Are you going to get an **u**mbrella?"

Definite: I lost *the* bottle that belongs to me.

Indefinite: Does anyone have *a* bottle to share?

Review Video: Function of Articles
Visit mometrix.com/academy and enter code: 449383

Comparison with Adjectives

Some adjectives are relative and other adjectives are absolute. Adjectives that are **relative** can show the comparison between things. **Absolute** adjectives can also show comparison, but they do so in a different way. Let's say that you are reading two books. You think that one book is perfect, and the other book is not exactly perfect. It is not possible for one book to be more perfect than the other. Either you think that the book is perfect, or you think that the book is imperfect. In this case, perfect and imperfect are absolute adjectives.

Relative adjectives will show the different **degrees** of something or someone to something else or someone else. The three degrees of adjectives include positive, comparative, and superlative.

The **positive** degree is the normal form of an adjective.

Example: This work is *difficult.* | She is *smart.*

The **comparative** degree compares one person or thing to another person or thing.

Example: This work is *more difficult* than your work. | She is *smarter* than me.

The **superlative** degree compares more than two people or things.

Example: This is the *most difficult* work of my life. | She is the *smartest* lady in school.

Review Video: What is an Adjective?
Visit mometrix.com/academy and enter code: 470154

Adverbs

An **adverb** is a word that is used to **modify** a verb, adjective, or another adverb. Usually, adverbs answer one of these questions: *When? Where? How?* and *Why?* The negatives *not* and *never* are considered adverbs. Adverbs that modify adjectives or other adverbs **strengthen** or **weaken** the words that they modify.

Examples:

He walks *quickly* through the crowd.

The water flows *smoothly* on the rocks.

Note: Adverbs are usually indicated by the morpheme *-ly*, which has been added to the root word. For instance, *quick* can be made into an adverb by adding *-ly* to construct *quickly*. Some words that end in *-ly* do not follow this rule and can behave as other parts of speech. Examples of adjectives ending in *-ly* include: *early, friendly, holy, lonely, silly*, and *ugly*. To know if a word that ends in *-ly* is an adjective or adverb, check your dictionary. Also, while many adverbs end in *-ly*, you need to remember that not all adverbs end in *-ly*.

Examples:

He is *never* angry.

You walked *across* the bridge.

Review Video: What is an Adverb?
Visit mometrix.com/academy and enter code: 713951

Review Video: Adverbs that Modify Adjectives
Visit mometrix.com/academy and enter code: 122570

COMPARISON WITH ADVERBS

The rules for comparing adverbs are the same as the rules for adjectives.

The **positive** degree is the standard form of an adverb.

Example: He arrives *soon.* | She speaks *softly* to her friends.

The **comparative** degree compares one person or thing to another person or thing.

Example: He arrives *sooner* than Sarah. | She speaks *more softly* than him.

The **superlative** degree compares more than two people or things.

Example: He arrives *soonest* of the group. | She speaks the *most softly* of any of her friends.

PREPOSITIONS

A **preposition** is a word placed before a noun or pronoun that shows the relationship between an object and another word in the sentence.

Common prepositions:

about	before	during	on	under
after	beneath	for	over	until
against	between	from	past	up
among	beyond	in	through	with
around	by	of	to	within
at	down	off	toward	without

Examples:

The napkin is *in* the drawer.

The Earth rotates *around* the Sun.

The needle is *beneath* the haystack.

Can you find "me" *among* the words?

Review Video: Prepositions
Visit mometrix.com/academy and enter code: 946763

Conjunctions

Conjunctions join words, phrases, or clauses and they show the connection between the joined pieces. **Coordinating conjunctions** connect equal parts of sentences. **Correlative conjunctions** show the connection between pairs. **Subordinating conjunctions** join subordinate (i.e., dependent) clauses with independent clauses.

Coordinating Conjunctions

The **coordinating conjunctions** include: *and, but, yet, or, nor, for,* and *so*

Examples:

> The rock was small, *but* it was heavy.
>
> She drove in the night, *and* he drove in the day.

Correlative Conjunctions

The **correlative conjunctions** are: *either...or* | *neither...nor* | *not only...but also*

Examples:

> *Either* you are coming *or* you are staying.
>
> He *not only* ran three miles *but also* swam 200 yards.

Review Video: Coordinating and Correlative Conjunctions
Visit mometrix.com/academy and enter code: 390329

Review Video: Adverb Equal Comparisons
Visit mometrix.com/academy and enter code: 231291

Subordinating Conjunctions

Common **subordinating conjunctions** include:

after	since	whenever
although	so that	where
because	unless	wherever
before	until	whether
in order that	when	while

Examples:

> I am hungry *because* I did not eat breakfast.
>
> He went home *when* everyone left.

Review Video: Subordinating Conjunctions
Visit mometrix.com/academy and enter code: 958913

Interjections

Interjections are words of exclamation (i.e., audible expression of great feeling) that are used alone or as a part of a sentence. Often, they are used at the beginning of a sentence for an introduction. Sometimes, they can be used in the middle of a sentence to show a change in thought or attitude.

> Common Interjections: Hey! | Oh, | Ouch! | Please! | Wow!

Agreement and Sentence Structure

Subjects and Predicates

Subjects

The **subject** of a sentence names who or what the sentence is about. The subject may be directly stated in a sentence, or the subject may be the implied *you*. The **complete subject** includes the simple subject and all of its modifiers. To find the complete subject, ask *Who* or *What* and insert the verb to complete the question. The answer, including any modifiers (adjectives, prepositional phrases, etc.), is the complete subject. To find the **simple subject**, remove all of the modifiers in the complete subject. Being able to locate the subject of a sentence helps with many problems, such as those involving sentence fragments and subject-verb agreement.

Examples:

simple subject: car

The small, red car is the one that he wants for Christmas.

complete subject: The small, red car

simple subject: artist

The young artist is coming over for dinner.

complete subject: The young artist

Review Video: Subjects in English
Visit mometrix.com/academy and enter code: 444771

In **imperative** sentences, the verb's subject is understood (e.g., [You] Run to the store), but is not actually present in the sentence. Normally, the subject comes before the verb. However, the subject comes after the verb in sentences that begin with *There are* or *There was.*

Direct:

John knows the way to the park.	Who knows the way to the park?	John
The cookies need ten more minutes.	What needs ten minutes?	The cookies
By five o'clock, Bill will need to leave.	Who needs to leave?	Bill
There are five letters on the table for him.	What is on the table?	Five letters
There were coffee and doughnuts in the house.	What was in the house?	Coffee and doughnuts

Implied:

Go to the post office for me.	Who is going to the post office?	You
Come and sit with me, please?	Who needs to come and sit?	You

Predicates

In a sentence, you always have a predicate and a subject. The subject tells what the sentence is about, and the **predicate** explains or describes the subject.

Think about the sentence *He sings.* In this sentence, we have a subject (He) and a predicate (sings). This is all that is needed for a sentence to be complete. Most sentences contain more information, but if this is all the information that you are given, then you have a complete sentence.

Now, let's look at another sentence: *John and Jane sing on Tuesday nights at the dance hall.*

subject: John and Jane | predicate: sing on Tuesday nights at the dance hall.

Subject-Verb Agreement

Verbs **agree** with their subjects in number. In other words, singular subjects need singular verbs. Plural subjects need plural verbs. **Singular** is for **one** person, place, or thing. **Plural** is for **more than one** person, place, or thing. Subjects and verbs must also share the same point of view, as in first, second, or third person. The present tense ending *-s* is used on a verb if its subject is third person singular; otherwise, the verb's ending is not modified.

Review Video: Subject-Verb Agreement
Visit mometrix.com/academy and enter code: 479190

Number Agreement Examples:

Single Subject and Verb: Dan (singular subject) calls (singular verb) home.

Dan is one person. So, the singular verb *calls* is needed.

Plural Subject and Verb: Dan and Bob (plural subject) call (plural verb) home.

More than one person needs the plural verb *call.*

Person Agreement Examples:

First Person: I *am* walking.

Second Person: You *are* walking.

Third Person: He *is* walking.

Complications with Subject-Verb Agreement

Words Between Subject and Verb

Words that come between the simple subject and the verb have no bearing on subject-verb agreement.

Examples:

The joy (singular subject) of my life returns (singular verb) home tonight.

The phrase *of my life* does not influence the verb *returns.*

The question (singular subject) that still remains unanswered is (singular verb) "Who are you?"

Don't let the phrase "*that still remains…*" trouble you. The subject *question* goes with *is.*

Compound Subjects

A compound subject is formed when two or more nouns joined by *and*, *or*, or *nor* jointly act as the subject of the sentence.

Joined by And

When a compound subject is joined by *and*, it is treated as a plural subject and requires a plural verb.

Examples:

(plural subject) (plural verb)
You and Jon are invited to come to my house.

(plural subject) (plural verb)
The pencil and paper belong to me.

Joined by Or/Nor

For a compound subject joined by *or* or *nor*, the verb must agree in number with the part of the subject that is closest to the verb (italicized in the examples below).

Examples:

(subject) (verb)
Today or tomorrow is the day.

(subject) (verb)
Stan or Phil wants to read the book.

(subject) (verb)
Neither the pen nor the book is on the desk.

(subject) (verb)
Either the blanket or pillows arrive this afternoon.

Indefinite Pronouns as Subject

An indefinite pronoun is a pronoun that does not refer to a specific noun. Different indefinite pronouns may only function as a singular noun, only function as a plural noun, or change depending on how they are used.

Always Singular

Pronouns such as *each*, *either*, *everybody*, *anybody*, *somebody*, and *nobody* are always singular.

Examples:

(singular subject) (singular verb)
Each of the runners has a different bib number.

(singular verb) (singular subject)
Is either of you ready for the game?

Note: The words *each* and *either* can also be used as adjectives (e.g., *each* person is unique). When one of these adjectives modifies the subject of a sentence, it is always a singular subject.

(singular subject) (singular verb)
Everybody grows a day older every day.

(singular subject) (singular verb)
Anybody is welcome to bring a tent.

ALWAYS PLURAL

Pronouns such as *both*, *several*, and *many* are always plural.

Examples:

> plural subject — Both; plural verb — were
>
> Both of the siblings were too tired to argue.
>
> plural subject — Many; plural verb — have tried
>
> Many have tried, but none have succeeded.

DEPEND ON CONTEXT

Pronouns such as *some*, *any*, *all*, *none*, *more*, and *most* can be either singular or plural depending on what they are representing in the context of the sentence.

Examples:

> singular subject — All; singular verb — was
>
> All of my dog's food was still there in his bowl.
>
> plural subject — all; plural verb — were
>
> By the end of the night, all of my guests were already excited about coming to my next party.

OTHER CASES INVOLVING PLURAL OR IRREGULAR FORM

Some nouns are **singular in meaning but plural in form**: news, mathematics, physics, and economics.

> The *news is* coming on now.
>
> *Mathematics is* my favorite class.

Some nouns are plural in form and meaning, and have **no singular equivalent**: scissors and pants.

> Do these *pants come* with a shirt?
>
> The *scissors are* for my project.

Mathematical operations are **irregular** in their construction, but are normally considered to be **singular in meaning**.

> *One plus one is* two.
>
> *Three times three is* nine.

Note: Look to your **dictionary** for help when you aren't sure whether a noun with a plural form has a singular or plural meaning.

COMPLEMENTS

A complement is a noun, pronoun, or adjective that is used to give more information about the subject or verb in the sentence.

Direct Objects

A direct object is a noun or pronoun that takes or receives the **action** of a verb. (Remember: a complete sentence does not need a direct object, so not all sentences will have them. A sentence needs only a subject and a verb.) When you are looking for a direct objcct, find the verb and ask *who* or *what.*

Examples:

> I took *the blanket.*
>
> Jane read *books.*

Indirect Objects

An indirect object is a word or group of words that show how an action had an **influence** on someone or something. If there is an indirect object in a sentence, then you always have a direct object in the sentence. When you are looking for the indirect object, find the verb and ask *to/for whom or what.*

Examples:

> indirect object: the old dog; direct object: a new trick
> We taught the old dog a new trick.
>
> indirect object: them; direct object: a math lesson
> I gave them a math lesson.

Review Video: Direct and Indirect Objects
Visit mometrix.com/academy and enter code: 817385

Predicate Nominatives and Predicate Adjectives

As we looked at previously, verbs may be classified as either action verbs or linking verbs. A linking verb is so named because it links the subject to words in the predicate that describe or define the subject. These words are called predicate nominatives (if nouns or pronouns) or predicate adjectives (if adjectives).

Examples:

> subject: father; predicate nominative: lawyer
> My father is a lawyer.
>
> subject: mother; predicate adjective: patient
> Your mother is patient.

Pronoun Usage

The **antecedent** is the noun that has been replaced by a pronoun. A pronoun and its antecedent **agree** when they have the same number (singular or plural) and gender (male, female, or neutral).

Examples:

> antecedent: John; pronoun: he
> **Singular agreement**: John came into town, and he played for us.
>
> antecedent: John and Rick; pronoun: they
> **Plural agreement**: John and Rick came into town, and they played for us.

To determine which is the correct pronoun to use in a compound subject or object, try each pronoun **alone** in place of the compound in the sentence. Your knowledge of pronouns will tell you which one is correct.

Example:

> Bob and (I, me) will be going.
>
> Test: (1) *I will be going* or (2) *Me will be going*. The second choice cannot be correct because *me* cannot be used as the subject of a sentence. Instead, *me* is used as an object.
>
> **Answer**: Bob and I will be going.

When a pronoun is used with a noun immediately following (as in "we boys"), try the sentence **without the added noun**.

Example:

> (We/Us) boys played football last year.
>
> Test: (1) *We played football last ye*ar or (2) *Us played football last year*. Again, the second choice cannot be correct because *us* cannot be used as a subject of a sentence. Instead, *us* is used as an object.
>
> **Answer**: We boys played football last year.

Review Video: Pronoun Usage
Visit mometrix.com/academy and enter code: 666500

Review Video: What is Pronoun-Antecedent Agreement?
Visit mometrix.com/academy and enter code: 919704

A pronoun should point clearly to the **antecedent**. Here is how a pronoun reference can be unhelpful if it is puzzling or not directly stated.

> **Unhelpful**: Ron and Jim (antecedent) went to the store, and he (pronoun) bought soda.
>
> Who bought soda? Ron or Jim?
>
> **Helpful**: Jim (antecedent) went to the store, and he (pronoun) bought soda.
>
> The sentence is clear. Jim bought the soda.

Some pronouns change their form by their placement in a sentence. A pronoun that is a **subject** in a sentence comes in the **subjective case**. Pronouns that serve as **objects** appear in the **objective case**. Finally, the pronouns that are used as **possessives** appear in the **possessive case**.

Examples:

> **Subjective case**: *He* is coming to the show.
>
> The pronoun *He* is the subject of the sentence.
>
> **Objective case**: Josh drove *him* to the airport.
>
> The pronoun *him* is the object of the sentence.

Possessive case: The flowers are *mine*.

The pronoun *mine* shows ownership of the flowers.

The word *who* is a subjective-case pronoun that can be used as a **subject**. The word *whom* is an objective-case pronoun that can be used as an **object**. The words *who* and *whom* are common in subordinate clauses or in questions.

Examples:

subject: who; verb: wants

He knows who wants to come.

object: whom; verb: want

He knows the man whom we want at the party.

Clauses

A clause is a group of words that contains both a subject and a predicate (verb). There are two types of clauses: independent and dependent. An **independent clause** contains a complete thought, while a **dependent (or subordinate) clause** does not. A dependent clause includes a subject and a verb, and may also contain objects or complements, but it cannot stand as a complete thought without being joined to an independent clause. Dependent clauses function within sentences as adjectives, adverbs, or nouns.

Example:

independent clause: I am running; dependent clause: because I want to stay in shape.

I am running because I want to stay in shape.

The clause *I am running* is an independent clause: it has a subject and a verb, and it gives a complete thought. The clause *because I want to stay in shape* is a dependent clause: it has a subject and a verb, but it does not express a complete thought. It adds detail to the independent clause to which it is attached.

> **Review Video: What is a Clause?**
> Visit mometrix.com/academy and enter code: 940170
>
> **Review Video: Independent and Dependent Clauses**
> Visit mometrix.com/academy and enter code: 556903

Types of Dependent Clauses

Adjective Clauses

An **adjective clause** is a dependent clause that modifies a noun or a pronoun. Adjective clauses begin with a relative pronoun (*who, whose, whom, which,* and *that*) or a relative adverb (*where, when,* and *why*).

Also, adjective clauses come after the noun that the clause needs to explain or rename. This is done to have a clear connection to the independent clause.

Examples:

independent clause: I learned the reason; adjective clause: why I won the award.

I learned the reason why I won the award.

independent clause: This is the place; adjective clause: where I started my first job.

This is the place where I started my first job.

An adjective clause can be an essential or nonessential clause. An essential clause is very important to the sentence. **Essential clauses** explain or define a person or thing. **Nonessential clauses** give more information about a person or thing but are not necessary to define them. Nonessential clauses are set off with commas while essential clauses are not.

Examples:

essential clause

A person who works hard at first can often rest later in life.

nonessential clause

Neil Armstrong, who walked on the moon, is my hero.

Review Video: Adjective Clauses and Phrases
Visit mometrix.com/academy and enter code: 520888

Adverb Clauses

An **adverb clause** is a dependent clause that modifies a verb, adjective, or adverb. In sentences with multiple dependent clauses, adverb clauses are usually placed immediately before or after the independent clause. An adverb clause is introduced with words such as *after, although, as, before, because, if, since, so, unless, when, where*, and *while*.

Examples:

adverb clause

When you walked outside, I called the manager.

adverb clause

I will go with you unless you want to stay.

Noun Clauses

A **noun clause** is a dependent clause that can be used as a subject, object, or complement. Noun clauses begin with words such as *how, that, what, whether, which, who,* and *why*. These words can also come with an adjective clause. Unless the noun clause is being used as the subject of the sentence, it should come after the verb of the independent clause.

Examples:

noun clause

The real mystery is how you avoided serious injury.

noun clause

What you learn from each other depends on your honesty with others.

Subordination

When two related ideas are not of equal importance, the ideal way to combine them is to make the more important idea an independent clause and the less important idea a dependent or subordinate clause. This is called **subordination**.

Example:

> **Separate ideas**: The team had a perfect regular season. The team lost the championship.
>
> **Subordinated**: Despite having a perfect regular season, *the team lost the championship*.

Phrases

A phrase is a group of words that functions as a single part of speech, usually a noun, adjective, or adverb. A **phrase** is not a complete thought, but it adds detail or explanation to a sentence, or renames something within the sentence.

Prepositional Phrases

One of the most common types of phrases is the prepositional phrase. A **prepositional phrase** begins with a preposition and ends with a noun or pronoun that is the object of the preposition. Normally, the prepositional phrase functions as an **adjective** or an **adverb** within the sentence.

Examples:

> The picnic is on the blanket. (prepositional phrase: "on the blanket")
>
> I am sick with a fever today. (prepositional phrase: "with a fever")
>
> Among the many flowers, John found a four-leaf clover. (prepositional phrase: "Among the many flowers")

Verbal Phrases

A **verbal** is a word or phrase that is formed from a verb but does not function as a verb. Depending on its particular form, it may be used as a noun, adjective, or adverb. A verbal does **not** replace a verb in a sentence.

Examples:

> Correct: Walk a mile daily. (verb: "Walk")
>
> This is a complete sentence with the implied subject *you*.
>
> Incorrect: To walk a mile. (verbal: "To walk")
>
> This is not a sentence since there is no functional verb.

There are three types of verbal: **participles**, **gerunds**, and **infinitives**. Each type of verbal has a corresponding **phrase** that consists of the verbal itself along with any complements or modifiers.

Participles

A **participle** is a type of verbal that always functions as an adjective. The present participle always ends with -*ing*. Past participles end with *-d, -ed, -n,* or *-t.*

> Examples: dance (verb) | dancing (present participle) | danced (past participle)

Participial phrases most often come right before or right after the noun or pronoun that they modify.

Examples:

participial phrase
Shipwrecked on an island, the boys started to fish for food.

participial phrase
Having been seated for five hours, we got out of the car to stretch our legs.

participial phrase
Praised for their work, the group accepted the first-place trophy.

Gerunds

A **gerund** is a type of verbal that always functions as a **noun**. Like present participles, gerunds always end with *-ing*, but they can be easily distinguished from one another by the part of speech they represent (participles always function as adjectives). Since a gerund or gerund phrase always functions as a noun, it can be used as the subject of a sentence, the predicate nominative, or the object of a verb or preposition.

Examples:

gerund
We want to be known for teaching the poor.
object of preposition

gerund
Coaching this team is the best job of my life.
subject

gerund
We like practicing our songs in the basement.
object of verb

Infinitives

An **infinitive** is a type of verbal that can function as a noun, an adjective, or an adverb. An infinitive is made of the word *to* and the basic form of the verb. As with all other types of verbal phrases, an infinitive phrase includes the verbal itself and all of its complements or modifiers.

Examples:

infinitive
To join the team is my goal in life.
noun

infinitive
The animals have enough food to eat for the night.
adjective

infinitive
People lift weights to exercise their muscles.
adverb

Review Video: Gerunds, Infinitives, and Participles
Visit mometrix.com/academy and enter code: 634263

APPOSITIVE PHRASES

An **appositive** is a word or phrase that is used to explain or rename nouns or pronouns. Noun phrases, gerund phrases, and infinitive phrases can all be used as appositives.

Examples:

appositive

Terriers, hunters at heart, have been dressed up to look like lap dogs.

The noun phrase *hunters at heart* renames the noun *terriers*.

appositive

His plan, to save and invest his money, was proven as a safe approach.

The infinitive phrase explains what the plan is.

Appositive phrases can be **essential** or **nonessential**. An appositive phrase is essential if the person, place, or thing being described or renamed is too general for its meaning to be understood without the appositive.

Examples:

essential

Two of America's Founding Fathers, George Washington and Thomas Jefferson, served as presidents.

nonessential

George Washington and Thomas Jefferson, two Founding Fathers, served as presidents.

ABSOLUTE PHRASES

An absolute phrase is a phrase that consists of **a noun followed by a participle**. An absolute phrase provides **context** to what is being described in the sentence, but it does not modify or explain any particular word; it is essentially independent.

Examples:

noun participle

The alarm ringing, he pushed the snooze button.

absolute phrase

noun participle

The music paused, she continued to dance through the crowd.

absolute phrase

PARALLELISM

When multiple items or ideas are presented in a sentence in series, such as in a list, the items or ideas must be stated in grammatically equivalent ways. In other words, if one idea is stated in gerund form, the second cannot be stated in infinitive form. For example, to write, *I enjoy reading and to study* would be incorrect. An infinitive and a gerund are not equivalent. Instead, you should write *I enjoy reading and studying*. In lists of more than two, all items must be parallel.

Example:

Incorrect: He stopped at the office, grocery store, and the pharmacy before heading home.

The first and third items in the list of places include the article *the*, so the second item needs it as well.

Correct: He stopped at the office, *the* grocery store, and the pharmacy before heading home.

Example:

Incorrect: While vacationing in Europe, she went biking, skiing, and climbed mountains.

The first and second items in the list are gerunds, so the third item must be as well.

Correct: While vacationing in Europe, she went biking, skiing, and *mountain climbing*.

Review Video: Parallel Sentence Construction
Visit mometrix.com/academy and enter code: 831988

Sentence Purpose

There are four types of sentences: declarative, imperative, interrogative, and exclamatory.

A **declarative** sentence states a fact and ends with a period.

The football game starts at seven o'clock.

An **imperative** sentence tells someone to do something and generally ends with a period. An urgent command might end with an exclamation point instead.

Don't forget to buy your ticket.

An **interrogative** sentence asks a question and ends with a question mark.

Are you going to the game on Friday?

An **exclamatory** sentence shows strong emotion and ends with an exclamation point.

I can't believe we won the game!

Review Video: Functions of a Sentence
Visit mometrix.com/academy and enter code: 475974

Sentence Structure

Sentences are classified by structure based on the type and number of clauses present. The four classifications of sentence structure are the following:

Simple: A simple sentence has one independent clause with no dependent clauses. A simple sentence may have **compound elements** (i.e., compound subject or verb).

Examples:

single subject | single verb

Judy watered the lawn.

compound subject | single verb

Judy and Alan watered the lawn.

single subject | compound verb | compound verb

Judy watered the lawn and pulled weeds.

compound subject | compound verb | compound verb

Judy and Alan watered the lawn and pulled weeds.

Compound: A compound sentence has two or more independent clauses with no dependent clauses. Usually, the independent clauses are joined with a comma and a coordinating conjunction or with a semicolon.

Examples:

independent clause | independent clause

The time has come, and we are ready.

independent clause | independent clause

I woke up at dawn; the sun was just coming up.

Complex: A complex sentence has one independent clause and at least one dependent clause.

Examples:

dependent clause | independent clause

Although he had the flu, Harry went to work.

independent clause | dependent clause

Marcia got married, after she finished college.

Compound-Complex: A compound-complex sentence has at least two independent clauses and at least one dependent clause.

Examples:

independent clause | dependent clause | independent clause

John is my friend who went to India, and he brought back souvenirs.

independent clause | independent clause | dependent clause

You may not realize this, but we heard the music that you played last night.

Review Video: Sentence Structure
Visit mometrix.com/academy and enter code: 700478

Sentence variety is important to consider when writing an essay or speech. A variety of sentence lengths and types creates rhythm, makes a passage more engaging, and gives writers an opportunity to demonstrate their writing style. Writing that uses the same length or type of sentence without variation can be boring or difficult to read. To evaluate a passage for effective sentence variety, it is helpful to note whether the passage contains diverse sentence structures and lengths. It is also important to pay attention to the way each sentence starts and avoid beginning with the same words or phrases.

SENTENCE FRAGMENTS

Recall that a group of words must contain at least one **independent clause** in order to be considered a sentence. If it doesn't contain even one independent clause, it is called a **sentence fragment**.

The appropriate process for **repairing** a sentence fragment depends on what type of fragment it is. If the fragment is a dependent clause, it can sometimes be as simple as removing a subordinating word (e.g., when, because, if) from the beginning of the fragment. Alternatively, a dependent clause can be incorporated into a closely related neighboring sentence. If the fragment is missing some required part, like a subject or a verb, the fix might be as simple as adding the missing part.

Examples:

> **Fragment**: Because he wanted to sail the Mediterranean.
>
> **Removed subordinating word**: He wanted to sail the Mediterranean.
>
> **Combined with another sentence**: Because he wanted to sail the Mediterranean, he booked a Greek island cruise.

RUN-ON SENTENCES

Run-on sentences consist of multiple independent clauses that have not been joined together properly. Run-on sentences can be corrected in several different ways:

Join clauses properly: This can be done with a comma and coordinating conjunction, with a semicolon, or with a colon or dash if the second clause is explaining something in the first.

Example:

> **Incorrect**: I went on the trip, we visited lots of castles.
>
> **Corrected**: I went on the trip, and we visited lots of castles.

Split into separate sentences: This correction is most effective when the independent clauses are very long or when they are not closely related.

Example:

> **Incorrect**: The drive to New York takes ten hours, my uncle lives in Boston.
>
> **Corrected**: The drive to New York takes ten hours. My uncle lives in Boston.

Make one clause dependent: This is the easiest way to make the sentence correct and more interesting at the same time. It's often as simple as adding a subordinating word between the two clauses or before the first clause.

Example:

> **Incorrect**: I finally made it to the store and I bought some eggs.
>
> **Corrected**: When I finally made it to the store, I bought some eggs.

Reduce to one clause with a compound verb: If both clauses have the same subject, remove the subject from the second clause, and you now have just one clause with a compound verb.

Example:

> **Incorrect**: The drive to New York takes ten hours, it makes me very tired.
>
> **Corrected**: The drive to New York takes ten hours and makes me very tired.

Note: While these are the simplest ways to correct a run-on sentence, often the best way is to completely reorganize the thoughts in the sentence and rewrite it.

> **Review Video: Fragments and Run-on Sentences**
> Visit mometrix.com/academy and enter code: 541989

DANGLING AND MISPLACED MODIFIERS

DANGLING MODIFIERS

A dangling modifier is a dependent clause or verbal phrase that does not have a clear logical connection to a word in the sentence.

Example:

> dangling modifier
>
> **Incorrect**: Reading each magazine article, the stories caught my attention.
>
> The word *stories* cannot be modified by *Reading each magazine article*. People can read, but stories cannot read. Therefore, the subject of the sentence must be a person.
>
> dependent clause
>
> **Corrected**: Reading each magazine article, I was entertained by the stories.

Example:

> dangling modifier
>
> **Incorrect**: Ever since childhood, my grandparents have visited me for Christmas.
>
> The speaker in this sentence can't have been visited by her grandparents when *they* were children, since she wouldn't have been born yet. Either the modifier should be clarified or the sentence should be rearranged to specify whose childhood is being referenced.
>
> dependent clause
>
> **Clarified**: Ever since I was a child, my grandparents have visited for Christmas.
>
> dependent clause
>
> **Rearranged**: I have enjoyed my grandparents visiting for Christmas, ever since childhood.

MISPLACED MODIFIERS

Because modifiers are grammatically versatile, they can be put in many different places within the structure of a sentence. The danger of this versatility is that a modifier can accidentally be placed where it is modifying the wrong word or where it is not clear which word it is modifying.

Example:

modifier

Incorrect: She read the book to a crowd that was filled with beautiful pictures.

The book was filled with beautiful pictures, not the crowd.

modifier

Corrected: She read the book that was filled with beautiful pictures to a crowd.

Example:

modifier

Ambiguous: Derek saw a bus nearly hit a man on his way to work.

Was Derek on his way to work or was the other man?

modifier

Derek: On his way to work, Derek saw a bus nearly hit a man.

modifier

The other man: Derek saw a bus nearly hit a man who was on his way to work.

Split Infinitives

A split infinitive occurs when a modifying word comes between the word *to* and the verb that pairs with *to*.

Example: To *clearly* explain vs. *To explain* clearly | To *softly* sing vs. *To sing* softly

Though considered improper by some, split infinitives may provide better clarity and simplicity in some cases than the alternatives. As such, avoiding them should not be considered a universal rule.

Double Negatives

Standard English allows **two negatives** only when a **positive** meaning is intended. For example, *The team was not displeased with their performance.* Double negatives to emphasize negation are not used in standard English.

Negative modifiers (e.g., never, no, and not) should not be paired with other negative modifiers or negative words (e.g., none, nobody, nothing, or neither). The modifiers *hardly, barely,* and *scarcely* are also considered negatives in standard English, so they should not be used with other negatives.

Punctuation

END PUNCTUATION

PERIODS

Use a period to end all sentences except direct questions and exclamations. Periods are also used for abbreviations.

> Examples: 3 p.m. | 2 a.m. | Mr. Jones | Mrs. Stevens | Dr. Smith | Bill, Jr. | Pennsylvania Ave.

Note: An abbreviation is a shortened form of a word or phrase.

QUESTION MARKS

Question marks should be used following a **direct question**. A polite request can be followed by a period instead of a question mark.

> **Direct Question**: What is for lunch today? | How are you? | Why is that the answer?
>
> **Polite Requests**: Can you please send me the item tomorrow. | Will you please walk with me on the track.

Review Video: Question Marks
Visit mometrix.com/academy and enter code: 118471

EXCLAMATION MARKS

Exclamation marks are used after a word group or sentence that shows much feeling or has special importance. Exclamation marks should not be overused. They are saved for proper **exclamatory interjections**.

> Example: We're going to the finals! | You have a beautiful car! | "That's crazy!" she yelled.

Review Video: Exclamation Points
Visit mometrix.com/academy and enter code: 199367

COMMAS

The comma is a punctuation mark that can help you understand connections in a sentence. Not every sentence needs a comma. However, if a sentence needs a comma, you need to put it in the right place. A comma in the wrong place (or an absent comma) will make a sentence's meaning unclear. These are some of the rules for commas:

Use Case	Example
Before a **coordinating conjunction** joining independent clauses	Bob caught three fish, and I caught two fish.
After an **introductory phrase**	After the final out, we went to a restaurant to celebrate.
After an **adverbial clause**	Studying the stars, I was awed by the beauty of the sky.
Between **items in a series**	I will bring the turkey, the pie, and the coffee.
For **interjections**	Wow, you know how to play this game.
After ***yes* and *no* responses**	No, I cannot come tomorrow.
Separate **nonessential modifiers**	John Frank, who coaches the team, was promoted today.
Separate **nonessential appositives**	Thomas Edison, an American inventor, was born in Ohio.
Separate **nouns of direct address**	You, John, are my only hope in this moment.
Separate **interrogative tags**	This is the last time, correct?
Separate **contrasts**	You are my friend, not my enemy.
Writing **dates**	July 4, 1776, is an important date to remember.
Writing **addresses**	He is meeting me at 456 Delaware Avenue, Washington, D.C., tomorrow morning.
Writing **geographical names**	Paris, France, is my favorite city.
Writing **titles**	John Smith, PhD, will be visiting your class today.
Separate **expressions like *he said***	"You can start," she said, "with an apology."

Also, you can use a comma **between coordinate adjectives** not joined with *and*. However, not all adjectives are coordinate (i.e., equal or parallel).

Incorrect: The kind, brown dog followed me home.

Correct: The kind, loyal dog followed me home.

There are two simple ways to know if your adjectives are coordinate. One, you can join the adjectives with *and*: *The kind and loyal dog*. Two, you can change the order of the adjectives: *The loyal, kind dog*.

Review Video: When to Use a Comma
Visit mometrix.com/academy and enter code: 786797

SEMICOLONS

The semicolon is used to connect major sentence pieces of equal value. Some rules for semicolons include:

Use Case	Example
Between closely connected independent clauses **not connected with a coordinating conjunction**	You are right; we should go with your plan.
Between independent clauses **linked with a transitional word**	I think that we can agree on this; however, I am not sure about my friends.
Between items in a **series that has internal punctuation**	I have visited New York, New York; Augusta, Maine; and Baltimore, Maryland.

Review Video: How to Use Semicolons
Visit mometrix.com/academy and enter code: 370605

Colons

The colon is used to call attention to the words that follow it. A colon must come after a **complete independent clause**. The rules for colons are as follows:

Use Case	Example
After an independent clause to **make a list**	I want to learn many languages: Spanish, German, and Italian.
For **explanations**	There is one thing that stands out on your resume: responsibility.
To give a **quote**	He started with an idea: "We are able to do more than we imagine."
After the **greeting in a formal letter**	To Whom It May Concern:
Show **hours and minutes**	It is 3:14 p.m.
Separate a **title and subtitle**	The essay is titled "America: A Short Introduction to a Modern Country."

Review Video: Colons
Visit mometrix.com/academy and enter code: 868673

Parentheses

Parentheses are used for additional information. Also, they can be used to put labels for letters or numbers in a series. Parentheses should be not be used very often. If they are overused, parentheses can be a distraction instead of a help.

Examples:

Extra Information: The rattlesnake (see Image 2) is a dangerous snake of North and South America.

Series: Include in the email (1) your name, (2) your address, and (3) your question for the author.

Review Video: Parentheses
Visit mometrix.com/academy and enter code: 947743

Quotation Marks

Use quotation marks to close off **direct quotations** of a person's spoken or written words. Do not use quotation marks around indirect quotations. An indirect quotation gives someone's message without using the person's exact words. Use **single quotation marks** to close off a quotation inside a quotation.

Direct Quote: Nancy said, "I am waiting for Henry to arrive."

Indirect Quote: Henry said that he is going to be late to the meeting.

Quote inside a Quote: The teacher asked, "Has everyone read 'The Gift of the Magi'?"

Quotation marks should be used around the titles of **short works**: newspaper and magazine articles, poems, short stories, songs, television episodes, radio programs, and subdivisions of books or websites.

Examples:

"Rip Van Winkle" (short story by Washington Irving)

"O Captain! My Captain!" (poem by Walt Whitman)

Although it is not standard usage, quotation marks are sometimes used to highlight **irony** or the use of words to mean something other than their dictionary definition. This type of usage should be employed sparingly, if at all.

Examples:

The boss warned Frank that he was walking on "thin ice."	Frank is not walking on real ice. Instead, he is being warned to avoid mistakes.
The teacher thanked the young man for his "honesty."	The quotation marks around *honesty* show that the teacher does not believe the young man's explanation.

Review Video: Quotation Marks
Visit mometrix.com/academy and enter code: 884918

Periods and commas are put **inside** quotation marks. Colons and semicolons are put **outside** the quotation marks. Question marks and exclamation points are placed inside quotation marks when they are part of a quote. When the question or exclamation mark goes with the whole sentence, the mark is left outside of the quotation marks.

Examples:

Period and comma	We read "The Gift of the Magi," "The Skylight Room," and "The Cactus."
Semicolon	They watched "The Nutcracker"; then, they went home.
Exclamation mark that is a part of a quote	The crowd cheered, "Victory!"
Question mark that goes with the whole sentence	Is your favorite short story "The Tell-Tale Heart"?

APOSTROPHES

An apostrophe is used to show **possession** or the **deletion of letters in contractions**. An apostrophe is not needed with the possessive pronouns *his, hers, its, ours, theirs, whose,* and *yours.*

Singular Nouns: David's car | a book's theme | my brother's board game

Plural Nouns that end with -*s*: the scissors' handle | boys' basketball

Plural Nouns that end without -*s*: Men's department | the people's adventure

Review Video: When to Use an Apostrophe
Visit mometrix.com/academy and enter code: 213068

Review Video: Punctuation Errors in Possessive Pronouns
Visit mometrix.com/academy and enter code: 221438

Hyphens

Hyphens are used to **separate compound words**. Use hyphens in the following cases:

Use Case	Example
Compound numbers from 21 to 99 when written out in words	This team needs twenty-five points to win the game.
Written-out fractions that are used as adjectives	The recipe says that we need a three-fourths cup of butter.
Compound adjectives that come before a noun	The well-fed dog took a nap.
Unusual compound words that would be hard to read or easily confused with other words	This is the best anti-itch cream on the market.

Note: This is not a complete set of the rules for hyphens. A dictionary is the best tool for knowing if a compound word needs a hyphen.

Review Video: Hyphens
Visit mometrix.com/academy and enter code: 981632

Dashes

Dashes are used to show a **break** or a **change in thought** in a sentence or to act as parentheses in a sentence. When typing, use two hyphens to make a dash. Do not put a space before or after the dash. The following are the functions of dashes:

Use Case	Example
Set off parenthetical statements or an **appositive with internal punctuation**	The three trees—oak, pine, and magnolia—are coming on a truck tomorrow.
Show a **break or change in tone or thought**	The first question—how silly of me—does not have a correct answer.

Ellipsis Marks

The ellipsis mark has **three** periods (...) to show when **words have been removed** from a quotation. If a **full sentence or more** is removed from a quoted passage, you need to use **four** periods to show the removed text and the end punctuation mark. The ellipsis mark should not be used at the beginning of a quotation. The ellipsis mark should also not be used at the end of a quotation unless some words have been deleted from the end of the final sentence.

Example:

> "Then he picked up the groceries...paid for them...later he went home."

Brackets

There are two main reasons to use brackets:

Use Case	Example
Placing **parentheses inside of parentheses**	The hero of this story, Paul Revere (a silversmith and industrialist [see Ch. 4]), rode through towns of Massachusetts to warn of advancing British troops.
Adding **clarification or detail to a quotation** that is not part of the quotation	The father explained, "My children are planning to attend my alma mater [State University]."

Review Video: Brackets
Visit mometrix.com/academy and enter code: 727546

Common Usage Mistakes

Word Confusion

Which, That, and Who

The words *which*, *that*, and *who* can act as **relative pronouns** to help clarify or describe a noun.

Which is used for things only.

Example: Andrew's car, *which is old and rusty,* broke down last week.

That is used for people or things. *That* is usually informal when used to describe people.

Example: Is this the only book *that Louis L'Amour wrote?*

Example: Is Louis L'Amour the author *that wrote Western novels?*

Who is used for people or for animals that have an identity or personality.

Example: Mozart was the composer *who wrote those operas.*

Example: John's dog, *who is called Max,* is large and fierce.

Homophones

Homophones are words that sound alike (or similar) but have different **spellings** and **definitions**. A homophone is a type of **homonym**, which is a pair or group of words that are pronounced or spelled the same, but do not mean the same thing.

To, Too, and Two

To can be an adverb or a preposition for showing direction, purpose, and relationship. See your dictionary for the many other ways to use *to* in a sentence.

Examples: I went to the store. | I want to go with you.

Too is an adverb that means *also, as well, very,* or *in excess.*

Examples: I can walk a mile too. | You have eaten too much.

Two is a number.

Example: You have two minutes left.

There, Their, and They're

There can be an adjective, adverb, or pronoun. Often, *there* is used to show a place or to start a sentence.

Examples: I went there yesterday. | There is something in his pocket.

Their is a pronoun that is used to show ownership.

Examples: He is their father. | This is their fourth apology this week.

They're is a contraction of *they are.*

Example: Did you know that they're in town?

Knew and New

Knew is the past tense of *know*.

Example: I knew the answer.

New is an adjective that means something is current, has not been used, or is modern.

Example: This is my new phone.

Then and Than

Then is an adverb that indicates sequence or order:

Example: I'm going to run to the library and then come home.

Than is special-purpose word used only for comparisons:

Example: Susie likes chips more than candy.

Its and It's

Its is a pronoun that shows ownership.

Example: The guitar is in its case.

It's is a contraction of *it is*.

Example: It's an honor and a privilege to meet you.

Note: The *h* in honor is silent, so *honor* starts with the vowel sound *o*, which must have the article *an*.

Your and You're

Your is a pronoun that shows ownership.

Example: This is your moment to shine.

You're is a contraction of *you are*.

Example: Yes, you're correct.

Saw and Seen

Saw is the past-tense form of *see*.

Example: I saw a turtle on my walk this morning.

Seen is the past participle of *see*.

Example: I have seen this movie before.

Affect and Effect

There are two main reasons that *affect* and *effect* are so often confused: 1) both words can be used as either a noun or a verb, and 2) unlike most homophones, their usage and meanings are closely related to each other. Here is a quick rundown of the four usage options:

Affect (n): feeling, emotion, or mood that is displayed

Example: The patient had a flat *affect*. (i.e., his face showed little or no emotion)

Affect (v): to alter, to change, to influence

Example: The sunshine *affects* the plant's growth.

Effect (n): a result, a consequence

Example: What *effect* will this weather have on our schedule?

Effect (v): to bring about, to cause to be

Example: These new rules will *effect* order in the office.

The noun form of *affect* is rarely used outside of technical medical descriptions, so if a noun form is needed on the test, you can safely select *effect*. The verb form of *effect* is not as rare as the noun form of *affect*, but it's still not all that likely to show up on your test. If you need a verb and you can't decide which to use based on the definitions, choosing *affect* is your best bet.

HOMOGRAPHS

Homographs are words that share the same spelling, but have different meanings and sometimes different pronunciations. To figure out which meaning is being used, you should bc looking for context clues. The context clues give hints to the meaning of the word. For example, the word *spot* has many meanings. It can mean "a place" or "a stain or blot." In the sentence "After my lunch, I saw a spot on my shirt," the word *spot* means "a stain or blot." The context clues of "After my lunch" and "on my shirt" guide you to this decision. A homograph is another type of homonym.

BANK

(noun): an establishment where money is held for savings or lending

(verb): to collect or pile up

CONTENT

(noun): the topics that will be addressed within a book

(adjective): pleased or satisfied

(verb): to make someone pleased or satisfied

FINE

(noun): an amount of money that acts a penalty for an offense

(adjective): very small or thin

(adverb): in an acceptable way

(verb): to make someone pay money as a punishment

INCENSE

(noun): a material that is burned in religious settings and makes a pleasant aroma

(verb): to frustrate or anger

LEAD

(noun): the first or highest position

(noun): a heavy metallic element

(verb): to direct a person or group of followers

(adjective): containing lead

Object

(noun): a lifeless item that can be held and observed

(verb): to disagree

Produce

(noun): fruits and vegetables

(verb): to make or create something

Refuse

(noun): garbage or debris that has been thrown away

(verb): to not allow

Subject

(noun): an area of study

(verb): to force or subdue

Tear

(noun): a fluid secreted by the eyes

(verb): to separate or pull apart

The Writing Process

Brainstorming

Brainstorming is a technique that is used to find a creative approach to a subject. This can be accomplished by simple **free-association** with a topic. For example, with paper and pen, write every thought that you have about the topic in a word or phrase. This is done without critical thinking. You should put everything that comes to your mind about the topic on your scratch paper. Then, you need to read the list over a few times. Next, look for patterns, repetitions, and clusters of ideas. This allows a variety of fresh ideas to come as you think about the topic.

Free Writing

Free writing is a more structured form of brainstorming. The method involves taking a limited amount of time (e.g., 2 to 3 minutes) to write everything that comes to mind about the topic in complete sentences. When time expires, review everything that has been written down. Many of your sentences may make little or no sense, but the insights and observations that can come from free writing make this method a valuable approach. Usually, free writing results in a fuller expression of ideas than brainstorming because thoughts and associations are written in complete sentences. However, both techniques can be used to complement each other.

Planning

Planning is the process of organizing a piece of writing before composing a draft. Planning can include creating an outline or a graphic organizer, such as a Venn diagram, a spider-map, or a flowchart. These methods should help the writer identify their topic, main ideas, and the general organization of the composition. Preliminary research can also take place during this stage. Planning helps writers organize all of their ideas and decide if they have enough material to begin their first draft. However, writers should remember that the decisions they make during this step will likely change later in the process, so their plan does not have to be perfect.

Drafting

Writers may then use their plan, outline, or graphic organizer to compose their first draft. They may write subsequent drafts to improve their writing. Writing multiple drafts can help writers consider different ways to communicate their ideas and address errors that may be difficult to correct without rewriting a section or the whole composition. Most writers will vary in how many drafts they choose to write, as there is no "right" number of drafts. Writing drafts also takes away the pressure to write perfectly on the first try, as writers can improve with each draft they write.

Revising, Editing, and Proofreading

Once a writer completes a draft, they can move on to the revising, editing, and proofreading steps to improve their draft. These steps begin with making broad changes that may apply to large sections of a composition and then making small, specific corrections. **Revising** is the first and broadest of these steps. Revising involves ensuring that the composition addresses an appropriate audience, includes all necessary material, maintains focus throughout, and is organized logically. Revising may occur after the first draft to ensure that the following drafts improve upon errors from the first draft. Some revision should occur between each draft to avoid repeating these errors. The **editing** phase of writing is narrower than the revising phase. Editing a composition should include steps such as improving transitions between paragraphs, ensuring each paragraph is on topic, and improving the flow of the text. The editing phase may also include correcting grammatical errors that cannot be fixed without significantly altering the text. **Proofreading** involves fixing misspelled words, typos, other grammatical errors, and any remaining surface-level flaws in the composition.

Recursive Writing Process

However you approach writing, you may find comfort in knowing that the revision process can occur in any order. The **recursive writing process** is not as difficult as the phrase may make it seem. Simply put, the recursive writing process means that you may need to revisit steps after completing other steps. It also implies that the steps are not required to take place in any certain order. Indeed, you may find that planning, drafting, and revising can all take place at about the same time. The writing process involves moving back and forth between planning, drafting, and revising, followed by more planning, more drafting, and more revising until the writing is satisfactory.

Review Video: Recursive Writing Process
Visit mometrix.com/academy and enter code: 951611

Technology in the Writing Process

Modern technology has yielded several tools that can be used to make the writing process more convenient and organized. Word processors and online tools, such as databases and plagiarism detectors, allow much of the writing process to be completed in one place, using one device.

Technology for Planning and Drafting

For the planning and drafting stages of the writing process, word processors are a helpful tool. These programs also feature formatting tools, allowing users to create their own planning tools or create digital outlines that can be easily converted into sentences, paragraphs, or an entire essay draft. Online databases and references also complement the planning process by providing convenient access to information and sources for research. Word processors also allow users to keep up with their work and update it more easily than if they wrote their work by hand. Online word processors often allow users to collaborate, making group assignments more convenient. These programs also allow users to include illustrations or other supplemental media in their compositions.

Technology for Revising, Editing, and Proofreading

Word processors also benefit the revising, editing, and proofreading stages of the writing process. Most of these programs indicate errors in spelling and grammar, allowing users to catch minor errors and correct them quickly. There are also websites designed to help writers by analyzing text for deeper errors, such as poor sentence structure, inappropriate complexity, lack of sentence variety, and style issues. These websites can help users fix errors they may not know to look for or may have simply missed. As writers finish these steps, they may benefit from checking their work for any plagiarism. There are several websites and programs that compare text to other documents and publications across the internet and detect any similarities within the text. These websites show the source of the similar information, so users know whether or not they referenced the source and unintentionally plagiarized its contents.

Technology for Publishing

Technology also makes managing written work more convenient. Digitally storing documents keeps everything in one place and is easy to reference. Digital storage also makes sharing work easier, as documents can be attached to an email or stored online. This also allows writers to publish their work easily, as they can electronically submit it to other publications or freely post it to a personal blog, profile, or website.

Outlining and Organizing Ideas

Main Ideas, Supporting Details, and Outlining a Topic

A writer often begins the first paragraph of a paper by stating the **main idea** or point, also known as the **topic sentence**. The rest of the paragraph supplies particular details that develop and support the main point. One way to visualize the relationship between the main point and supporting information is by considering a table: the tabletop is the main point, and each of the table's legs is a supporting detail or group of details. Both professional authors and students can benefit from planning their writing by first making an outline of the topic. Outlines facilitate quick identification of the main point and supporting details without having to wade through the additional language that will exist in the fully developed essay, article, or paper. Outlining can also help readers to analyze a piece of existing writing for the same reason. The outline first summarizes the main idea in one sentence. Then, below that, it summarizes the supporting details in a numbered list. Writing the paper then consists of filling in the outline with detail, writing a paragraph for each supporting point, and adding an introduction and conclusion.

Introduction

The purpose of the introduction is to capture the reader's attention and announce the essay's main idea. Normally, the introduction contains 50-80 words, or 3-5 sentences. An introduction can begin with an interesting quote, a question, or a strong opinion—something that will **engage** the reader's interest and prompt them to keep reading. If you are writing your essay to a specific prompt, your introduction should include a **restatement or summarization** of the prompt so that the reader will have some context for your essay. Finally, your introduction should briefly state your **thesis or main idea**: the primary thing you hope to communicate to the reader through your essay. Don't try to include all of the details and nuances of your thesis, or all of your reasons for it, in the introduction. That's what the rest of the essay is for!

Review Video: Introduction
Visit mometrix.com/academy and enter code: 961328

Thesis Statement

The thesis is the main idea of the essay. A temporary thesis, or working thesis, should be established early in the writing process because it will serve to keep the writer focused as ideas develop. This temporary thesis is subject to change as you continue to write.

The temporary thesis has two parts: a **topic** (i.e., the focus of your essay based on the prompt) and a **comment**. The comment makes an important point about the topic. A temporary thesis should be interesting and specific. Also, you need to limit the topic to a manageable scope. These three questions are useful tools to measure the effectiveness of any temporary thesis:

- Does the focus of my essay have enough interest to hold an audience?
- Is the focus of my essay specific enough to generate interest?
- Is the focus of my essay manageable for the time limit? Too broad? Too narrow?

The thesis should be a generalization rather than a fact because the thesis prepares readers for facts and details that support the thesis. The process of bringing the thesis into sharp focus may help in outlining major sections of the work. Once the thesis and introduction are complete, you can address the body of the work.

Review Video: Thesis Statements
Visit mometrix.com/academy and enter code: 691033

Supporting the Thesis

Throughout your essay, the thesis should be **explained clearly and supported** adequately by additional arguments. The thesis sentence needs to contain a clear statement of the purpose of your essay and a comment about the thesis. With the thesis statement, you have an opportunity to state what is noteworthy of this particular treatment of the prompt. Each sentence and paragraph should build on and support the thesis.

When you respond to the prompt, use parts of the passage to support your argument or defend your position. Using supporting evidence from the passage strengths your argument because readers can see your attention to the entire passage and your response to the details and facts within the passage. You can use facts, details, statistics, and direct quotations from the passage to uphold your position. Be sure to point out which information comes from the original passage and base your argument around that evidence.

Body

In an essay's introduction, the writer establishes the thesis and may indicate how the rest of the piece will be structured. In the body of the piece, the writer **elaborates** upon, **illustrates**, and **explains** the **thesis statement**. How writers arrange supporting details and their choices of paragraph types are development techniques. Writers may give examples of the concept introduced in the thesis statement. If the subject includes a cause-and-effect relationship, the author may explain its causality. A writer will explain or analyze the main idea of the piece throughout the body, often by presenting arguments for the veracity or credibility of the thesis statement. Writers may use development to define or clarify ambiguous terms. Paragraphs within the body may be organized using natural sequences, like space and time. Writers may employ **inductive reasoning**, using multiple details to establish a generalization or causal relationship, or **deductive reasoning**, proving a generalized hypothesis or proposition through a specific example or case.

Review Video: Drafting Body Paragraphs
Visit mometrix.com/academy and enter code: 724590

Paragraphs

After the introduction of a passage, a series of body paragraphs will carry a message through to the conclusion. Each paragraph should be **unified around a main point**. Normally, a good topic sentence summarizes the paragraph's main point. A topic sentence is a general sentence that gives an introduction to the paragraph.

The sentences that follow support the topic sentence. However, though it is usually the first sentence, the topic sentence can come as the final sentence to the paragraph if the earlier sentences give a clear explanation of the paragraph's topic. This allows the topic sentence to function as a concluding sentence. Overall, the paragraphs need to stay true to the main point. This means that any unnecessary sentences that do not advance the main point should be removed.

The main point of a paragraph requires adequate development (i.e., a substantial paragraph that covers the main point). A paragraph of two or three sentences does not cover a main point. This is especially true when the main point of the paragraph gives strong support to the argument of the thesis. An occasional short paragraph is fine as a transitional device. However, a well-developed argument will have paragraphs with more than a few sentences.

Methods of Developing Paragraphs

Common methods of adding substance to paragraphs include examples, illustrations, analogies, and cause and effect.

- **Examples** are supporting details to the main idea of a paragraph or a passage. When authors write about something that their audience may not understand, they can provide an example to show their point. When authors write about something that is not easily accepted, they can give examples to prove their point.
- **Illustrations** are extended examples that require several sentences. Well-selected illustrations can be a great way for authors to develop a point that may not be familiar to their audience.

- **Analogies** make comparisons between items that appear to have nothing in common. Analogies are employed by writers to provoke fresh thoughts about a subject. These comparisons may be used to explain the unfamiliar, to clarify an abstract point, or to argue a point. Although analogies are effective literary devices, they should be used carefully in arguments. Two things may be alike in some respects but completely different in others.
- **Cause and effect** is an excellent device to explain the connection between an action or situation and a particular result. One way that authors can use cause and effect is to state the effect in the topic sentence of a paragraph and add the causes in the body of the paragraph. This method can give an author's paragraphs structure, which always strengthens writing.

Types of Paragraphs

A **paragraph of narration** tells a story or a part of a story. Normally, the sentences are arranged in chronological order (i.e., the order that the events happened). However, flashbacks (i.e., an anecdote from an earlier time) can be included.

A **descriptive paragraph** makes a verbal portrait of a person, place, or thing. When specific details are used that appeal to one or more of the senses (i.e., sight, sound, smell, taste, and touch), authors give readers a sense of being present in the moment.

A **process paragraph** is related to time order (i.e., First, you open the bottle. Second, you pour the liquid, etc.). Usually, this describes a process or teaches readers how to perform a process.

Comparing two things draws attention to their similarities and indicates a number of differences. When authors contrast, they focus only on differences. Both comparing and contrasting may be done point-by-point, noting both the similarities and differences of each point, or in sequential paragraphs, where you discuss all the similarities and then all the differences, or vice versa.

Breaking Text into Paragraphs

For most forms of writing, you will need to use multiple paragraphs. As such, determining when to start a new paragraph is very important. Reasons for starting a new paragraph include:

- To mark off the introduction and concluding paragraphs
- To signal a shift to a new idea or topic
- To indicate an important shift in time or place
- To explain a point in additional detail
- To highlight a comparison, contrast, or cause and effect relationship

Paragraph Length

Most readers find that their comfort level for a paragraph is between 100 and 200 words. Shorter paragraphs cause too much starting and stopping and give a choppy effect. Paragraphs that are too long often test the attention span of readers. Two notable exceptions to this rule exist. In scientific or scholarly papers, longer paragraphs suggest seriousness and depth. In journalistic writing, constraints are placed on paragraph size by the narrow columns in a newspaper format.

The first and last paragraphs of a text will usually be the introduction and conclusion. These special-purpose paragraphs are likely to be shorter than paragraphs in the body of the work. Paragraphs in the body of the essay follow the subject's outline (e.g., one paragraph per point in short essays and a group of paragraphs per point in longer works). Some ideas require more development than others, so it is good for a writer to remain flexible. A paragraph of excessive length may be divided, and shorter ones may be combined.

Coherent Paragraphs

A smooth flow of sentences and paragraphs without gaps, shifts, or bumps will lead to paragraph **coherence**. Ties between old and new information can be smoothed using several methods:

- **Linking ideas clearly**, from the topic sentence to the body of the paragraph, is essential for a smooth transition. The topic sentence states the main point, and this should be followed by specific details, examples, and illustrations that support the topic sentence. The support may be direct or indirect. In **indirect support**, the illustrations and examples may support a sentence that in turn supports the topic directly.
- The **repetition of key words** adds coherence to a paragraph. To avoid dull language, variations of the key words may be used.
- **Parallel structures** are often used within sentences to emphasize the similarity of ideas and connect sentences giving similar information.
- Maintaining a **consistent verb tense** throughout the paragraph helps. Shifting tenses affects the smooth flow of words and can disrupt the coherence of the paragraph.

Review Video: How to Write a Good Paragraph
Visit mometrix.com/academy and enter code: 682127

Sequence Words and Phrases

When a paragraph opens with the topic sentence, the second sentence may begin with a phrase like *first of all*, introducing the first supporting detail or example. The writer may introduce the second supporting item with words or phrases like *also, in addition*, and *besides*. The writer might introduce succeeding pieces of support with wording like, *another thing, moreover, furthermore*, or *not only that, but*. The writer may introduce the last piece of support with *lastly, finally*, or *last but not least*. Writers get off the point by presenting off-target items not supporting the main point. For example, a main point *my dog is not smart* is supported by the statement, *he's six years old and still doesn't answer to his name*. But *he cries when I leave for school* is not supportive, as it does not indicate lack of intelligence. Writers stay on point by presenting only supportive statements that are directly relevant to and illustrative of their main point.

Review Video: Sequence
Visit mometrix.com/academy and enter code: 489027

Transitions

Transitions between sentences and paragraphs guide readers from idea to idea and indicate relationships between sentences and paragraphs. Writers should be judicious in their use of transitions, inserting them sparingly. They should also be selected to fit the author's purpose—transitions can indicate time, comparison, and conclusion, among other purposes. Tone is also important to consider when using transitional phrases, varying the tone for different audiences. For example, in a scholarly essay, *in summary* would be preferable to the more informal *in short*.

When working with transitional words and phrases, writers usually find a natural flow that indicates when a transition is needed. In reading a draft of the text, it should become apparent where the flow is disrupted. At this point, the writer can add transitional elements during the revision process. Revising can also afford an opportunity to delete transitional devices that seem heavy handed or unnecessary.

Review Video: Transitions in Writing
Visit mometrix.com/academy and enter code: 233246

Types of Transitional Words

Time	Afterward, immediately, earlier, meanwhile, recently, lately, now, since, soon, when, then, until, before, etc.
Sequence	too, first, second, further, moreover, also, again, and, next, still, besides, finally
Comparison	similarly, in the same way, likewise, also, again, once more
Contrasting	but, although, despite, however, instead, nevertheless, on the one hand... on the other hand, regardless, yet, in contrast.
Cause and Effect	because, consequently, thus, therefore, then, to this end, since, so, as a result, if... then, accordingly
Examples	for example, for instance, such as, to illustrate, indeed, in fact, specifically
Place	near, far, here, there, to the left/right, next to, above, below, beyond, opposite, beside
Concession	granted that, naturally, of course, it may appear, although it is true that
Repetition, Summary, or Conclusion	as mentioned earlier, as noted, in other words, in short, on the whole, to summarize, therefore, as a result, to conclude, in conclusion
Addition	and, also, furthermore, moreover
Generalization	in broad terms, broadly speaking, in general

Review Video: Transitional Words and Phrases
Visit mometrix.com/academy and enter code: 197796

Review Video: What are Transition Words?
Visit mometrix.com/academy and enter code: 707563

Review Video: How to Effectively Connect Sentences
Visit mometrix.com/academy and enter code: 948325

Conclusion

Two important principles to consider when writing a conclusion are strength and closure. A strong conclusion gives the reader a sense that the author's main points are meaningful and important, and that the supporting facts and arguments are convincing, solid, and well developed. When a conclusion achieves closure, it gives the impression that the writer has stated all necessary information and points and completed the work, rather than simply stopping after a specified length. Some things to avoid when writing concluding paragraphs include:

- Introducing a completely new idea
- Beginning with obvious or unoriginal phrases like "In conclusion" or "To summarize"
- Apologizing for one's opinions or writing
- Repeating the thesis word for word rather than rephrasing it
- Believing that the conclusion must always summarize the piece

Review Video: Drafting Conclusions
Visit mometrix.com/academy and enter code: 209408

Writing Style and Form

Writing Style and Linguistic Form

Linguistic form encodes the literal meanings of words and sentences. It comes from the phonological, morphological, syntactic, and semantic parts of a language. **Writing style** consists of different ways of encoding the meaning and indicating figurative and stylistic meanings. An author's writing style can also be referred to as his or her **voice**.

Writers' stylistic choices accomplish three basic effects on their audiences:

- They **communicate meanings** beyond linguistically dictated meanings,
- They communicate the **author's attitude**, such as persuasive or argumentative effects accomplished through style, and
- They communicate or **express feelings**.

Within style, component areas include:

- Narrative structure
- Viewpoint
- Focus
- Sound patterns
- Meter and rhythm
- Lexical and syntactic repetition and parallelism
- Writing genre
- Representational, realistic, and mimetic effects
- Representation of thought and speech
- Meta-representation (representing representation)
- Irony
- Metaphor and other indirect meanings
- Representation and use of historical and dialectal variations
- Gender-specific and other group-specific speech styles, both real and fictitious
- Analysis of the processes for inferring meaning from writing

Level of Formality

The relationship between writer and reader is important in choosing a **level of formality** as most writing requires some degree of formality. **Formal writing** is for addressing a superior in a school or work environment. Business letters, textbooks, and newspapers use a moderate to high level of formality. **Informal writing** is appropriate for private letters, personal emails, and business correspondence between close associates.

For your exam, you will want to be aware of informal and formal writing. One way that this can be accomplished is to watch for shifts in point of view in the essay. For example, unless writers are using a personal example, they will rarely refer to themselves (e.g., "*I* think that *my* point is very clear.") to avoid being informal when they need to be formal.

Also, be mindful of an author who addresses his or her audience **directly** in their writing (e.g., "Readers, *like you*, will understand this argument.") as this can be a sign of informal writing. Good writers understand the need to be consistent with their level of formality. Shifts in levels of formality or point of view can confuse readers and cause them to discount the message.

Clichés

Clichés are phrases that have been **overused** to the point that the phrase has no importance or has lost the original meaning. These phrases have no originality and add very little to a passage. Therefore, most writers will avoid the use of clichés. Another option is to make changes to a cliché so that it is not predictable and empty of meaning.

Examples:

When life gives you lemons, make lemonade.

Every cloud has a silver lining.

Jargon

Jargon is **specialized vocabulary** that is used among members of a certain trade or profession. Since jargon is understood by only a small audience, writers will use jargon in passages that will only be read by a specialized audience. For example, medical jargon should be used in a medical journal but not in a New York Times article. Jargon includes exaggerated language that tries to impress rather than inform. Sentences filled with jargon are not precise and are difficult to understand.

Examples:

"He is going to *toenail* these frames for us." (Toenail is construction jargon for nailing at an angle.)

"They brought in a *kip* of material today." (Kip refers to 1000 pounds in architecture and engineering.)

Slang

Slang is an **informal** and sometimes private language that is understood by some individuals. Slang terms have some usefulness, but they can have a small audience. So, most formal writing will not include this kind of language.

Examples:

"Yes, the event was a blast!" (In this sentence, *blast* means that the event was a great experience.)

"That attempt was an epic fail." (By *epic fail*, the speaker means that his or her attempt was not a success.)

Colloquialism

A colloquialism is a word or phrase that is found in informal writing. Unlike slang, **colloquial language** will be familiar to a greater range of people. However, colloquialisms are still considered inappropriate for formal writing. Colloquial language can include some slang, but these are limited to contractions for the most part.

Examples:

"Can *y'all* come back another time?" (Y'all is a contraction of "you all.")

"Will you stop him from building this *castle in the air*?" (A "castle in the air" is an improbable or unlikely event.)

Academic Language

In educational settings, students are often expected to use academic language in their schoolwork. Academic language is also commonly found in dissertations and theses, texts published by academic journals, and other forms of academic research. Academic language conventions may vary between fields, but general academic language is free of slang, regional terminology, and noticeable grammatical errors. Specific terms may also be used in academic language, and it is important to understand their proper usage. A writer's command of academic language impacts their ability to communicate in an academic or professional context. While it is acceptable to use colloquialisms, slang, improper grammar, or other forms of informal speech in social settings or at home, it is inappropriate to practice non-academic language in academic contexts.

TONE

Tone may be defined as the writer's **attitude** toward the topic, and to the audience. This attitude is reflected in the language used in the writing. The tone of a work should be **appropriate to the topic** and to the intended audience. While it may be fine to use slang or jargon in some pieces, other texts should not contain such terms. Tone can range from humorous to serious and any level in between. It may be more or less formal, depending on the purpose of the writing and its intended audience. All these nuances in tone can flavor the entire writing and should be kept in mind as the work evolves.

WORD SELECTION

A writer's choice of words is a signature of their style. Careful thought about the use of words can improve a piece of writing. A passage can be an exciting piece to read when attention is given to the use of vivid or specific nouns rather than general ones.

Example:

> General: His kindness will never be forgotten.
>
> Specific: His thoughtful gifts and bear hugs will never be forgotten.

Attention should also be given to the kind of verbs that are used in sentences. Active verbs (e.g., run, swim) are about an action. Whenever possible, an **active verb should replace a linking verb** to provide clear examples for arguments and to strengthen a passage overall. When using an active verb, one should be sure that the verb is used in the active voice instead of the passive voice. Verbs are in the active voice when the subject is the one doing the action. A verb is in the passive voice when the subject is the recipient of an action.

Example:

> Passive: The winners were called to the stage by the judges.
>
> Active: The judges called the winners to the stage.

CONCISENESS

Conciseness is writing that communicates a message in the fewest words possible. Writing concisely is valuable because short, uncluttered messages allow the reader to understand the author's message more easily and efficiently. Planning is important in writing concise messages. If you have in mind what you need to write beforehand, it will be easier to make a message short and to the point. Do not state the obvious.

Revising is also important. After the message is written, make sure you have effective, pithy sentences that efficiently get your point across. When reviewing the information, imagine a conversation taking place, and concise writing will likely result.

APPROPRIATE KINDS OF WRITING FOR DIFFERENT TASKS, PURPOSES, AND AUDIENCES

When preparing to write a composition, consider the audience and purpose to choose the best type of writing. Three common types of writing are persuasive, expository, and narrative. **Persuasive**, or argumentative writing, is used to convince the audience to take action or agree with the author's claims. **Expository** writing is meant to inform the audience of the author's observations or research on a topic. **Narrative** writing is used to tell the audience a story and often allows more room for creativity. While task, purpose, and audience inform a writer's mode of writing, these factors also impact elements such as tone, vocabulary, and formality.

For example, students who are writing to persuade their parents to grant them some additional privilege, such as permission for a more independent activity, should use more sophisticated vocabulary and diction that sounds more mature and serious to appeal to the parental audience. However, students who are writing for younger children should use simpler vocabulary and sentence structure, as well as choose words that are more vivid and entertaining. They should treat their topics more lightly, and include humor when appropriate. Students who are writing for their classmates may use language that is more informal, as well as age-appropriate.

Review Video: Writing Purpose and Audience
Visit mometrix.com/academy and enter code: 146627

Modes of Writing

Essays

Essays usually focus on one topic, subject, or goal. There are several types of essays, including informative, persuasive, and narrative. An essay's structure and level of formality depend on the type of essay and its goal. While narrative essays typically do not include outside sources, other types of essays often require some research and the integration of primary and secondary sources.

The basic format of an essay typically has three major parts: the introduction, the body, and the conclusion. The body is further divided into the writer's main points. Short and simple essays may have three main points, while essays covering broader ranges and going into more depth can have almost any number of main points, depending on length.

An essay's introduction should answer three questions:

1. What is the **subject** of the essay?

   If a student writes an essay about a book, the answer would include the title and author of the book and any additional information needed—such as the subject or argument of the book.

2. How does the essay **address** the subject?

   To answer this, the writer identifies the essay's organization by briefly summarizing main points and the evidence supporting them.

3. What will the essay **prove**?

   This is the thesis statement, usually the opening paragraph's last sentence, clearly stating the writer's message.

The body elaborates on all the main points related to the thesis, introducing one main point at a time, and includes supporting evidence with each main point. Each body paragraph should state the point in a topic sentence, which is usually the first sentence in the paragraph. The paragraph should then explain the point's meaning, support it with quotations or other evidence, and then explain how this point and the evidence are related to the thesis. The writer should then repeat this procedure in a new paragraph for each additional main point.

The conclusion reiterates the content of the introduction, including the thesis, to remind the reader of the essay's main argument or subject. The essay writer may also summarize the highlights of the argument or description contained in the body of the essay, following the same sequence originally used in the body. For example, a conclusion might look like: Point 1 + Point 2 + Point 3 = Thesis, or Point 1 → Point 2 → Point 3 → Thesis Proof. Good organization makes essays easier for writers to compose and provides a guide for readers to follow. Well-organized essays hold attention better and are more likely to get readers to accept their theses as valid.

Informative vs. Persuasive Writing

Informative writing, also called explanatory or expository writing, begins with the basis that something is true or factual, while **persuasive** writing strives to prove something that may or may not be true or factual. Whereas argumentative text is written to **persuade** readers to agree with the author's position, informative text merely **provides information and insight** to readers. Informative writing concentrates on **informing** readers about why or how something is as it is. This can include offering new information, explaining how a process works, and developing a concept for readers. To accomplish these objectives, the essay may name and distinguish various things within a category, provide definitions, provide details about the parts of something, explain a particular function or behavior, and give readers explanations for why a fact, object, event, or process exists or occurs.

Narrative Writing

Put simply, **narrative** writing tells a story. The most common examples of literary narratives are novels. Non-fictional biographies, autobiographies, memoirs, and histories are also narratives. Narratives should tell stories in such a way that the readers learn something or gain insight or understanding. Students can write more interesting narratives by describing events or experiences that were meaningful to them. Narratives should start with the story's actions or events, rather than long descriptions or introductions. Students should ensure that there is a point to each story by describing what they learned from the experience they narrate. To write an effective description, students should include sensory details, asking themselves what they saw, heard, felt or touched, smelled, and tasted during the experiences they describe. In narrative writing, the details should be **concrete** rather than **abstract**. Using concrete details enables readers to imagine everything that the writer describes.

Review Video: Narratives
Visit mometrix.com/academy and enter code: 280100

Sensory Details

Students need to use vivid descriptions when writing descriptive essays. Narratives should also include descriptions of characters, things, and events. Students should remember to describe not only the visual detail of what someone or something looks like, but details from other senses, as well. For example, they can contrast the feeling of a sea breeze to that of a mountain breeze, describe how they think something inedible would taste, and compare sounds they hear in the same location at different times of day and night. Readers have trouble visualizing images or imagining sensory impressions and feelings from abstract descriptions, so concrete descriptions make these more real.

Concrete vs. Abstract Descriptions in Narrative

Concrete language provides information that readers can grasp and may empathize with, while **abstract language**, which is more general, can leave readers feeling disconnected, empty, or even confused. "It was a lovely day" is abstract, but "The sun shone brightly, the sky was blue, the air felt warm, and a gentle breeze wafted across my skin" is concrete. "Ms. Couch was a good teacher" uses abstract language, giving only a general idea of the writer's opinion. But "Ms. Couch is excellent at helping us take our ideas and turn them into good essays and stories" uses concrete language, giving more specific examples of what makes Ms. Couch a good teacher. "I like writing poems but not essays" gives readers a general idea that the student prefers one genre over another, but not why. But when reading, "I like writing short poems with rhythm and rhyme, but I hate writing five-page essays that go on and on about the same ideas," readers understand that the student prefers the brevity, rhyme, and meter of short poetry over the length and redundancy of longer prose.

Autobiographical Narratives

Autobiographical narratives are narratives written by an author about an event or period in their life. Autobiographical narratives are written from one person's perspective, in first person, and often include the author's thoughts and feelings alongside their description of the event or period. Structure, style, or theme varies between different autobiographical narratives, since each narrative is personal and specific to its author and his or her experience.

Reflective Essay

A less common type of essay is the reflective essay. **Reflective essays** allow the author to reflect, or think back, on an experience and analyze what they recall. They should consider what they learned from the experience, what they could have done differently, what would have helped them during the experience, or anything else that they have realized from looking back on the experience. Reflection essays incorporate both objective reflection on one's own actions and subjective explanation of thoughts and feelings. These essays can be written for a number of experiences in a formal or informal context.

Journals and Diaries

A **journal** is a personal account of events, experiences, feelings, and thoughts. Many people write journals to express their feelings and thoughts or to help them process experiences they have had. Since journals are **private documents** not meant to be shared with others, writers may not be concerned with grammar, spelling, or other mechanics. However, authors may write journals that they expect or hope to publish someday; in this case, they not only express their thoughts and feelings and process their experiences, but they also attend to their craft in writing them. Some authors compose journals to record a particular time period or a series of related events, such as a cancer diagnosis, treatment, surviving the disease, and how these experiences have changed or affected them. Other experiences someone might include in a journal are recovering from addiction, journeys of spiritual exploration and discovery, time spent in another country, or anything else someone wants to personally document. Journaling can also be therapeutic, as some people use journals to work through feelings of grief over loss or to wrestle with big decisions.

Examples of Diaries in Literature

The Diary of a Young Girl by Dutch Jew Anne Frank (1947) contains her life-affirming, nonfictional diary entries from 1942-1944 while her family hid in an attic from World War II's genocidal Nazis. *Go Ask Alice* (1971) by Beatrice Sparks is a cautionary, fictional novel in the form of diary entries by Alice, an unhappy, rebellious teen who takes LSD, runs away from home and lives with hippies, and eventually returns home. Frank's writing reveals an intelligent, sensitive, insightful girl, raised by intellectual European parents—a girl who believes in the goodness of human nature despite surrounding atrocities. Alice, influenced by early 1970s counterculture, becomes less optimistic. However, similarities can be found between them: Frank dies in a Nazi concentration camp while the fictitious Alice dies from a drug overdose. Both young women are also unable to escape their surroundings. Additionally, adolescent searches for personal identity are evident in both books.

Review Video: Journals, Diaries, Letters, and Blogs
Visit mometrix.com/academy and enter code: 432845

Letters

Letters are messages written to other people. In addition to letters written between individuals, some writers compose letters to the editors of newspapers, magazines, and other publications, while some write "Open Letters" to be published and read by the general public. Open letters, while intended for everyone to read, may also identify a group of people or a single person whom the letter directly addresses. In everyday use, the most-used forms are business letters and personal or friendly letters. Both kinds share common elements: business or personal letterhead stationery; the writer's return address at the top; the addressee's address next; a salutation, such as "Dear [name]" or some similar opening greeting, followed by a colon in business letters or a comma in personal letters; the body of the letter, with paragraphs as indicated; and a closing, like "Sincerely/Cordially/Best regards/etc." or "Love," in intimate personal letters.

Early Letters

The Greek word for "letter" is *epistolē*, which became the English word "epistle." The earliest letters were called epistles, including the New Testament's epistles from the apostles to the Christians. In ancient Egypt, the writing curriculum in scribal schools included the epistolary genre. Epistolary novels frame a story in the form of letters. Examples of noteworthy epistolary novels include:

- *Pamela* (1740), by 18th-century English novelist Samuel Richardson
- *Shamela* (1741), Henry Fielding's satire of *Pamela* that mocked epistolary writing.
- *Lettres persanes* (1721) by French author Montesquieu
- *The Sorrows of Young Werther* (1774) by German author Johann Wolfgang von Goethe
- *The History of Emily Montague* (1769), the first Canadian novel, by Frances Brooke
- *Dracula* (1897) by Bram Stoker

- *Frankenstein* (1818) by Mary Shelley
- *The Color Purple* (1982) by Alice Walker

Blogs

The word "blog" is derived from "weblog" and refers to writing done exclusively on the internet. Readers of reputable newspapers expect quality content and layouts that enable easy reading. These expectations also apply to blogs. For example, readers can easily move visually from line to line when columns are narrow, while overly wide columns cause readers to lose their places. Blogs must also be posted with layouts enabling online readers to follow them easily. However, because the way people read on computer, tablet, and smartphone screens differs from how they read print on paper, formatting and writing blog content is more complex than writing newspaper articles. Two major principles are the bases for blog-writing rules: The first is while readers of print articles skim to estimate their length, online they must scroll down to scan; therefore, blog layouts need more subheadings, graphics, and other indications of what information follows. The second is onscreen reading can be harder on the eyes than reading printed paper, so legibility is crucial in blogs.

Rules and Rationales for Writing Blogs

1. Format all posts for smooth page layout and easy scanning.
2. Column width should not be too wide, as larger lines of text can be difficult to read
3. Headings and subheadings separate text visually, enable scanning or skimming, and encourage continued reading.
4. Bullet-pointed or numbered lists enable quick information location and scanning.
5. Punctuation is critical, so beginners should use shorter sentences until confident in their knowledge of punctuation rules.
6. Blog paragraphs should be far shorter—two to six sentences each—than paragraphs written on paper to enable "chunking" because reading onscreen is more difficult.
7. Sans-serif fonts are usually clearer than serif fonts, and larger font sizes are better.
8. Highlight important material and draw attention with **boldface**, but avoid overuse. Avoid hard-to-read *italics* and ALL CAPITALS.
9. Include enough blank spaces: overly busy blogs tire eyes and brains. Images not only break up text but also emphasize and enhance text and can attract initial reader attention.
10. Use background colors judiciously to avoid distracting the eye or making it difficult to read.
11. Be consistent throughout posts, since people read them in different orders.
12. Tell a story with a beginning, middle, and end.

Specialized Modes of Writing

Editorials

Editorials are articles in newspapers, magazines, and other serial publications. Editorials express an opinion or belief belonging to the majority of the publication's leadership. This opinion or belief generally refers to a specific issue, topic, or event. These articles are authored by a member, or a small number of members, of the publication's leadership and are often written to affect their readers, such as persuading them to adopt a stance or take a particular action.

Resumes

Resumes are brief, but formal, documents that outline an individual's experience in a certain area. Resumes are most often used for job applications. Such resumes will list the applicant's work experience, certification, and achievements or qualifications related to the position. Resumes should only include the most pertinent information. They should also use strategic formatting to highlight the applicant's most impressive experiences and achievements, to ensure the document can be read quickly and easily, and to eliminate both visual clutter and excessive negative space.

Reports

Reports summarize the results of research, new methodology, or other developments in an academic or professional context. Reports often include details about methodology and outside influences and factors. However, a report should focus primarily on the results of the research or development. Reports are objective and deliver information efficiently, sacrificing style for clear and effective communication.

Memoranda

A memorandum, also called a memo, is a formal method of communication used in professional settings. Memoranda are printed documents that include a heading listing the sender and their job title, the recipient and their job title, the date, and a specific subject line. Memoranda often include an introductory section explaining the reason and context for the memorandum. Next, a memorandum includes a section with details relevant to the topic. Finally, the memorandum will conclude with a paragraph that politely and clearly defines the sender's expectations of the recipient.

Vocabulary and Word Relationships

Synonyms and Antonyms

When you understand how words relate to each other, you will discover more in a passage. This is explained by understanding **synonyms** (e.g., words that mean the same thing) and **antonyms** (e.g., words that mean the opposite of one another). As an example, *dry* and *arid* are synonyms, and *dry* and *wet* are antonyms.

There are many pairs of words in English that can be considered synonyms, despite having slightly different definitions. For instance, the words *friendly* and *collegial* can both be used to describe a warm interpersonal relationship, and one would be correct to call them synonyms. However, *collegial* (kin to *colleague*) is often used in reference to professional or academic relationships, and *friendly* has no such connotation.

If the difference between the two words is too great, then they should not be called synonyms. *Hot* and *warm* are not synonyms because their meanings are too distinct. A good way to determine whether two words are synonyms is to substitute one word for the other word and verify that the meaning of the sentence has not changed. Substituting *warm* for *hot* in a sentence would convey a different meaning. Although warm and hot may seem close in meaning, warm generally means that the temperature is moderate, and hot generally means that the temperature is excessively high.

Antonyms are words with opposite meanings. *Light* and *dark*, *up* and *down*, *right* and *left*, *good* and *bad*: these are all sets of antonyms. Be careful to distinguish between antonyms and pairs of words that are simply different. *Black* and *gray*, for instance, are not antonyms because gray is not the opposite of black. *Black* and *white*, on the other hand, are antonyms.

Not every word has an antonym. For instance, many nouns do not. What would be the antonym of *chair*? During your exam, the questions related to antonyms are more likely to concern adjectives. You will recall that adjectives are words that describe a noun. Some common adjectives include *purple*, *fast*, *skinny*, and *sweet*. From those four adjectives, *purple* is the item that lacks a group of obvious antonyms.

Review Video: What Are Synonyms and Antonyms?
Visit mometrix.com/academy and enter code: 105612

Affixes

Affixes in the English language are morphemes that are added to words to create related but different words. Derivational affixes form new words based on and related to the original words. For example, the affix *–ness* added to the end of the adjective *happy* forms the noun *happiness.* Inflectional affixes form different grammatical versions of words. For example, the plural affix *–s* changes the singular noun *book* to the plural noun *books*, and the past tense affix *–ed* changes the present tense verb *look* to the past tense *looked.* Prefixes are affixes placed in front of words. For example, *heat* means to make hot; *preheat* means to heat in advance. Suffixes are affixes placed at the ends of words. The *happiness* example above contains the suffix *–ness.* Circumfixes add parts both before and after words, such as how *light* becomes *enlighten* with the prefix *en-* and the suffix *–en.* Interfixes create compound words via central affixes: *speed* and *meter* become *speedometer* via the interfix *–o–*.

Review Video: Affixes
Visit mometrix.com/academy and enter code: 782422

Word Roots, Prefixes, and Suffixes to Help Determine Meanings of Words

Many English words were formed from combining multiple sources. For example, the Latin *habēre* means "to have," and the prefixes *in-* and *im-* mean a lack or prevention of something, as in *insufficient* and *imperfect.* Latin combined *in-* with *habēre* to form *inhibēre,* whose past participle was *inhibitus.* This is the origin of the English word *inhibit,* meaning to prevent from having. Hence by knowing the meanings of both the prefix and the root, one can decipher the word meaning. In Greek, the root *enkephalo-* refers to the brain. Many medical terms are based on this root, such as encephalitis and hydrocephalus. Understanding the prefix and suffix meanings (*-itis* means inflammation; *hydro-* means water) allows a person to deduce that encephalitis refers to brain inflammation and hydrocephalus refers to water (or other fluid) in the brain.

Review Video: Determining Word Meanings
Visit mometrix.com/academy and enter code: 894894

Review Video: Root Words in English
Visit mometrix.com/academy and enter code: 896380

Prefixes

While knowing prefix meanings helps ESL and beginning readers learn new words, other readers take for granted the meanings of known words. However, prefix knowledge will also benefit them for determining meanings or definitions of unfamiliar words. For example, native English speakers and readers familiar with recipes know what *preheat* means. Knowing that *pre-* means in advance can also inform them that *presume* means to assume in advance, that *prejudice* means advance judgment, and that this understanding can be applied to many other words beginning with *pre-*. Knowing that the prefix *dis-* indicates opposition informs the meanings of words like *disbar, disagree, disestablish,* and many more. Knowing *dys-* means bad, impaired, abnormal, or difficult informs *dyslogistic, dysfunctional, dysphagia,* and *dysplasia.*

Suffixes

In English, certain suffixes generally indicate both that a word is a noun, and that the noun represents a state of being or quality. For example, *-ness* is commonly used to change an adjective into its noun form, as with *happy* and *happiness, nice* and *niceness,* and so on. The suffix *–tion* is commonly used to transform a verb into its noun form, as with *converse* and *conversation or move* and *motion*. Thus, if readers are unfamiliar with the second form of a word, knowing the meaning of the transforming suffix can help them determine meaning.

Prefixes for Numbers

Prefix	Definition	Examples
bi-	two	bisect, biennial
mono-	one, single	monogamy, monologue
poly-	many	polymorphous, polygamous
semi-	half, partly	semicircle, semicolon
uni-	one	uniform, unity

Prefixes for Time, Direction, and Space

Prefix	Definition	Examples
a-	in, on, of, up, to	abed, afoot
ab-	from, away, off	abdicate, abjure
ad-	to, toward	advance, adventure
ante-	before, previous	antecedent, antedate
anti-	against, opposing	antipathy, antidote
cata-	down, away, thoroughly	catastrophe, cataclysm
circum-	around	circumspect, circumference
com-	with, together, very	commotion, complicate
contra-	against, opposing	contradict, contravene
de-	from	depart
dia-	through, across, apart	diameter, diagnose
dis-	away, off, down, not	dissent, disappear
epi-	upon	epilogue
ex-	out	extract, excerpt
hypo-	under, beneath	hypodermic, hypothesis
inter-	among, between	intercede, interrupt
intra-	within	intramural, intrastate
ob-	against, opposing	objection
per-	through	perceive, permit
peri-	around	periscope, perimeter
post-	after, following	postpone, postscript
pre-	before, previous	prevent, preclude
pro-	forward, in place of	propel, pronoun
retro-	back, backward	retrospect, retrograde
sub-	under, beneath	subjugate, substitute
super-	above, extra	supersede, supernumerary
trans-	across, beyond, over	transact, transport
ultra-	beyond, excessively	ultramodern, ultrasonic

Negative Prefixes

Prefix	Definition	Examples
a-	without, lacking	atheist, agnostic
in-	not, opposing	incapable, ineligible
non-	not	nonentity, nonsense
un-	not, reverse of	unhappy, unlock

EXTRA PREFIXES

Prefix	Definition	Examples
belli-	war, warlike	bellicose
bene-	well, good	benefit, benefactor
equi-	equal	equivalent, equilibrium
for-	away, off, from	forget, forswear
fore-	previous	foretell, forefathers
homo-	same, equal	homogenized, homonym
hyper-	excessive, over	hypercritical, hypertension
in-	in, into	intrude, invade
magn-	large	magnitude, magnify
mal-	bad, poorly, not	malfunction, malpractice
mis-	bad, poorly, not	misspell, misfire
mor-	death	mortality, mortuary
neo-	new	Neolithic, neoconservative
omni-	all, everywhere	omniscient, omnivore
ortho-	right, straight	orthogonal, orthodox
over-	above	overbearing, oversight
pan-	all, entire	panorama, pandemonium
para-	beside, beyond	parallel, paradox
phil-	love, like	philosophy, philanthropic
prim-	first, early	primitive, primary
re-	backward, again	revoke, recur
sym-	with, together	sympathy, symphony
vis-	to see	visage, visible

Below is a list of common suffixes and their meanings:

ADJECTIVE SUFFIXES

Suffix	Definition	Examples
-able (-ible)	capable of being	toler*able*, ed*ible*
-esque	in the style of, like	picturesque, grotesque
-ful	filled with, marked by	thankful, zestful
-ific	make, cause	terrific, beatific
-ish	suggesting, like	churlish, childish
-less	lacking, without	hopeless, countless
-ous	marked by, given to	religious, riotous

Noun Suffixes

Suffix	Definition	Examples
-acy	state, condition	accuracy, privacy
-ance	act, condition, fact	acceptance, vigilance
-ard	one that does excessively	drunkard, sluggard
-ation	action, state, result	occupation, starvation
-dom	state, rank, condition	serfdom, wisdom
-er (-or)	office, action	teach*er*, elevat*or*, hon*or*
-ess	feminine	waitress, duchess
-hood	state, condition	manhood, statehood
-ion	action, result, state	union, fusion
-ism	act, manner, doctrine	barbarism, socialism
-ist	worker, follower	monopolist, socialist
-ity (-ty)	state, quality, condition	acid*ity*, civil*ity*, twen*ty*
-ment	result, action	Refreshment
-ness	quality, state	greatness, tallness
-ship	position	internship, statesmanship
-sion (-tion)	state, result	revi*sion*, expedi*tion*
-th	act, state, quality	warmth, width
-tude	quality, state, result	magnitude, fortitude

Verb Suffixes

Suffix	Definition	Examples
-ate	having, showing	separate, desolate
-en	cause to be, become	deepen, strengthen
-fy	make, cause to have	glorify, fortify
-ize	cause to be, treat with	sterilize, mechanize

Denotative vs. Connotative Meaning

The **denotative** meaning of a word is the literal meaning. The **connotative** meaning goes beyond the denotative meaning to include the emotional reaction that a word may invoke. The connotative meaning often takes the denotative meaning a step further due to associations the reader makes with the denotative meaning. Readers can differentiate between the denotative and connotative meanings by first recognizing how authors use each meaning. Most non-fiction, for example, is fact-based and authors do not use flowery, figurative language. The reader can assume that the writer is using the denotative meaning of words. In fiction, the author may use the connotative meaning. Readers can determine whether the author is using the denotative or connotative meaning of a word by implementing context clues.

Review Video: Connotation and Denotation
Visit mometrix.com/academy and enter code: 310092

Nuances of Word Meaning Relative to Connotation, Denotation, Diction, and Usage

A word's denotation is simply its objective dictionary definition. However, its connotation refers to the subjective associations, often emotional, that specific words evoke in listeners and readers. Two or more words can have the same dictionary meaning, but very different connotations. Writers use diction (word choice) to convey various nuances of thought and emotion by selecting synonyms for other words that best communicate the associations they want to trigger for readers. For example, a car engine is naturally greasy; in this sense, "greasy" is a neutral term. But when a person's smile, appearance, or clothing is described as "greasy," it has a negative connotation. Some words have even gained additional or different meanings over time. For example, *awful* used to be used to describe things that evoked a sense of awe. When *awful* is separated into its root word, awe, and suffix, -ful, it can be understood to mean "full of awe." However, the word is now commonly used to describe things that evoke repulsion, terror, or another intense, negative reaction.

Review Video: Word Usage in Sentences
Visit mometrix.com/academy and enter code: 197863

Context Clues

Readers of all levels will encounter words that they have either never seen or have encountered only on a limited basis. The best way to define a word in **context** is to look for nearby words that can assist in revealing the meaning of the word. For instance, unfamiliar nouns are often accompanied by examples that provide a definition. Consider the following sentence: *Dave arrived at the party in hilarious garb: a leopard-print shirt, buckskin trousers, and bright green sneakers.* If a reader was unfamiliar with the meaning of garb, he or she could read the examples (i.e., a leopard-print shirt, buckskin trousers, and high heels) and quickly determine that the word means *clothing*. Examples will not always be this obvious. Consider this sentence: *Parsley, lemon, and flowers were just a few of the items he used as garnishes.* Here, the word *garnishes* is exemplified by parsley, lemon, and flowers. Readers who have eaten in a variety of restaurants will probably be able to identify a garnish as something used to decorate a plate.

Review Video: Context Clues
Visit mometrix.com/academy and enter code: 613660

Using Contrast in Context Clues

In addition to looking at the context of a passage, readers can use contrast to define an unfamiliar word in context. In many sentences, the author will not describe the unfamiliar word directly; instead, he or she will describe the opposite of the unfamiliar word. Thus, you are provided with some information that will bring you closer to defining the word. Consider the following example: *Despite his intelligence, Hector's low brow and bad posture made him look obtuse.* The author writes that Hector's appearance does not convey intelligence. Therefore, *obtuse* must mean unintelligent. Here is another example: *Despite the horrible weather, we were beatific about our trip to Alaska*. The word *despite* indicates that the speaker's feelings were at odds with the weather. Since the weather is described as *horrible*, then *beatific* must mean something positive.

Substitution to Find Meaning

In some cases, there will be very few contextual clues to help a reader define the meaning of an unfamiliar word. When this happens, one strategy that readers may employ is **substitution**. A good reader will brainstorm some possible synonyms for the given word, and he or she will substitute these words into the sentence. If the sentence and the surrounding passage continue to make sense, then the substitution has revealed at least some information about the unfamiliar word. Consider the sentence: *Frank's admonition rang in her ears as she climbed the mountain.* A reader unfamiliar with *admonition* might come up with some substitutions like *vow, promise, advice, complaint*, or *compliment.* All of these words make general sense of the sentence, though their meanings are diverse. However, this process has suggested that an admonition is some sort of message. The substitution strategy is rarely able to pinpoint a precise definition, but this process can be effective as a last resort.

Occasionally, you will be able to define an unfamiliar word by looking at the descriptive words in the context. Consider the following sentence: *Fred dragged the recalcitrant boy kicking and screaming up the stairs.* The words *dragged, kicking*, and *screaming* all suggest that the boy does not want to go up the stairs. The reader may assume that *recalcitrant* means something like unwilling or protesting. In this example, an unfamiliar adjective was identified.

Additionally, using description to define an unfamiliar noun is a common practice compared to unfamiliar adjectives, as in this sentence: *Don's wrinkled frown and constantly shaking fist identified him as a curmudgeon of the first order*. Don is described as having a *wrinkled frown and constantly shaking fist*, suggesting that a *curmudgeon* must be a grumpy person. Contrasts do not always provide detailed information about the unfamiliar word, but they at least give the reader some clues.

Words with Multiple Meanings

When a word has more than one meaning, readers can have difficulty determining how the word is being used in a given sentence. For instance, the verb *cleave*, can mean either *join* or *separate*. When readers come upon this word, they will have to select the definition that makes the most sense. Consider the following sentence: *Hermione's knife cleaved the bread cleanly*. Since a knife cannot join bread together, the word must indicate separation. A slightly more difficult example would be the sentence: *The birds cleaved to one another as they flew from the oak tree.* Immediately, the presence of the words *to one another* should suggest that in this sentence *cleave* is being used to mean *join*. Discovering the intent of a word with multiple meanings requires the same tricks as defining an unknown word: look for contextual clues and evaluate the substituted words.

Context Clues to Help Determine Meanings of Words

If readers simply bypass unknown words, they can reach unclear conclusions about what they read. However, looking for the definition of every unfamiliar word in the dictionary can slow their reading progress. Moreover, the dictionary may list multiple definitions for a word, so readers must search the word's context for meaning. Hence context is important to new vocabulary regardless of reader methods. Four types of context clues are examples, definitions, descriptive words, and opposites. Authors may use a certain word, and then follow it with several different examples of what it describes. Sometimes authors actually supply a definition of a word they use, which is especially true in informational and technical texts. Authors may use descriptive words that elaborate upon a vocabulary word they just used. Authors may also use opposites with negation that help define meaning.

Examples and Definitions

An author may use a word and then give examples that illustrate its meaning. Consider this text: "Teachers who do not know how to use sign language can help students who are deaf or hard of hearing understand certain instructions by using gestures instead, like pointing their fingers to indicate which direction to look or go; holding up a hand, palm outward, to indicate stopping; holding the hands flat, palms up, curling a finger toward oneself in a beckoning motion to indicate 'come here'; or curling all fingers toward oneself repeatedly to indicate 'come on', 'more', or 'continue.'" The author of this text has used the word "gestures" and then followed it with examples, so a reader unfamiliar with the word could deduce from the examples that "gestures" means "hand motions." Readers can find examples by looking for signal words "for example," "for instance," "like," "such as," and "e.g."

While readers sometimes have to look for definitions of unfamiliar words in a dictionary or do some work to determine a word's meaning from its surrounding context, at other times an author may make it easier for readers by defining certain words. For example, an author may write, "The company did not have sufficient capital, that is, available money, to continue operations." The author defined "capital" as "available money," and heralded the definition with the phrase "that is." Another way that authors supply word definitions is with appositives. Rather than being introduced by a signal phrase like "that is," "namely," or "meaning," an appositive comes after the vocabulary word it defines and is enclosed within two commas. For example, an author may write, "The Indians introduced the Pilgrims to pemmican, cakes they made of lean meat dried and mixed with fat, which proved greatly beneficial to keep settlers from starving while trapping." In this example, the appositive phrase following "pemmican" and preceding "which" defines the word "pemmican."

Descriptions

When readers encounter a word they do not recognize in a text, the author may expand on that word to illustrate it better. While the author may do this to make the prose more picturesque and vivid, the reader can also take advantage of this description to provide context clues to the meaning of the unfamiliar word. For example, an author may write, "The man sitting next to me on the airplane was obese. His shirt stretched across his vast expanse of flesh, strained almost to bursting." The descriptive second sentence elaborates on and helps to define the previous sentence's word "obese" to mean extremely fat. A reader unfamiliar with the word "repugnant" can decipher its meaning through an author's accompanying description: "The way the child grimaced and shuddered as he swallowed the medicine showed that its taste was particularly repugnant."

OPPOSITES

Text authors sometimes introduce a contrasting or opposing idea before or after a concept they present. They may do this to emphasize or heighten the idea they present by contrasting it with something that is the reverse. However, readers can also use these context clues to understand familiar words. For example, an author may write, "Our conversation was not cheery. We sat and talked very solemnly about his experience and a number of similar events." The reader who is not familiar with the word "solemnly" can deduce by the author's preceding use of "not cheery" that "solemn" means the opposite of cheery or happy, so it must mean serious or sad. Or if someone writes, "Don't condemn his entire project because you couldn't find anything good to say about it," readers unfamiliar with "condemn" can understand from the sentence structure that it means the opposite of saying anything good, so it must mean reject, dismiss, or disapprove. "Entire" adds another context clue, meaning total or complete rejection.

SYNTAX TO DETERMINE PART OF SPEECH AND MEANINGS OF WORDS

Syntax refers to sentence structure and word order. Suppose that a reader encounters an unfamiliar word when reading a text. To illustrate, consider an invented word like "splunch." If this word is used in a sentence like "Please splunch that ball to me," the reader can assume from syntactic context that "splunch" is a verb. We would not use a noun, adjective, adverb, or preposition with the object "that ball," and the prepositional phrase "to me" further indicates "splunch" represents an action. However, in the sentence, "Please hand that splunch to me," the reader can assume that "splunch" is a noun. Demonstrative adjectives like "that" modify nouns. Also, we hand someone some*thing*—a thing being a noun; we do not hand someone a verb, adjective, or adverb. Some sentences contain further clues. For example, from the sentence, "The princess wore the glittering splunch on her head," the reader can deduce that it is a crown, tiara, or something similar from the syntactic context, without knowing the word.

SYNTAX TO INDICATE DIFFERENT MEANINGS OF SIMILAR SENTENCES

The syntax, or structure, of a sentence affords grammatical cues that aid readers in comprehending the meanings of words, phrases, and sentences in the texts that they read. Seemingly minor differences in how the words or phrases in a sentence are ordered can make major differences in meaning. For example, two sentences can use exactly the same words but have different meanings based on the word order:

- "The man with a broken arm sat in a chair."
- "The man sat in a chair with a broken arm."

While both sentences indicate that a man sat in a chair, differing syntax indicates whether the man's or chair's arm was broken.

DETERMINING MEANING OF PHRASES AND PARAGRAPHS

Like unknown words, the meanings of phrases, paragraphs, and entire works can also be difficult to discern. Each of these can be better understood with added context. However, for larger groups of words, more context is needed. Unclear phrases are similar to unclear words, and the same methods can be used to understand their meaning. However, it is also important to consider how the individual words in the phrase work together. Paragraphs are a bit more complicated. Just as words must be compared to other words in a sentence, paragraphs must be compared to other paragraphs in a composition or a section.

DETERMINING MEANING IN VARIOUS TYPES OF COMPOSITIONS

To understand the meaning of an entire composition, the type of composition must be considered. **Expository writing** is generally organized so that each paragraph focuses on explaining one idea, or part of an idea, and its relevance. **Persuasive writing** uses paragraphs for different purposes to organize the parts of the argument.

Unclear paragraphs must be read in the context of the paragraphs around them for their meaning to be fully understood. The meaning of full texts can also be unclear at times. The purpose of composition is also important for understanding the meaning of a text. To quickly understand the broad meaning of a text, look to the introductory and concluding paragraphs. Fictional texts are different. Some fictional works have implicit meanings, but some do not. The target audience must be considered for understanding texts that do have an implicit meaning, as most children's fiction will clearly state any lessons or morals. For other fiction, the application of literary theories and criticism may be helpful for understanding the text.

Additional Resources for Determining Word Meaning and Usage

While these strategies are useful for determining the meaning of unknown words and phrases, sometimes additional resources are needed to properly use the terms in different contexts. Some words have multiple definitions, and some words are inappropriate in particular contexts or modes of writing. The following tools are helpful for understanding all meanings and proper uses for words and phrases.

- **Dictionaries** provide the meaning of a multitude of words in a language. Many dictionaries include additional information about each word, such as its etymology, its synonyms, or variations of the word.
- **Glossaries** are similar to dictionaries, as they provide the meanings of a variety of terms. However, while dictionaries typically feature an extensive list of words and comprise an entire publication, glossaries are often included at the end of a text and only include terms and definitions that are relevant to the text they follow.
- **Spell Checkers** are used to detect spelling errors in typed text. Some spell checkers may also detect the misuse of plural or singular nouns, verb tenses, or capitalization. While spell checkers are a helpful tool, they are not always reliable or attuned to the author's intent, so it is important to review the spell checker's suggestions before accepting them.
- **Style Manuals** are guidelines on the preferred punctuation, format, and grammar usage according to different fields or organizations. For example, the Associated Press Stylebook is a style guide often used for media writing. The guidelines within a style guide are not always applicable across different contexts and usages, as the guidelines often cover grammatical or formatting situations that are not objectively correct or incorrect.

Literary Elements

Literary Terminology

- In works of prose such as novels, a group of connected sentences covering one main topic is termed a **paragraph**.
- In works of poetry, a group of verses similarly connected is called a **stanza**.
- In drama, when early works used verse, these were also divided into stanzas or **couplets**.
- Drama evolved to use predominantly prose. Overall, whether prose or verse, the conversation in a play is called **dialogue**.
- Large sections of dialogue spoken by one actor are called **soliloquies** or **monologues**.
- Dialogue that informs audiences but is unheard by other characters is called an **aside**.
- Novels and plays share certain common elements, such as:
    - **Characters** - the people in the story.
    - **Plot** - the action of the story.
    - **Climax** - when action or dramatic tension reaches its highest point.
    - **Denouement** - the resolution following the climax.
- Sections dividing novels are called **chapters**, while sections of plays are called **acts**.
- Subsections of plays' acts are called **scenes**. Novel chapters usually do not have subsections. However, some novels do include groups of chapters that form different sections.

Literary Analysis

The best literary analysis shows special insight into at least one important aspect of a text. When analyzing literary texts, it can be difficult to find a starting place. Many texts can be analyzed several different ways, often leaving an overwhelming number of options for writers to consider. However, narrowing the focus to a particular element of literature can be helpful when preparing to analyze a text. Symbolism, themes, and motifs are common starting points for literary analysis. These three methods of analysis can lead to a holistic analysis of a text, since they involve elements that are often distributed throughout the text. However, not all texts feature these elements in a way that facilitates a strong analysis, if they are present at all. It is also common to focus on character or plot development for analysis. These elements are compatible with theme, symbolism, and allusion. Setting and imagery, figurative language, and any external contexts can also contribute to analysis or complement one of these other elements. The application of a critical, or literary, theory to a text can also provide a thorough and strong analysis.

Setting and Time Frame

A literary text has both a setting and time frame. A **setting** is the place in which the story as a whole is set. The **time frame** is the period in which the story is set. This may refer to the historical period the story takes place in or if the story takes place over a single day. Both setting and time frame are relevant to a text's meaning because they help the reader place the story in time and space. An author uses setting and time frame to anchor a text, create a mood, and enhance its meaning. This helps a reader understand why a character acts the way he does, or why certain events in the story are important. The setting impacts the **plot** and character **motivations**, while the time frame helps place the story in **chronological context**.

Example

Read the following excerpt from The Adventures of Huckleberry Finn by Mark Twain and analyze the relevance of setting to the text's meaning:

> We said there warn't no home like a raft, after all. Other places do seem so cramped up and smothery, but a raft don't. You feel mighty free and easy and comfortable on a raft.

This excerpt from *The Adventures of Huckleberry Finn* by Mark Twain reveals information about the **setting** of the book. By understanding that the main character, Huckleberry Finn, lives on a raft, the reader can place the story on a river, in this case, the Mississippi River in the South before the Civil War. The information about the setting also gives the reader clues about the **character** of Huck Finn: he clearly values independence and freedom, and he likes the outdoors. The information about the setting in the quote helps the reader to better understand the rest of the text.

THEME

The **theme** of a passage is what the reader learns from the text or the passage. It is the lesson or **moral** contained in the passage. It also is a unifying idea that is used throughout the text; it can take the form of a common setting, idea, symbol, design, or recurring event. A passage can have two or more themes that convey its overall idea. The theme or themes of a passage are often based on **universal themes**. They can frequently be expressed using well-known sayings about life, society, or human nature, such as "Hard work pays off" or "Good triumphs over evil." Themes are not usually stated **explicitly**. The reader must figure them out by carefully reading the passage. Themes are often the reason why passages are written; they give a passage unity and meaning. Themes are created through **plot development**. The events of a story help shape the themes of a passage.

EXAMPLE

Explain why "Take care of what you care about" accurately describes the theme of the following excerpt.

> Luca collected baseball cards, but he wasn't very careful with them. He left them around the house. His dog liked to chew. One day, Luca and his friend Bart were looking at his collection. Then they went outside. When Luca got home, he saw his dog chewing on his cards. They were ruined.

This excerpt tells the story of a boy who is careless with his baseball cards and leaves them lying around. His dog ends up chewing them and ruining them. The lesson is that if you care about something, you need to take care of it. This is the theme, or point, of the story. Some stories have more than one theme, but this is not really true of this excerpt. The reader needs to figure out the theme based on what happens in the story. Sometimes, as in the case of fables, the theme is stated directly in the text. However, this is not usually the case.

Review Video: Themes in Literature
Visit mometrix.com/academy and enter code: 732074

PLOT AND STORY STRUCTURE

The **plot** includes the events that happen in a story and the order in which they are told to the reader. There are several types of plot structures, as stories can be told in many ways. The most common plot structure is the chronological plot, which presents the events to the reader in the same order they occur for the characters in the story. Chronological plots usually have five main parts, the **exposition**, **rising action**, the **climax**, **falling action**, and the **resolution**. This type of plot structure guides the reader through the story's events as the characters experience them and is the easiest structure to understand and identify. While this is the most common plot structure, many stories are nonlinear, which means the plot does not sequence events in the same order the characters experience them. Such stories might include elements like flashbacks that cause the story to be nonlinear.

Review Video: How to Make a Story Map
Visit mometrix.com/academy and enter code: 261719

EXPOSITION

The **exposition** is at the beginning of the story and generally takes place before the rising action begins. The purpose of the exposition is to give the reader context for the story, which the author may do by introducing one or more characters, describing the setting or world, or explaining the events leading up to the point where the story begins. The exposition may still include events that contribute to the plot, but the **rising action** and main conflict of the story are not part of the exposition. Some narratives skip the exposition and begin the story with the beginning of the rising action, which causes the reader to learn the context as the story intensifies.

CONFLICT

A **conflict** is a problem to be solved. Literary plots typically include one conflict or more. Characters' attempts to resolve conflicts drive the narrative's forward movement. **Conflict resolution** is often the protagonist's primary occupation. Physical conflicts like exploring, wars, and escapes tend to make plots most suspenseful and exciting. Emotional, mental, or moral conflicts tend to make stories more personally gratifying or rewarding for many audiences. Conflicts can be external or internal. A major type of internal conflict is some inner personal battle, or **man versus self**. Major types of external conflicts include **man versus nature**, **man versus man**, and **man versus society**. Readers can identify conflicts in literary plots by identifying the protagonist and antagonist and asking why they conflict, what events develop the conflict, where the climax occurs, and how they identify with the characters.

Read the following paragraph and discuss the type of conflict present:

> Timothy was shocked out of sleep by the appearance of a bear just outside his tent. After panicking for a moment, he remembered some advice he had read in preparation for this trip: he should make noise so the bear would not be startled. As Timothy started to hum and sing, the bear wandered away.

There are three main types of conflict in literature: **man versus man**, **man versus nature**, and **man versus self**. This paragraph is an example of man versus nature. Timothy is in conflict with the bear. Even though no physical conflict like an attack exists, Timothy is pitted against the bear. Timothy uses his knowledge to "defeat" the bear and keep himself safe. The solution to the conflict is that Timothy makes noise, the bear wanders away, and Timothy is safe.

Review Video: Conflict
Visit mometrix.com/academy and enter code: 559550

Review Video: Determining Relationships in a Story
Visit mometrix.com/academy and enter code: 929925

RISING ACTION

The **rising action** is the part of the story where conflict **intensifies**. The rising action begins with an event that prompts the main conflict of the story. This may also be called the **inciting incident**. The main conflict generally occurs between the protagonist and an antagonist, but this is not the only type of conflict that may occur in a narrative. After this event, the protagonist works to resolve the main conflict by preparing for an altercation, pursuing a goal, fleeing an antagonist, or doing some other action that will end the conflict. The rising action is composed of several additional events that increase the story's tension. Most often, other developments will occur alongside the growth of the main conflict, such as character development or the development of minor conflicts. The rising action ends with the **climax**, which is the point of highest tension in the story.

CLIMAX

The **climax** is the event in the narrative that marks the height of the story's conflict or tension. The event that takes place at the story's climax will end the rising action and bring about the results of the main conflict. If the conflict was between a good protagonist and an evil antagonist, the climax may be a final battle between the two characters. If the conflict is an adventurer looking for heavily guarded treasure, the climax may be the adventurer's encounter with the final obstacle that protects the treasure. The climax may be made of multiple scenes, but can usually be summarized as one event. Once the conflict and climax are complete, the **falling action** begins.

Falling Action

The **falling action** shows what happens in the story between the climax and the resolution. The falling action often composes a much smaller portion of the story than the rising action does. While the climax includes the end of the main conflict, the falling action may show the results of any minor conflicts in the story. For example, if the protagonist encountered a troll on the way to find some treasure, and the troll demanded the protagonist share the treasure after retrieving it, the falling action would include the protagonist returning to share the treasure with the troll. Similarly, any unexplained major events are usually made clear during the falling action. Once all significant elements of the story are resolved or addressed, the story's resolution will occur. The **resolution** is the end of the story, which shows the final result of the plot's events and shows what life is like for the main characters once they are no longer experiencing the story's conflicts.

Resolution

The way the conflict is **resolved** depends on the type of conflict. The plot of any book starts with the lead up to the conflict, then the conflict itself, and finally the solution, or **resolution**, to the conflict. In **man versus man** conflicts, the conflict is often resolved by two parties coming to some sort of agreement or by one party triumphing over the other party. In **man versus nature** conflicts, the conflict is often resolved by man coming to some realization about some aspect of nature. In **man versus self** conflicts, the conflict is often resolved by the character growing or coming to an understanding about part of himself.

Syntax and Word Choice

Authors use words and **syntax**, or sentence structure, to make their texts unique, convey their own writing style, and sometimes to make a point or emphasis. They know that word choice and syntax contribute to the reader's understanding of the text as well as to the tone and mood of a text.

Review Video: What is Syntax?
Visit mometrix.com/academy and enter code: 242280

Allusion

An allusion is an uncited but recognizable reference to something else. Authors use language to make allusions to places, events, artwork, and other books in order to make their own text richer. For example, an author may allude to a very important text in order to make his own text seem more important. Martin Luther King, Jr. started his "I Have a Dream" speech by saying "Five score years ago…" This is a clear allusion to President Abraham Lincoln's "Gettysburg Address" and served to remind people of the significance of the event. An author may allude to a place to ground his text or make a cultural reference to make readers feel included. There are many reasons that authors make allusions.

Review Video: Allusions
Visit mometrix.com/academy and enter code: 294065

Comic Relief

Comic relief is the use of comedy by an author to break up a dramatic or tragic scene and infuse it with a bit of **lightheartedness**. In William Shakespeare's *Hamlet*, two gravediggers digging the grave for Ophelia share a joke while they work. The death and burial of Ophelia are tragic moments that directly follow each other. Shakespeare uses an instance of comedy to break up the tragedy and give his audience a bit of a break from the tragic drama. Authors sometimes use comic relief so that their work will be less depressing; other times they use it to create irony or contrast between the darkness of the situation and the lightness of the joke. Often, authors will use comedy to parallel what is happening in the tragic scenes.

Review Video: What is Comic Relief?
Visit mometrix.com/academy and enter code: 779604

Mood and Tone

Mood is a story's atmosphere, or the feelings the reader gets from reading it. The way authors set the mood in writing is comparable to the way filmmakers use music to set the mood in movies. Instead of music, though, writers judiciously select descriptive words to evoke certain **moods**. The mood of a work may convey joy, anger, bitterness, hope, gloom, fear, apprehension, or any other emotion the author wants the reader to feel. In addition to vocabulary choices, authors also use figurative expressions, particular sentence structures, and choices of diction that project and reinforce the moods they want to create. Whereas mood is the reader's emotions evoked by reading what is written, **tone** is the emotions and attitudes of the writer that she or he expresses in the writing. Authors use the same literary techniques to establish tone as they do to establish mood. An author may use a humorous tone, an angry or sad tone, a sentimental or unsentimental tone, or something else entirely.

Mood and Tone in The Great Gatsby

To understand the difference between mood and tone, look at this excerpt from F. Scott Fitzgerald's *The Great Gatsby*. In this passage, Nick Caraway, the novel's narrator, is describing his affordable house, which sits in a neighborhood full of expensive mansions.

> "I lived at West Egg, the—well the less fashionable of the two, though this is a most superficial tag to express the bizarre and not a little sinister contrast between them. My house was at the very tip of the egg, only fifty yard from the Sound, and squeezed between two huge places that rented for twelve or fifteen thousand a season ... My own house was an eyesore, but it was a small eyesore, and it had been overlooked, so I had a view of the water, a partial view of my neighbor's lawn, and the consoling proximity of millionaires—all for eighty dollars a month."

In this description, the mood created for the reader does not match the tone created through the narrator. The mood in this passage is one of dissatisfaction and inferiority. Nick compares his home to his neighbors', saying he lives in the "less fashionable" neighborhood and that his house is "overlooked," an "eyesore," and "squeezed between two huge" mansions. He also adds that his placement allows him the "consoling proximity of millionaires." A literal reading of these details leads the reader to have negative feelings toward Nick's house and his economic inferiority to his neighbors, creating the mood.

However, Fitzgerald also conveys an opposing attitude, or tone, through Nick's description. Nick calls the distinction between the neighborhoods "superficial," showing a suspicion of the value suggested by the neighborhoods' titles, properties, and residents. Nick also undermines his critique of his own home by calling it "a small eyesore" and claiming it has "been overlooked." However, he follows these statements with a description of his surroundings, claiming that he has "a view of the water" and can see some of his wealthy neighbor's property from his home, and a comparison between the properties' rent. While the mental image created for the reader depicts a small house shoved between looming mansions, the tone suggests that Nick enjoys these qualities about his home, or at least finds it charming. He acknowledges its shortcomings, but includes the benefits of his home's unassuming appearance.

Review Video: Style, Tone, and Mood
Visit mometrix.com/academy and enter code: 416961

Character Development

When depicting characters or figures in a written text, authors generally use actions, dialogue, and descriptions as characterization techniques. Characterization can occur in both fiction and nonfiction and is used to show a character or figure's personality, demeanor, and thoughts. This helps create a more engaging experience for the reader by providing a more concrete picture of a character or figure's tendencies and features. Characterizations also gives authors the opportunity to integrate elements such as dialects, activities, attire, and attitudes into their writing.

To understand the meaning of a story, it is vital to understand the characters as the author describes them. We can look for contradictions in what a character thinks, says, and does. We can notice whether the author's observations about a character differ from what other characters in the story say about that character. A character may be dynamic, meaning they change significantly during the story, or static, meaning they remain the same from beginning to end. Characters may be two-dimensional, not fully developed, or may be well developed with characteristics that stand out vividly. Characters may also symbolize universal properties. Additionally, readers can compare and contrast characters to analyze how each one developed.

A well-known example of character development can be found in Charles Dickens's *Great Expectations*. The novel's main character, Pip, is introduced as a young boy, and he is depicted as innocent, kind, and humble. However, as Pip grows up and is confronted with the social hierarchy of Victorian England, he becomes arrogant and rejects his loved ones in pursuit of his own social advancement. Once he achieves his social goals, he realizes the merits of his former lifestyle, and lives with the wisdom he gained in both environments and life stages. Dickens shows Pip's ever-changing character through his interactions with others and his inner thoughts, which evolve as his personal values and personality shift.

Review Video: Character Changes
Visit mometrix.com/academy and enter code: 408719

Dialogue

Effectively written dialogue serves at least one, but usually several, purposes. It advances the story and moves the plot, develops the characters, sheds light on the work's theme or meaning, and can, often subtly, account for the passage of time not otherwise indicated. It can alter the direction that the plot is taking, typically by introducing some new conflict or changing existing ones. **Dialogue** can establish a work's narrative voice and the characters' voices and set the tone of the story or of particular characters. When fictional characters display enlightenment or realization, dialogue can give readers an understanding of what those characters have discovered and how. Dialogue can illuminate the motivations and wishes of the story's characters. By using consistent thoughts and syntax, dialogue can support character development. Skillfully created, it can also represent real-life speech rhythms in written form. Via conflicts and ensuing action, dialogue also provides drama.

Dialogue in Fiction

In fictional works, effectively written dialogue does more than just break up or interrupt sections of narrative. While **dialogue** may supply exposition for readers, it must nonetheless be believable. Dialogue should be dynamic, not static, and it should not resemble regular prose. Authors should not use dialogue to write clever similes or metaphors, or to inject their own opinions. Nor should they use dialogue at all when narrative would be better. Most importantly, dialogue should not slow the plot movement. Dialogue must seem natural, which means careful construction of phrases rather than actually duplicating natural speech, which does not necessarily translate well to the written word. Finally, all dialogue must be pertinent to the story, rather than just added conversation.

Foreshadowing

Foreshadowing is a device authors use to give readers **hints** about events that will take place later in a story. Foreshadowing most often takes place through a character's dialogue or actions. Sometimes the character will know what is going to happen and will purposefully allude to future events. For example, consider a protagonist who is about to embark on a journey through the woods. Just before the protagonist begins the trip, another character says, "Be careful, you never know what could be out in those woods!" This alerts the reader that the woods may be dangerous and prompts the reader to expect something to attack the protagonist in the woods. This is an example of foreshadowing through warning. Alternatively, a character may unknowingly foreshadow later events. For example, consider a story where a brother and sister run through their house and knock over a vase and break it. The brother says, "Don't worry, we'll clean it up! Mom will never know!" However, the reader knows that their mother will most likely find out what they have done, so the reader expects the siblings to later get in trouble for running, breaking the vase, and hiding it from their mother.

Symbolism

Symbolism describes an author's use of a **symbol**, an element of the story that **represents** something else. Symbols can impact stories in many ways, including deepening the meaning of a story or its elements, comparing a story to another work, or foreshadowing later events in a story. Symbols can be objects, characters, colors, numbers, or anything else the author establishes as a symbol. Symbols can be clearly established through direct comparison or repetition, but they can also be established subtly or gradually over a large portion of the story. Another form of symbolism is **allusion**, which is when something in a story is used to prompt the reader to think about another work. Many well-known works use **Biblical allusions**, which are allusions to events or details in the Bible that inform a work or an element within it.

Point of View

Another element that impacts a text is the author's point of view. The **point of view** of a text is the perspective from which a passage is told. An author will always have a point of view about a story before he or she draws up a plot line. The author will know what events they want to take place, how they want the characters to interact, and how they want the story to resolve. An author will also have an opinion on the topic or series of events which is presented in the story that is based on their prior experience and beliefs.

The two main points of view that authors use, especially in a work of fiction, are first person and third person. If the narrator of the story is also the main character, or *protagonist*, the text is written in first-person point of view. In first person, the author writes from the perspective of *I*. Third-person point of view is probably the most common that authors use in their passages. Using third person, authors refer to each character by using *he* or *she*. In third-person omniscient, the narrator is not a character in the story and tells the story of all of the characters at the same time.

Review Video: Point of View
Visit mometrix.com/academy and enter code: 383336

First-Person Narration

First-person narratives let narrators express inner feelings and thoughts, especially when the narrator is the protagonist as Lemuel Gulliver is in Jonathan Swift's *Gulliver's Travels.* The narrator may be a close friend of the protagonist, like Dr. Watson in Sir Arthur Conan Doyle's *Sherlock Holmes.* Or, the narrator can be less involved with the main characters and plot, like Nick Carraway in F. Scott Fitzgerald's *The Great Gatsby.* When a narrator reports others' narratives, she or he is a "**frame narrator**," like the nameless narrator of Joseph Conrad's *Heart of Darkness* or Mr. Lockwood in Emily Brontë's *Wuthering Heights.* **First-person plural** is unusual but can be effective. Isaac Asimov's *I, Robot*, William Faulkner's *A Rose for Emily*, Maxim Gorky's *Twenty-Six Men and a Girl*, and Jeffrey Eugenides' *The Virgin Suicides* all use first-person plural narration. Author Kurt Vonnegut is the first-person narrator in his semi-autobiographical novel *Timequake.* Also unusual, but effective, is a **first-person omniscient** (rather than the more common third-person omniscient) narrator, like Death in Markus Zusak's *The Book Thief* and the ghost in Alice Sebold's *The Lovely Bones.*

Second-Person Narration

While **second-person** address is very commonplace in popular song lyrics, it is the least used form of narrative voice in literary works. Popular serial books of the 1980s like *Fighting Fantasy* or *Choose Your Own Adventure* employed second-person narratives. In some cases, a narrative combines both second-person and first-person voices, using the pronouns *you* and *I*. This can draw readers into the story, and it can also enable the authors to compare directly "your" and "my" feelings, thoughts, and actions. When the narrator is also a character in the story, as in Edgar Allan Poe's short story "The Tell-Tale Heart" or Jay McInerney's novel *Bright Lights, Big City,* the narrative is better defined as first-person despite it also addressing "you."

Third-Person Narration

Narration in the third person is the most prevalent type, as it allows authors the most flexibility. It is so common that readers simply assume without needing to be informed that the narrator is not a character in the story, or involved in its events. **Third-person singular** is used more frequently than **third-person plural**, though some authors have also effectively used plural. However, both singular and plural are most often included in stories according to which characters are being described. The third-person narrator may be either objective or subjective, and either omniscient or limited. **Objective third-person** narration does not include what the characters described are thinking or feeling, while **subjective third-person** narration does. The **third-person omniscient** narrator knows everything about all characters, including their thoughts and emotions, and all related places, times, and events. However, the **third-person limited** narrator may know everything about a particular character, but is limited to that character. In other words, the narrator cannot speak about anything that character does not know.

Alternating-Person Narration

Although authors more commonly write stories from one point of view, there are also instances wherein they alternate the narrative voice within the same book. For example, they may sometimes use an omniscient third-person narrator and a more intimate first-person narrator at other times. In J. K. Rowling's series of *Harry Potter* novels, she often writes in a third-person limited narrative, but sometimes changes to narration by characters other than the protagonist. George R. R. Martin's series *A Song of Ice and Fire* changes the point of view to coincide with divisions between chapters. The same technique is used by Erin Hunter (a pseudonym for several authors of the *Warriors, Seekers,* and *Survivors* book series). Authors using first-person narrative sometimes switch to third-person to describe significant action scenes, especially those where the narrator was absent or uninvolved, as Barbara Kingsolver does in her novel *The Poisonwood Bible.*

Historical and Social Context

Fiction that is heavily influenced by a historical or social context cannot be comprehended as the author intended if the reader does not keep this context in mind. Many important elements of the text will be influenced by any context, including symbols, allusions, settings, and plot events. These contexts, as well as the identity of the work's author, can help to inform the reader about the author's concerns and intended meanings. For example, George Orwell published his novel *1984* in the year 1949, soon after the end of World War II. At that time, following the defeat of the Nazis, the Cold War began between the Western Allied nations and the Eastern Soviet Communists. People were therefore concerned about the conflict between the freedoms afforded by Western democracies versus the oppression represented by Communism. Orwell had also previously fought in the Spanish Civil War against a Spanish regime that he and his fellows viewed as oppressive. From this information, readers can infer that Orwell was concerned about oppression by totalitarian governments. This informs *1984*'s story of Winston Smith's rebellion against the oppressive "Big Brother" government, of the fictional dictatorial state of Oceania, and his capture, torture, and ultimate conversion by that government. Some literary theories also seek to use historical and social contexts to reveal deeper meanings and implications in a text.

Textual Evidence

No literary analysis is complete without textual evidence. Summaries, paraphrases, and quotes are all forms of textual evidence, but direct quotes from the text are the most effective form of evidence. The best textual evidence is relevant, accurate, and clearly supports the writer's claim. This can include pieces of descriptions, dialogue, or exposition that shows the applicability of the analysis to the text. Analysis that is average, or sufficient, shows an understanding of the text; contains supporting textual evidence that is relevant and accurate, if not strong; and shows a specific and clear response. Analysis that partially meets criteria also shows understanding, but the textual evidence is generalized, incomplete, only partly relevant or accurate, or connected only weakly. Inadequate analysis is vague, too general, or incorrect. It may give irrelevant or incomplete textual evidence, or may simply summarize the plot rather than analyzing the work. It is important to incorporate textual evidence from the work being analyzed and any supplemental materials and to provide appropriate attribution for these sources.

Chapter Quiz

1. Which of the following is the least used form of narration used in literature?

a. First-person
b. Second-person
c. Third-person limited
d. Third-person omniscient

2. Which of the following lists the terms of chronological plots in order from first to last?

a. Exposition, rising action, climax, falling action, resolution
b. Rising action, exposition, falling action, climax, resolution
c. Rising action, exposition, climax, falling action, resolution
d. Resolution, exposition, climax, falling action, rising action

3. If a writer alludes to another piece of literature, that writer is doing which of the following?

a. Admiring it
b. Criticizing it
c. Defending its conclusions
d. Referencing it

Chapter Quiz Answer Key

1. B: While second-person address is very commonplace in popular song lyrics, it is the least used form of narrative voice in literary works. Popular serial books of the 1980s like *Fighting Fantasy* or *Choose Your Own Adventure* employed second-person narratives. In some cases, a narrative combines both second-person and first-person voices, using the pronouns *you* and *I*. This can draw readers into the story, and it can also enable the authors to compare directly "your" and "my" feelings, thoughts, and actions. When the narrator is also a character in the story, as in Edgar Allan Poe's short story "The Tell-Tale Heart" or Jay McInerney's novel *Bright Lights, Big City,* the narrative is better defined as first-person despite it also addressing "you."

2. A: The most common plot structure is the chronological plot, which presents the events to the reader in the same order they occur for the characters in the story. Chronological plots usually have five main parts: the exposition, rising action, the climax, falling action, and the resolution. This type of plot structure guides the reader through the story's events as the characters experience them and is the easiest structure to understand and identify.

3. D: An allusion is an uncited but recognizable reference to something else. Authors use language to make allusions to places, events, artwork, and other books in order to make their own text richer. For example, an author may allude to a very important text in order to make his own text seem more important.

Reading Comprehension

Understanding a Passage

One of the most important skills in reading comprehension is the identification of **topics** and **main ideas**. There is a subtle difference between these two features. The topic is the subject of a text (i.e., what the text is all about). The main idea, on the other hand, is the most important point being made by the author. The topic is usually expressed in a few words at the most while the main idea often needs a full sentence to be completely defined. As an example, a short passage might be written on the topic of penguins, and the main idea could be written as *Penguins are different from other birds in many ways*. In most nonfiction writing, the topic and the main idea will be **stated directly** and often appear in a sentence at the very beginning or end of the text. When being tested on an understanding of the author's topic, you may be able to skim the passage for the general idea by reading only the first sentence of each paragraph. A body paragraph's first sentence is often—but not always—the main **topic sentence** which gives you a summary of the content in the paragraph.

However, there are cases in which the reader must figure out an **unstated** topic or main idea. In these instances, you must read every sentence of the text and try to come up with an overarching idea that is supported by each of those sentences.

Note: The main idea should not be confused with the thesis statement. While the main idea gives a brief, general summary of a text, the thesis statement provides a **specific perspective** on an issue that the author supports with evidence.

Review Video: Topics and Main Ideas
Visit mometrix.com/academy and enter code: 407801

Supporting details are smaller pieces of evidence that provide backing for the main point. In order to show that a main idea is correct or valid, an author must add details that prove their point. All texts contain details, but they are only classified as supporting details when they serve to reinforce some larger point. Supporting details are most commonly found in informative and persuasive texts. In some cases, they will be clearly indicated with terms like *for example* or *for instance*, or they will be enumerated with terms like *first*, *second*, and *last*. However, you need to be prepared for texts that do not contain those indicators. As a reader, you should consider whether the author's supporting details really back up his or her main point. Details can be factual and correct, yet they may not be **relevant** to the author's point. Conversely, details can be relevant, but be ineffective because they are based on opinion or assertions that cannot be proven.

Review Video: Supporting Details
Visit mometrix.com/academy and enter code: 396297

An example of a main idea is: *Giraffes live in the Serengeti of Africa*. A supporting detail about giraffes could be: *A giraffe in this region benefits from a long neck by reaching twigs and leaves on tall trees.* The main idea gives the general idea that the text is about giraffes. The supporting detail gives a specific fact about how the giraffes eat.

Organization of the Text

The way a text is organized can help readers understand the author's intent and his or her conclusions. There are various ways to organize a text, and each one has a purpose and use. Usually, authors will organize information logically in a passage so the reader can follow and locate the information within the text. However, since not all passages are written with the same logical structure, you need to be familiar with several different types of passage structure.

Review Video: Organizational Methods to Structure Text
Visit mometrix.com/academy and enter code: 606263

Review Video: Sequence of Events in a Story
Visit mometrix.com/academy and enter code: 807512

Chronological

When using **chronological** order, the author presents information in the order that it happened. For example, biographies are typically written in chronological order. The subject's birth and childhood are presented first, followed by their adult life, and lastly the events leading up to the person's death.

Cause and Effect

One of the most common text structures is **cause and effect**. A **cause** is an act or event that makes something happen, and an **effect** is the thing that happens as a result of the cause. A cause-and-effect relationship is not always explicit, but there are some terms in English that signal causes, such as *since*, *because*, and *due to*. Furthermore, terms that signal effects include *consequently, therefore, this leads to*. As an example, consider the sentence *Because the sky was clear, Ron did not bring an umbrella*. The cause is the clear sky, and the effect is that Ron did not bring an umbrella. However, readers may find that sometimes the cause-and-effect relationship will not be clearly noted. For instance, the sentence *He was late and missed the meeting* does not contain any signaling words, but the sentence still contains a cause (he was late) and an effect (he missed the meeting).

Review Video: Cause and Effect
Visit mometrix.com/academy and enter code: 868099

Multiple Effects

Be aware of the possibility for a single cause to have **multiple effects.** (e.g., *Single cause*: Because you left your homework on the table, your dog engulfed the assignment. *Multiple effects*: As a result, you receive a failing grade, your parents do not allow you to go out with your friends, you miss out on the new movie, and one of your classmates spoils it for you before you have another chance to watch it).

Multiple Causes

Also, there is the possibility for a single effect to have **multiple causes.** (e.g., *Single effect*: Alan has a fever. *Multiple causes*: An unexpected cold front came through the area, and Alan forgot to take his multi-vitamin to avoid getting sick.) Additionally, an effect can in turn be the cause of another effect, in what is known as a cause-and-effect chain. (e.g., As a result of her disdain for procrastination, Lynn prepared for her exam. This led to her passing her test with high marks. Hence, her resume was accepted and her application was approved.)

Cause and Effect in Persuasive Essays

Persuasive essays, in which an author tries to make a convincing argument and change the minds of readers, usually include cause-and-effect relationships. However, these relationships should not always be taken at face value. Frequently, an author will assume a cause or take an effect for granted. To read a persuasive essay effectively, readers need to judge the cause-and-effect relationships that the author is presenting. For instance, imagine an author wrote the following: *The parking deck has been unprofitable because people would prefer to ride their bikes.* The relationship is clear: the cause is that people prefer to ride their bikes, and the effect is that the parking deck has been unprofitable. However, readers should consider whether this argument is conclusive. Perhaps there are other reasons for the failure of the parking deck: a down economy, excessive fees, etc. Too often, authors present causal relationships as if they are fact rather than opinion. Readers should be on the alert for these dubious claims.

Problem-Solution

Some nonfiction texts are organized to **present a problem** followed by a solution. For this type of text, the problem is often explained before the solution is offered. In some cases, as when the problem is well known, the solution may be introduced briefly at the beginning. Other passages may focus on the solution, and the problem will be referenced only occasionally. Some texts will outline multiple solutions to a problem, leaving readers to choose among them. If the author has an interest or an allegiance to one solution, he or she may fail to mention or describe accurately some of the other solutions. Readers should be careful of the author's agenda when reading a problem-solution text. Only by understanding the author's perspective and interests can one develop a proper judgment of the proposed solution.

Compare and Contrast

Many texts follow the **compare-and-contrast** model in which the similarities and differences between two ideas or things are explored. Analysis of the similarities between ideas is called **comparison**. In an ideal comparison, the author places ideas or things in an equivalent structure, i.e., the author presents the ideas in the same way. If an author wants to show the similarities between cricket and baseball, then he or she may do so by summarizing the equipment and rules for each game. Be mindful of the similarities as they appear in the passage and take note of any differences that are mentioned. Often, these small differences will only reinforce the more general similarity.

Review Video: Compare and Contrast
Visit mometrix.com/academy and enter code: 798319

Thinking critically about ideas and conclusions can seem like a daunting task. One way to ease this task is to understand the basic elements of ideas and writing techniques. Looking at the ways different ideas relate to each other can be a good way for readers to begin their analysis. For instance, sometimes authors will write about two ideas that are in opposition to each other. Or, one author will provide his or her ideas on a topic, and another author may respond in opposition. The analysis of these opposing ideas is known as **contrast**. Contrast is often marred by the author's obvious partiality to one of the ideas. A discerning reader will be put off by an author who does not engage in a fair fight. In an analysis of opposing ideas, both ideas should be presented in clear and reasonable terms. If the author does prefer a side, you need to read carefully to determine the areas where the author shows or avoids this preference. In an analysis of opposing ideas, you should proceed through the passage by marking the major differences point by point with an eye that is looking for an explanation of each side's view. For instance, in an analysis of capitalism and communism, there is an importance in outlining each side's view on labor, markets, prices, personal responsibility, etc. Additionally, as you read through the passages, you should note whether the opposing views present each side in a similar manner.

Sequence

Readers must be able to identify a text's **sequence**, or the order in which things happen. Often, when the sequence is very important to the author, the text is indicated with signal words like *first*, *then*, *next*, and *last*. However, a sequence can be merely implied and must be noted by the reader. Consider the sentence *He walked through the garden and gave water and fertilizer to the plants*. Clearly, the man did not walk through the garden before he collected water and fertilizer for the plants. So, the implied sequence is that he first collected water, then he collected fertilizer, next he walked through the garden, and last he gave water or fertilizer as necessary to the plants. Texts do not always proceed in an orderly sequence from first to last. Sometimes they begin at the end and start over at the beginning. As a reader, you can enhance your understanding of the passage by taking brief notes to clarify the sequence.

Making Connections to Enhance Comprehension

Reading involves thinking. For good comprehension, readers make **text-to-self**, **text-to-text**, and **text-to-world connections**. Making connections helps readers understand text better and predict what might occur next based on what they already know, such as how characters in the story feel or what happened in another text. Text-to-self connections with the reader's life and experiences make literature more personally relevant and meaningful to readers. Readers can make connections before, during, and after reading—including whenever the text reminds them of something similar they have encountered in life or other texts. The genre, setting, characters, plot elements, literary structure and devices, and themes an author uses allow a reader to make connections to other works of literature or to people and events in their own lives. Venn diagrams and other graphic organizers help visualize connections. Readers can also make double-entry notes: key content, ideas, events, words, and quotations on one side, and the connections with these on the other.

Summarizing Literature to Support Comprehension

When reading literature, especially demanding works, **summarizing** helps readers identify important information and organize it in their minds. They can also identify themes, problems, and solutions, and can sequence the story. Readers can summarize before, during, and after they read. They should use their own words, as they do when describing a personal event or giving directions. Previewing a text's organization before reading by examining the book cover, table of contents, and illustrations also aids summarizing. Making notes of key words and ideas in a graphic organizer while reading can benefit readers in the same way. Graphic organizers are another useful method; readers skim the text to determine main ideas and then narrow the list with the aid of the organizer. Unimportant details should be omitted in summaries. Summaries can be organized using description, problem-solution, comparison-contrast, sequence, main ideas, or cause-and-effect.

Review Video: Summarizing Text
Visit mometrix.com/academy and enter code: 172903

Paraphrasing

Paraphrasing is another method that the reader can use to aid in comprehension. When paraphrasing, one puts what they have read into their own words by rephrasing what the author has written, or one "translates" all of what the author shared into their own words by including as many details as they can.

Making Predictions and Inferences

Making Predictions

When we read literature, **making predictions** about what will happen in the writing reinforces our purpose for reading and prepares us mentally. A **prediction** is a guess about what will happen next. Readers constantly make predictions based on what they have read and what they already know. We can make predictions before we begin reading and during our reading. Consider the following sentence: *Staring at the computer screen in shock, Kim blindly reached over for the brimming glass of water on the shelf to her side.* The sentence suggests that Kim is distracted, and that she is not looking at the glass that she is going to pick up. So, a reader might predict that Kim is going to knock over the glass. Of course, not every prediction will be accurate: perhaps Kim will pick the glass up cleanly. Nevertheless, the author has certainly created the expectation that the water might be spilled.

As we read on, we can test the accuracy of our predictions, revise them in light of additional reading, and confirm or refute our predictions. Predictions are always subject to revision as the reader acquires more information. A reader can make predictions by observing the title and illustrations; noting the structure, characters, and subject; drawing on existing knowledge relative to the subject; and asking "why" and "who" questions. Connecting reading to what we already know enables us to learn new information and construct meaning. For example, before third-graders read a book about Johnny Appleseed, they may start a KWL chart—a list of what they *Know*, what they *Want* to know or learn, and what they have *Learned* after reading. Activating existing background knowledge and thinking about the text before reading improves comprehension.

Review Video: Predictive Reading
Visit mometrix.com/academy and enter code: 437248

Test-taking tip: To respond to questions requiring future predictions, your answers should be based on evidence of past or present behavior and events.

Evaluating Predictions

When making predictions, readers should be able to explain how they developed their prediction. One way readers can defend their thought process is by citing textual evidence. Textual evidence to evaluate reader predictions about literature includes specific synopses of the work, paraphrases of the work or parts of it, and direct quotations from the work. These references to the text must support the prediction by indicating, clearly or unclearly, what will happen later in the story. A text may provide these indications through literary devices such as foreshadowing. Foreshadowing is anything in a text that gives the reader a hint about what is to come by emphasizing the likelihood of an event or development. Foreshadowing can occur through descriptions, exposition, and dialogue. Foreshadowing in dialogue usually occurs when a character gives a warning or expresses a strong feeling that a certain event will occur. Foreshadowing can also occur through irony. However, unlike other forms of foreshadowing, the events that seem the most likely are the opposite of what actually happens. Instances of foreshadowing and irony can be summarized, paraphrased, or quoted to defend a reader's prediction.

Review Video: Textual Evidence for Predictions
Visit mometrix.com/academy and enter code: 261070

Drawing Conclusions from Inferences

Inferences about literary text are logical conclusions that readers make based on their observations and previous knowledge. An inference is based on both what is found in a passage or a story and what is known from personal experience. For instance, a story may say that a character is frightened and can hear howling in the distance. Based on both what is in the text and personal knowledge, it is a logical conclusion that the character is frightened because he hears the sound of wolves. A good inference is supported by the information in a passage.

IMPLICIT AND EXPLICIT INFORMATION

By inferring, readers construct meanings from text that are personally relevant. By combining their own schemas or concepts and their background information pertinent to the text with what they read, readers interpret it according to both what the author has conveyed and their own unique perspectives. Inferences are different from **explicit information**, which is clearly stated in a passage. Authors do not always explicitly spell out every meaning in what they write; many meanings are implicit. Through inference, readers can comprehend implied meanings in the text, and also derive personal significance from it, making the text meaningful and memorable to them. Inference is a natural process in everyday life. When readers infer, they can draw conclusions about what the author is saying, predict what may reasonably follow, amend these predictions as they continue to read, interpret the import of themes, and analyze the characters' feelings and motivations through their actions.

EXAMPLE OF DRAWING CONCLUSIONS FROM INFERENCES

Read the excerpt and decide why Jana finally relaxed.

> Jana loved her job, but the work was very demanding. She had trouble relaxing. She called a friend, but she still thought about work. She ordered a pizza, but eating it did not help. Then, her kitten jumped on her lap and began to purr. Jana leaned back and began to hum a little tune. She felt better.

You can draw the conclusion that Jana relaxed because her kitten jumped on her lap. The kitten purred, and Jana leaned back and hummed a tune. Then she felt better. The excerpt does not explicitly say that this is the reason why she was able to relax. The text leaves the matter unclear, but the reader can infer or make a "best guess" that this is the reason she is relaxing. This is a logical conclusion based on the information in the passage. It is the best conclusion a reader can make based on the information he or she has read. Inferences are based on the information in a passage, but they are not directly stated in the passage.

Test-taking tip: While being tested on your ability to make correct inferences, you must look for **contextual clues**. An answer can be true, but not the best or most correct answer. The contextual clues will help you find the answer that is the **best answer** out of the given choices. Be careful in your reading to understand the context in which a phrase is stated. When asked for the implied meaning of a statement made in the passage, you should immediately locate the statement and read the **context** in which the statement was made. Also, look for an answer choice that has a similar phrase to the statement in question.

Review Video: Inference
Visit mometrix.com/academy and enter code: 379203

Review Video: How to Support a Conclusion
Visit mometrix.com/academy and enter code: 281653

Chapter Quiz

1. Which of the following describes logical conclusions that readers make based on their observations and previous knowledge?

a. Imperatives
b. Interrogatives
c. Inferences
d. Predictions

Chapter Quiz Answer Key

1. C: Inferences about literary text are logical conclusions that readers make based on their observations and previous knowledge. An inference is based on both what is found in a passage or a story and what is known from personal experience. For instance, a story may say that a character is frightened and can hear howling in the distance. Based on both what is in the text and personal knowledge, it is a logical conclusion that the character is frightened because they hear the sound of wolves. A good inference is supported by the information in a passage.

Interactions with Texts

Purposes for Writing

In order to be an effective reader, one must pay attention to the author's **position** and **purpose**. Even those texts that seem objective and impartial, like textbooks, have a position and bias. Readers need to take these positions into account when considering the author's message. When an author uses emotional language or clearly favors one side of an argument, his or her position is clear. However, the author's position may be evident not only in what he or she writes, but also in what he or she doesn't write. In a normal setting, a reader would want to review some other texts on the same topic in order to develop a view of the author's position. If this was not possible, then you would want to at least acquire some background about the author. However, since you are in the middle of an exam and the only source of information is the text, you should look for language and argumentation that seems to indicate a particular stance on the subject.

Review Video: Author's Position
Visit mometrix.com/academy and enter code: 827954

Usually, identifying the author's **purpose** is easier than identifying his or her position. In most cases, the author has no interest in hiding his or her purpose. A text that is meant to entertain, for instance, should be written to please the reader. Most narratives, or stories, are written to entertain, though they may also inform or persuade. Informative texts are easy to identify, while the most difficult purpose of a text to identify is persuasion because the author has an interest in making this purpose hard to detect. When a reader discovers that the author is trying to persuade, he or she should be skeptical of the argument. For this reason, persuasive texts often try to establish an entertaining tone and hope to amuse the reader into agreement. On the other hand, an informative tone may be implemented to create an appearance of authority and objectivity.

An author's purpose is evident often in the organization of the text (e.g., section headings in bold font points to an informative text). However, you may not have such organization available to you in your exam. Instead, if the author makes his or her main idea clear from the beginning, then the likely purpose of the text is to inform. If the author begins by making a claim and provides various arguments to support that claim, then the purpose is probably to persuade. If the author tells a story or wants to gain the reader's attention more than to push a particular point or deliver information, then his or her purpose is most likely to entertain. As a reader, you must judge authors on how well they accomplish their purpose. In other words, you need to consider the type of passage (e.g., technical, persuasive, etc.) that the author has written and if the author has followed the requirements of the passage type.

Making Logical Conclusions about a Passage

A reader should always be drawing conclusions from the text. Sometimes conclusions are **implied** from written information, and other times the information is **stated directly** within the passage. One should always aim to draw conclusions from information stated within a passage, rather than to draw them from mere implications. At times an author may provide some information and then describe a counterargument. Readers should be alert for direct statements that are subsequently rejected or weakened by the author. Furthermore, you should always read through the entire passage before drawing conclusions. Many readers are trained to expect the author's conclusions at either the beginning or the end of the passage, but many texts do not adhere to this format.

Drawing conclusions from information implied within a passage requires confidence on the part of the reader. **Implications** are things that the author does not state directly, but readers can assume based on what the author does say. Consider the following passage: *I stepped outside and opened my umbrella. By the time I got to work, the cuffs of my pants were soaked.* The author never states that it is raining, but this fact is clearly implied. Conclusions based on implication must be well supported by the text. In order to draw a solid conclusion, readers should have **multiple pieces of evidence**. If readers have only one piece, they must be assured that there is no other possible explanation than their conclusion. A good reader will be able to draw many conclusions from information implied by the text, which will be a great help on the exam.

Drawing Conclusions

A common type of inference that a reader has to make is **drawing a conclusion**. The reader makes this conclusion based on the information provided within a text. Certain facts are included to help a reader come to a specific conclusion. For example, a story may open with a man trudging through the snow on a cold winter day, dragging a sled behind him. The reader can logically **infer** from the setting of the story that the man is wearing heavy winter clothes in order to stay warm. Information is implied based on the setting of a story, which is why **setting** is an important element of the text. If the same man in the example was trudging down a beach on a hot summer day, dragging a surf board behind him, the reader would assume that the man is not wearing heavy clothes. The reader makes inferences based on their own experiences and the information presented to them in the story.

Test-taking tip: When asked to identify a conclusion that may be drawn, look for critical "hedge" phrases, such as *likely*, *may*, *can*, and *will often*, among many others. When you are being tested on this knowledge, remember the question that writers insert into these hedge phrases to cover every possibility. Often an answer will be wrong simply because there is no room for exception. Extreme positive or negative answers (such as always or never) are usually not correct. When answering these questions, the reader **should not** use any outside knowledge that is not gathered directly or reasonably inferred from the passage. Correct answers can be derived straight from the passage.

Example

Read the following sentence from *Little Women* by Louisa May Alcott and draw a conclusion based upon the information presented:

> *You know the reason Mother proposed not having any presents this Christmas was because it is going to be a hard winter for everyone; and she thinks we ought not to spend money for pleasure, when our men are suffering so in the army.*

Based on the information in the sentence, the reader can conclude, or **infer**, that the men are away at war while the women are still at home. The pronoun *our* gives a clue to the reader that the character is speaking about men she knows. In addition, the reader can assume that the character is speaking to a brother or sister, since the term "Mother" is used by the character while speaking to another person. The reader can also come to the conclusion that the characters celebrate Christmas, since it is mentioned in the **context** of the sentence. In the sentence, the mother is presented as an unselfish character who is opinionated and thinks about the wellbeing of other people.

Comparing Two Stories

When presented with two different stories, there will be **similarities** and **differences** between the two. A reader needs to make a list, or other graphic organizer, of the points presented in each story. Once the reader has written down the main point and supporting points for each story, the two sets of ideas can be compared. The reader can then present each idea and show how it is the same or different in the other story. This is called **comparing and contrasting ideas**.

The reader can compare ideas by stating, for example: "In Story 1, the author believes that humankind will one day land on Mars, whereas in Story 2, the author believes that Mars is too far away for humans to ever step foot on." Note that the two viewpoints are different in each story that the reader is comparing. A reader may state that: "Both stories discussed the likelihood of humankind landing on Mars." This statement shows how the viewpoint presented in both stories is based on the same topic, rather than how each viewpoint is different. The reader will complete a comparison of two stories with a conclusion.

Review Video: Comparing Two Stories
Visit mometrix.com/academy and enter code: 833765

Outlining a Passage

As an aid to drawing conclusions, **outlining** the information contained in the passage should be a familiar skill to readers. An effective outline will reveal the structure of the passage and will lead to solid conclusions. An effective outline will have a title that refers to the basic subject of the text, though the title does not need to restate the main idea. In most outlines, the main idea will be the first major section. Each major idea in the passage will be established as the head of a category. For instance, the most common outline format calls for the main ideas of the passage to be indicated with Roman numerals. In an effective outline of this kind, each of the main ideas will be represented by a Roman numeral and none of the Roman numerals will designate minor details or secondary ideas. Moreover, all supporting ideas and details should be placed in the appropriate place on the outline. An outline does not need to include every detail listed in the text, but it should feature all of those that are central to the argument or message. Each of these details should be listed under the corresponding main idea.

Review Video: Outlining
Visit mometrix.com/academy and enter code: 584445

Using Graphic Organizers

Ideas from a text can also be organized using **graphic organizers**. A graphic organizer is a way to simplify information and take key points from the text. A graphic organizer such as a timeline may have an event listed for a corresponding date on the timeline, while an outline may have an event listed under a key point that occurs in the text. Each reader needs to create the type of graphic organizer that works the best for him or her in terms of being able to recall information from a story. Examples include a spider-map, which takes a main idea from the story and places it in a bubble with supporting points branching off the main idea. An outline is useful for diagramming the main and supporting points of the entire story, and a Venn diagram compares and contrasts characteristics of two or more ideas.

Review Video: Graphic Organizers
Visit mometrix.com/academy and enter code: 665513

Summarizing

A helpful tool is the ability to **summarize** the information that you have read in a paragraph or passage format. This process is similar to creating an effective outline. First, a summary should accurately define the main idea of the passage, though the summary does not need to explain this main idea in exhaustive detail. The summary should continue by laying out the most important supporting details or arguments from the passage. All of the significant supporting details should be included, and none of the details included should be irrelevant or insignificant. Also, the summary should accurately report all of these details. Too often, the desire for brevity in a summary leads to the sacrifice of clarity or accuracy. Summaries are often difficult to read because they omit all of the graceful language, digressions, and asides that distinguish great writing. However, an effective summary should communicate the same overall message as the original text.

Evaluating a Passage

It is important to understand the logical conclusion of the ideas presented in an informational text. **Identifying a logical conclusion** can help you determine whether you agree with the writer or not. Coming to this conclusion is much like making an inference: the approach requires you to combine the information given by the text with what you already know and make a logical conclusion. If the author intended for the reader to draw a certain conclusion, then you can expect the author's argumentation and detail to be leading in that direction.

One way to approach the task of drawing conclusions is to make brief **notes** of all the points made by the author. When the notes are arranged on paper, they may clarify the logical conclusion. Another way to approach conclusions is to consider whether the reasoning of the author raises any pertinent questions. Sometimes you will be able to draw several conclusions from a passage. On occasion these will be conclusions that were never imagined by the author. Therefore, be aware that these conclusions must be **supported directly by the text**.

Evaluation of Summaries

A summary of a literary passage is a condensation in the reader's own words of the passage's main points. Several guidelines can be used in evaluating a summary. The summary should be complete yet concise. It should be accurate, balanced, fair, neutral, and objective, excluding the reader's own opinions or reactions. It should reflect in similar proportion how much each point summarized was covered in the original passage. Summary writers should include tags of attribution, like "Macaulay argues that" to reference the original author whose ideas are represented in the summary. Summary writers should not overuse quotations; they should only quote central concepts or phrases they cannot precisely convey in words other than those of the original author. Another aspect of evaluating a summary is considering whether it can stand alone as a coherent, unified composition. In addition, evaluation of a summary should include whether its writer has cited the original source of the passage they have summarized so that readers can find it.

Chapter Quiz

1. Which of the following is most important when drawing conclusions from a text?

a. The conclusions make sense to others.
b. The conclusions are supported directly by the text.
c. The conclusions agree with previous convictions.
d. The conclusions align with the author's purpose for writing the text.

2. All of the following are true about summaries, EXCEPT:

a. They should focus on the main point of the text rather than proportional to how much each point was covered in the passage.
b. They should be accurate, balanced, fair, neutral, and objective.
c. They should be complete and concise.
d. They should only quote central concepts or phrases that cannot be precisely conveyed in words other than those of the original author.

Chapter Quiz Answer Key

1. B: It is important to understand the logical conclusion of the ideas presented in an informational text. Identifying a logical conclusion can help readers determine whether they agree with the writer or not. Coming to this conclusion is much like making an inference: the approach requires readers to combine the information given by the text with what they already know and make a logical conclusion. If the author intended for the reader to draw a certain conclusion, then readers can expect the author's argumentation and detail to be leading in that direction. Sometimes a reader will be able to draw several conclusions from a passage. On occasion these will be conclusions that were never imagined by the author. Therefore, be aware that these conclusions must be supported directly by the text.

2. A: A summary of a literary passage is a condensation in the reader's own words of the passage's main points. Several guidelines can be used in evaluating a summary. The summary should be complete yet concise. It should be accurate, balanced, fair, neutral, and objective, excluding the reader's own opinions or reactions. It should reflect in similar proportion how much each point summarized was covered in the original passage. Summary writers should include tags of attribution, like "Macaulay argues that" to reference the original author whose ideas are represented in the summary. Summary writers should not overuse quotations, but only quote central concepts or phrases they cannot precisely convey in words other than those of the original author. Another aspect of evaluating a summary is considering whether it can stand alone as a coherent, unified composition. In addition, evaluation of a summary should include whether its writer has cited the original source of the passage they have summarized so that readers can find it.

Language and Dialect

Diversity and Situational Nature of Language

Language is a diverse tool that allows people to communicate. However, language is often impacted and molded by the culture that uses it. This can make it difficult to learn and use a new language, since not all native speakers of the language will use it or interpret it the same way. For example, English is spoken all over America, but Americans in various regions of the country speak using different **dialects**. Other differences in speech include **accents** and **rhythm of speech**. Language is also manipulated by situations. Some terms and phrases have multiple meanings. A word's meaning often depends on the **context** in which the word or phrase is used, meaning that non-native speakers must learn to interpret situations to understand messages.

Factors of Language and Communication

Influences on Language

While dialect and diction are heavily influenced by an individual's culture and the location and history of the place they live, other personal factors can also impact language. A person's ethnicity, religious beliefs or background, and gender can influence the way they use and understand language. **Ethnicity** impacts language by incorporating a group's communication norms into an individual's speech and behavior. These norms may affect a speaker's tone, volume, or pace. These factors may lead others outside of that group to misinterpret the speaker's message, depending on their understanding of how those factors are used in speech. A person's **religious beliefs** can also affect their use of language. Religious beliefs and practices may lead an individual to abstain from using certain terms and may change the context in which a speaker uses specific words, or change their understanding of the word's usage. Additionally, a person may use language differently depending on their gender. **Gender's** influence on communication varies by region and industry. A region or industry's treatment of gender roles often impacts language use among its members. This can lead members of one gender group to be more assertive or submissive or to use different terms and phrases.

Culture and Communication

Individuals from different countries and cultures communicate differently. Not only do many people speak different languages, but they also speak using different inflections, volumes, tones, and dialects. These factors can have a significant impact on communication, even if the communicators speak the same language. In different cultures, certain behaviors are associated with different meanings and implications. When communicators from different cultures have a conversation, these expectations and associations may lead to misunderstanding. For example, Americans are considered to be louder and more demonstrative than people from other countries. Someone from a country where people speak more quietly who is not aware of this characterization may perceive an American's volume or large gestures as an indication of anger, when in reality, the American speaker is calm. The American may similarly perceive the other person as sad or shy due to their quiet voice, when the speaker is actually happy and comfortable in the conversation. Awareness of these factors and effects promotes respect for others and helps speakers understand the reasons for differences in communication, rather than allowing these differences to create division or conflict.

Language vs. Dialect

Languages are distinct and structured forms of verbal communication. Languages have cohesive sets of rules and words that are shared between the majority of that language's users. The main identifier of a language is that members of one language group are incapable of communicating fluently with members of another language group. New languages are formed as different dialects grow further apart until the members of each dialect can no longer innately communicate with each other.

Dialects are subsets of languages that do not violate the rules of the language as a whole, but which vary from other dialects in vocabulary usage, grammar forms, pronunciation, and spelling. Two major groupings of dialects are American and British English. Most American English and British English speakers can communicate with relative ease with one another, though the pronunciation, vocabulary (torch vs. flashlight;

trunk vs. boot), spelling (meter vs. metre; color vs. colour), and grammar (in American English, collective nouns are always considered singular, but can be singular or plural in British English).

Development of Dialects over Time

Dialects are formed primarily through the influences of location and time, but can be the result of other elements of **social stratification** as well (economic, ethnic, religious, etc.). As one group of a language's speakers is separated from another, in British and American English speakers for example, the language develops in isolated locations at the same time, resulting in distinct dialects. Language changes continuously over time as new words and phrases are adopted and others are phased out. Eventually, these small changes result culminate into enough grammar and vocabulary changes that the speakers of the distinct dialects cannot easily communicate with one another. The dialects can then be recognized as distinct languages.

Use of Dialect in Media

Literary authors often use dialect when writing dialogue to illustrate the social and geographical backgrounds of specific characters, which supports character development. For example, in *The Adventures of Huckleberry Finn* (1885), Mark Twain's novel is written in the dialect of a young, uneducated, white, Southern character, opening with this sentence: "You don't know about me without you have read a book by the name of The Adventures of Tom Sawyer, but that ain't no matter." Twain uses a different and exaggerated dialect to represent the speech of the African-American slave Jim: "We's safe, Huck, we's safe! Jump up and crack yo' heels. Dat's de good ole Cairo at las', I jis knows it."

In *To Kill a Mockingbird,* author Harper Lee used dialect in the characters' dialogue to portray an uneducated boy in the American South: "Reckon I have. Almost died the first year I come to school and et them pecans—folks say he pizened 'em." Lee also uses many Southern regional expressions, such as "right stove up," "What in the sam holy hill?", "sit a spell," "fess" (meaning "confess"), "jim-dandy," and "hush your fussing." These contribute to Lee's characterization of the people she describes, who live in a small town in Alabama circa the 1930s. In *Wuthering Heights* (1847), Emily Bronte reproduces Britain's 18th–19th-century Yorkshire dialect in the speech of servant Joseph: "Running after t'lads, as usuald!... If I war yah, maister, I'd just slam t'boards i' their faces all on 'em, gentle and simple! Never a day ut yah're off, but yon cat o' Linton comes sneaking hither; and Miss Nelly, shoo's a fine lass!"

Dialect vs. Diction

When written as characters' dialogue in literary works, dialect represents the particular pronunciation, grammar, and figurative expressions used by certain groups of people based on their geographic region, social class, and cultural background. For example, when a character says, "There's gold up in them thar hills," the author is using dialect to add to the characterization of that individual. Diction is more related to individual characters than to groups of people. The way in which a specific character speaks, including his or her choice of words, manner of expressing himself or herself, and use of grammar all represent individual types of diction. For example, two characters in the same novel might describe the same action or event using different diction: One says "I'm heading uptown for the evening," and the other says "I'm going out for a night on the town." These convey the same literal meaning, but due to their variations in diction, the speakers are expressing themselves in slightly different ways.

Review Video: Dialogue, Paradox, and Dialect
Visit mometrix.com/academy and enter code: 684341

Influences on Regional Dialect

Linguistic researchers have identified regional variations in vocabulary choices, which have evolved because of differences in local climates and how they influence human behaviors. For example, in the Southern United States, the Linguistic Atlas of the Gulf States (LAGS) Project by Dr. Lee Pederson of Emory University discovered and documented that people living in the northern or Upland section of the Piedmont plateau region call the fungal infection commonly known as athlete's foot "toe itch," but people living in the southern or Lowland section call it "ground itch." The explanation for this difference is that in the north, temperatures are cooler and people wear shoes accordingly, so they associate the itching with the feet in their description, but in the south, temperatures are hotter and people often went barefoot, so they associated the itching with the ground that presumably transmitted the infection.

Using Dialect in Writing

Dialect is most appropriate for informal or creative writing. Using dialectal writing when communicating casually or informally, such as in a text message or a quick email to a peer, is acceptable. However, in academic and professional contexts, writing using indications of dialect is inappropriate and often unacceptable. If the audience includes individuals who have a higher rank than the author, or authority over the author, it is best not to write in a way that suggests a dialect.

Developmental Literacy

Literacy

Literacy is commonly understood as the **ability to read and write**. UNESCO, the United Nations Educational, Scientific, and Cultural Organization, has further defined literacy as the "ability to identify, understand, interpret, create, communicate, compute, and use printed and written materials associated with varying contexts." Under the UNESCO definition, understanding cultural, political, and historical contexts of communities falls under the definition of literacy. While **reading literacy** may be gauged simply by the ability to read a newspaper, **writing literacy** includes spelling, grammar, and sentence structure. To be literate in a foreign language, one would also need to be able to understand a language by listening and be able to speak the language. Some argue that visual representation and numeracy should be included in the requirements one must meet to be considered literate. **Computer literacy** refers to one's ability to utilize the basic functions of computers and other technologies. Subsets of reading literacy include phonological awareness, decoding, comprehension, and vocabulary.

Phonological Awareness

A subskill of literacy, phonological awareness is the ability to perceive sound structures in a spoken word, such as syllables and the individual phonemes within syllables. **Phonemes** are the sounds represented by the letters in the alphabet. The ability to separate, blend, and manipulate sounds is critical to developing reading and spelling skills. Phonological awareness is concerned with not only syllables, but also **onset sounds** (the initial sound in a word, such as /k/ in 'cat') and **rime** (the sounds that follow the onset in a word, such as /at/ in 'cat'). Phonological awareness is an auditory skill that does not necessarily involve print. It should be developed before the student has learned letter to sound correspondences. A student's phonological awareness is an indicator of future reading success.

Review Video: Phonological and Phonemic Awareness, and Phonics
Visit mometrix.com/academy and enter code: 197017

Review Video: Components of Oral Language Development
Visit mometrix.com/academy and enter code: 480589

Communication Development Normally Occurring Within a Child's First Five Years of Life

Language and communication development depend strongly on the language a child develops within the first five years of life. During this time, three developmental periods are observed. At birth, the first period begins. This period is characterized by infant crying and gazing. Babies communicate their sensations and emotions through these behaviors, so they are expressive; however, they are not yet intentional. They indirectly indicate their needs through expressing how they feel, and when these needs are met, these communicative behaviors are reinforced. These expressions and reinforcement are the foundations for the later development of intentional communication. This becomes possible in the second developmental period, between 6 and 18 months. At this time, infants become able to coordinate their attention visually with other people relative to things and events, enabling purposeful communication with adults. During the third developmental period, from 18 months on, children come to use language as their main way of communicating and learning. Preschoolers can carry on conversations, exercise self-control through language use, and conduct verbal negotiations.

Milestones of Normal Language Development by the 2 Years Old

By the time most children reach the age of 2 years, they have acquired a vocabulary of about 150 to 300 words. They can name various familiar objects found in their environments. They are able to use at least two prepositions in their speech (e.g., *in*, *on*, and/or *under*). Two-year-olds typically combine the words they know into short sentences. These sentences tend to be mostly noun-verb or verb-noun combinations (e.g., "Daddy work," "Watch this"). They may also include verb-preposition combinations (e.g., "Go out," "Come in"). By the age of 2 years, children use pronouns, such as *I*, *me*, and *you*. They typically can use at least two such pronouns correctly. A normally developing 2-year-old will respond to some commands, directions, or questions, such as "Show me your eyes" or "Where are your ears?"

Salient General Aspects of Human Language Abilities from Before Birth to 5 Years of Age

Language and communication abilities are integral parts of human life that are central to learning, successful school performance, successful social interactions, and successful living. Human language ability begins before birth: the developing fetus can hear not only internal maternal sounds, but also the mother's voice, others' voices, and other sounds outside the womb. Humans have a natural sensitivity to human sounds and languages from before they are born until they are about 4½ years old. These years are critical for developing language and communication. Babies and young children are predisposed to greater sensitivity to human sounds than other sounds, orienting them toward the language spoken around them. Children absorb their environmental language completely, including vocal tones, syntax, usage, and emphasis. This linguistic absorption occurs very rapidly. Children's first 2½ years particularly involve amazing abilities to learn language, including grammatical expression.

6 Months, 12 Months, and 18 Months

Individual differences dictate a broad range of language development that is still normal. However, parents observing noticeably delayed language development in their children should consult professionals. Typically, babies respond to hearing their names by 6 months of age, turn their heads and eyes toward the sources of human voices they hear, and respond accordingly to friendly and angry tones of voice. By the age of 12 months, toddlers can usually understand and follow simple directions, especially when these are accompanied by physical and/or vocal cues. They can intentionally use one or more words with the correct meaning. By the age of 18 months, a normally developing child usually has acquired a vocabulary of roughly 5 to 20 words. Eighteen-month-old children use nouns in their speech most of the time. They are very likely to repeat certain words and/or phrases over and over. At this age, children typically are able to follow simple verbal commands without needing as many visual or auditory cues as at 12 months.

Three Years

By the time they are 3 years old, most normally developing children have acquired vocabularies of between 900 and 1,000 words. Typically, they correctly use the pronouns *I*, *me*, and *you*. They use more verbs more frequently. They apply past tenses to some verbs and plurals to some nouns. 3-year-olds usually can use at least three prepositions; the most common are *in*, *on*, and *under*. The normally developing 3-year-old knows the major body parts and can name them. 3-year-olds typically use 3-word sentences with ease. Normally, parents should find approximately 75 to 100 percent of what a 3-year-old says to be intelligible, while strangers should find between 50 and 75 percent of a 3-year-old's speech intelligible. Children this age comprehend most simple questions about their activities and environments and can answer questions about what they should do when they are thirsty, hungry, sleepy, hot, or cold. They can tell about their experiences in ways that adults can generally follow. By the age of 3 years, children should also be able to tell others their name, age, and sex.

Four Years

When normally developing children are 4 years old, most know the names of animals familiar to them. They can use at least four prepositions in their speech (e.g., *in*, *on*, *under*, *to*, *from*, etc.). They can name familiar objects in pictures, and they know and can identify one color or more. Usually, they are able to repeat four-syllable words they hear. They verbalize as they engage in their activities, which Vygotsky dubbed "private speech." Private speech helps young children think through what they are doing, solve problems, make decisions, and reinforce the correct sequences in multistep activities. When presented with contrasting items, 4-year-olds can understand comparative concepts like bigger and smaller. At this age, they are able to comply with simple commands without the target stimuli being in their sight (e.g., "Put those clothes in the hamper" [upstairs]). Four-year-old children will also frequently repeat speech sounds, syllables, words, and phrases, similar to 18-month-olds' repetitions but at higher linguistic and developmental levels.

Five Years

Once most children have reached the age of 5 years, their speech has expanded from the emphasis of younger children on nouns, verbs, and a few prepositions, and is now characterized by many more descriptive words, including adjectives and adverbs. Five-year-olds understand common antonyms, such as big/little, heavy/light, long/short, and hot/cold. They can now repeat longer sentences they hear, up to about 9 words. When given three consecutive, uninterrupted commands, the typical 5-year-old can follow these without forgetting one or two. At age 5, most children have learned simple concepts of time like today, yesterday, and tomorrow; day, morning, afternoon, and night; and before, after, and later. Five-year-olds typically speak in relatively long sentences and normally should be incorporating some compound sentences (with more than one independent clause) and complex sentences (with one or more independent and dependent clauses). Five-year-old children's speech is also grammatically correct most of the time.

Activities That Teach Phonological Awareness

Classroom activities that teach phonological awareness include language play and exposure to a variety of sounds and the contexts of sounds. Activities that teach phonological awareness include:

- Clapping to the sounds of individual words, names, or all words in a sentence
- Practicing saying blended phonemes
- Singing songs that involve phoneme replacement (e.g., The Name Game)
- Reading poems, songs, and nursery rhymes out loud
- Reading patterned and predictable texts out loud
- Listening to environmental sounds or following verbal directions
- Playing games with rhyming chants or fingerplays
- Reading alliterative texts out loud
- Grouping objects by beginning sounds
- Reordering words in a well-known sentence or making silly phrases by deleting words from a well-known sentence (perhaps from a favorite storybook)

Teaching of Reading Through Phonics

Phonics is the process of learning to read by learning how spoken language is represented by letters. Students learn to read phonetically by sounding out the **phonemes** in words and then blending them together to produce the correct sounds in words. In other words, the student connects speech sounds with letters or groups of letters and blends the sounds together to determine the pronunciation of an unknown word. Phonics is a method commonly used to teach **decoding and reading**, but it has been challenged by other methods, such as the whole language approach. Despite the complexity of pronunciation and combined sounds in the English language, phonics is a highly effective way to teach reading. Being able to read or pronounce a word does not mean the student comprehends the meaning of the word, but context aids comprehension. When phonics is used as a foundation for decoding, children eventually learn to recognize words automatically and advance to decoding multisyllable words with practice.

Alphabetic Principle and Alphabet Writing Systems

The **alphabetic principle** refers to the use of letters and combinations of letters to represent speech sounds. The way letters are combined and pronounced is guided by a system of rules that establishes relationships between written and spoken words and their letter symbols. Alphabet writing systems are common around the world. Some are **phonological** in that each letter stands for an individual sound and words are spelled just as they sound. However, keep in mind that there are other writing systems as well, such as the Chinese **logographic** system and the Japanese **syllabic** system.

> **Review Video: Print Awareness and Alphabet Knowledge**
> Visit mometrix.com/academy and enter code: 541069

Facts Children Should Know About Letters

To be appropriately prepared to learn to read and write, a child should learn:

- That each letter is **distinct** in appearance
- What **direction and shape** must be used to write each letter
- That each letter has a **name**, which can be associated with the shape of a letter
- That there are **26** letters in the English alphabet, and letters are grouped in a certain order
- That letters represent **sounds of speech**
- That **words** are composed of letters and have meaning
- That one must be able to **correspond** letters and sounds to read

Development of Language Skills

Children learn language through interacting with others, by experiencing language in daily and relevant context, and through understanding that speaking and listening are necessary for effective communication. Teachers can promote **language development** by intensifying the opportunities a child has to experience and understand language.

Teachers can assist language development by:

- Modeling enriched vocabulary and teaching new words
- Using questions and examples to extend a child's descriptive language skills
- Providing ample response time to encourage children to practice speech
- Asking for clarification to provide students with the opportunity to develop communication skills
- Promoting conversations among children
- Providing feedback to let children know they have been heard and understood, and providing further explanation when needed

Relationship Between Oral and Written Language Development

Oral and written language development occur simultaneously. The acquisition of skills in one area supports the acquisition of skills in the other. However, oral language is not a prerequisite to written language. An immature form of oral language development is babbling, and an immature form of written language development is scribbling. **Oral language development** does not occur naturally, but does occur in a social context. This means it is best to include children in conversations rather than simply talk at them. **Written language development** can occur without direct instruction. In fact, reading and writing do not necessarily need to be taught through formal lessons if the child is exposed to a print-rich environment. A teacher can assist a child's language development by building on what the child already knows, discussing relevant and meaningful events and experiences, teaching vocabulary and literacy skills, and providing opportunities to acquire more complex language.

Print-Rich Environment

A teacher can provide a **print-rich environment** in the classroom in a number of ways. These include:

- **Displaying** the following in the classroom:
    - Children's names in print or cursive
    - Children's written work

- Newspapers and magazines
- Instructional charts
- Written schedules
- Signs and labels
- Printed songs, poems, and rhymes

- Using **graphic organizers** such as KWL charts or story road maps to:
    - Remind students about what was read and discussed
    - Expand on the lesson topic or theme
    - Show the relationships among books, ideas, and words
- Using **big books** to:
    - Point out features of print, such as specific letters and punctuation
    - Track print from right to left
    - Emphasize the concept of words and the fact that they are used to communicate

Benefits of Print and Book Awareness

Print and book awareness helps a child understand:

- That there is a **connection** between print and messages contained on signs, labels, and other print forms in the child's environment
- That reading and writing are ways to obtain information and communicate ideas
- That **print** written in English runs from left to right and from top to bottom
- That a book has **parts**, such as a title, a cover, a title page, and a table of contents
- That a book has an **author** and contains a **story**
- That **illustrations** can carry meaning
- That **letters and words** are different
- That **words and sentences** are separated by spaces and punctuation
- That different **text forms** are used for different functions
- That print represents **spoken language**
- How to **hold** a book

Decoding

Decoding is the method or strategy used to make sense of printed words and figure out how to correctly pronounce them. In order to **decode**, a student needs to know the relationships between letters and sounds, including letter patterns; that words are constructed from phonemes and phoneme blends; and that a printed word represents a word that can be spoken. This knowledge will help the student recognize familiar words and make informed guesses about the pronunciation of unfamiliar words. Decoding is not the same as comprehension. It does not require an understanding of the meaning of a word, only a knowledge of how to recognize and pronounce it. Decoding can also refer to the skills a student uses to determine the meaning of a **sentence**. These skills include applying knowledge of vocabulary, sentence structure, and context.

Role of Fluency in Literacy Development

Fluency is the goal of literacy development. It is the ability to read accurately and quickly. Evidence of fluency includes the ability to recognize words automatically and group words for comprehension. At this point, the student no longer needs to decode words except for complex, unfamiliar ones. He or she is able to move to the next level and understand the **meaning** of a text. The student should be able to self-check for comprehension and should feel comfortable expressing ideas in writing. Teachers can help students build fluency by continuing to provide:

- Reading experiences and discussions about text that gradually increase in level of difficulty
- Reading practice, both silently and out loud

- Word analysis practice
- Instruction on reading comprehension strategies
- Opportunities to express responses to readings through writing

Review Video: Fluency
Visit mometrix.com/academy and enter code: 531179

Role of Vocabulary in Literacy Development

When students do not know the meaning of words in a text, their comprehension is limited. As a result, the text becomes boring or confusing. The larger a student's **vocabulary** is, the better their reading comprehension will be. A larger vocabulary is also associated with an enhanced ability to **communicate** in speech and writing. It is the teacher's role to help students develop a good working vocabulary. Students learn most of the words they use and understand by listening to the world around them (adults, other students, media, etc.) They also learn from their reading experiences, which include being read to and reading independently. Carefully designed activities can also stimulate vocabulary growth, and should emphasize useful words that students see frequently, important words necessary for understanding text, and difficult words and phrases, such as idioms or words with more than one meaning.

Teaching Techniques Promoting Vocabulary Development

A student's **vocabulary** can be developed by:

- Calling upon a student's **prior knowledge** and making comparisons to that knowledge
- **Defining** a word and providing multiple examples of the use of the word in context
- Showing a student how to use **context clues** to discover the meaning of a word
- Providing instruction on **prefixes**, **roots**, and **suffixes** to help students break a word into its parts and decipher its meaning
- Showing students how to use a **dictionary and a thesaurus**
- Asking students to **practice** new vocabulary by using the words in their own writing
- Providing a **print-rich environment** with a word wall
- Studying a group of words related to a **single subject**, such as farm words, transportation words, etc. so that concept development is enhanced

Affixes, Prefixes, and Root Words

Affixes are syllables attached to the beginning or end of a word to make a derivative or inflectional form of a word. Both prefixes and suffixes are affixes. A **prefix** is a syllable that appears at the beginning of a word that creates a specific meaning in combination with the root or base word. For example, the prefix *mis* means wrong. When combined with the root word *spelling*, the word *misspelling* is created, which means wrong spelling. A **root word** is the base of a word to which affixes can be added. For example, the prefix *in-* or *pre-* can be added to the latin root word *vent* to create *invent* or *prevent*, respectively. The suffix *-er* can be added to the root word *manage* to create *manager*, which means one who manages. The suffix *-able*, meaning capable of, can be added to *manage* to create *managable*, which means capable of being managed.

Suffixes

A **suffix** is a syllable that appears at the end of a word that creates a specific meaning in combination with the root or base word. There are three types of suffixes:

- **Noun suffixes**—Noun suffixes can change a verb or adjective to a noun. They can denote the act of, state of, quality of, or result of something. For example, *-ment* added to *argue* becomes *argument*, which can be understood as the act the act of resulting state from arguing or the reasons given to prove an idea. Noun suffixes can also denote the doer, or one who acts. For example, *-eer* added to *auction* becomes *auctioneer*, meaning one who auctions. Other examples include *-hood*, *-ness*, *-tion*, *-ship*, and *-ism*.
- **Verb suffixes**—These change other words to verbs and denote to make or to perform the act of. For example, *-en* added to *soft* makes *soften*, which means to make soft. Other verb suffixes are *-ate* (perpetuate), *-fy* (dignify), and *-ize* (sterilize).
- **Adjectival suffixes**—These suffixes change other words to adjectives and include suffixes such as *-ful*, which means full of. When added to *care*, the word *careful* is formed, which means full of care. Other examples are *-ish* and *-less*.

Strategies to Improve Reading Comprehension

Teachers can model the strategies students can use on their own to better comprehend a text through a read-aloud. First, the teacher should do a walk-through of the story **illustrations** and ask, "What's happening here?" The teacher should then ask students to **predict** what the story will be about based on what they have seen. As the book is read, the teacher should ask open-ended questions such as, "Why do you think the character did this?" and "How do you think the character feels?" The teacher should also ask students if they can **relate** to the story or have background knowledge of something similar. After the reading, the teacher should ask the students to **retell** the story in their own words to check for comprehension. Possible methods of retelling include performing a puppet show or summarizing the story to a partner.

Review Video: The Link Between Grammar Skills and Reading Comprehension
Visit mometrix.com/academy and enter code: 411287

Role of Prior Knowledge in Determining Appropriate Literacy Education

Even preschool children have some literacy skills, and the extent and type of these skills have implications for instructional approaches. **Comprehension** results from relating two or more pieces of information. One piece comes from the text, and another piece might come from **prior knowledge** (something from a student's long-term memory). For a child, that prior knowledge comes from being read to at home; taking part in other literacy experiences, such as playing computer or word games; being exposed to a print-rich environment at home; and observing parents' reading habits. Children who have had **extensive literacy experience** are better prepared to further develop their literacy skills in school than children who have not been read to, have few books or magazines in their homes, are seldom exposed to high-level oral or written language activities, and seldom witness adults engaged in reading and writing. Children with a scant literacy background are at a disadvantage. The teacher must not make any assumptions about their prior knowledge, and should use intense, targeted instruction. Otherwise, the student may have trouble improving their reading comprehension.

English Language Learning

Theories of Language Development

Four theories of language development are:

- **Learning approach**—This theory assumes that language is first learned by imitating the speech of adults. It is then solidified in school through drills about the rules of language structures.
- **Linguistic approach**—Championed by Noam Chomsky in the 1950s, this theory proposes that the ability to use a language is innate. This is a biological approach rather than one based on cognition or social patterning.
- **Cognitive approach**—Developed in the 1970s and based on the work of Piaget, this theory states that children must develop appropriate cognitive skills before they can acquire language.
- **Sociocognitive approach**—In the 1970s, some researchers proposed that language development is a complex interaction of linguistic, social, and cognitive influences. This theory best explains the lack of language skills among children who are neglected, have uneducated parents, or live in poverty.

Classroom Practices Benefiting Second Language Acquisition

Since some students may have a limited understanding of English, a teacher should employ the following practices to promote second language acquisition:

- Make all instruction as **understandable** as possible and use simple and repeated terms.
- Relate instruction to the **cultures** of ESL children.
- Increase **interactive activities** and use gestures or nonverbal actions when modeling.
- Provide language and literacy development instruction in **all curriculum areas**.
- Establish **consistent routines** that help children connect words and events.
- Use a **schedule** so children know what will happen next and will not feel lost.
- Integrate ESL children into **group activities** with non-ESL children.
- Appoint bilingual students to act as **student translators**.
- Explain actions as activities happen so that a **word to action relationship** is established.
- Initiate opportunities for ESL children to **experiment** with and practice new language.
- Employ multisensory learning.

Teaching Strategies to Promote Listening Skills of ESL Students

Listening is a critical skill when learning a new language. Students spend a great deal more time listening than they do speaking, and far less time reading and writing than speaking. One way to encourage ESL students to listen is to talk about topics that are of **interest** to the ESL learner. Otherwise, students may tune out the speaker because they don't want to put in that much effort to learn about a topic they find boring. Another way to encourage ESL students to listen is to talk about content or give examples that are **easy** to understand or are **related** to a topic that is familiar to ESL students. Culturally relevant materials will be more interesting to ESL students, will make them feel more comfortable, and will contain vocabulary that they may already be familiar with.

Considerations Relevant to ESL Students Related to Learning by Listening

Listening is not a passive skill, but an **active** one. Therefore, a teacher needs to make the listening experience as rewarding as possible and provide as many auditory and visual clues as possible. Three ways that the teacher can make the listening experience rewarding for ESL students are:

- Avoid **colloquialisms** and **abbreviated or slang terms** that may be confusing to the ESL listener, unless there is enough time to define them and explain their use.
- Make the spoken English understandable by stopping to **clarify** points, **repeating** new or difficult words, and **defining** words that may not be known.

- Support the spoken word with as many **visuals** as possible. Pictures, diagrams, gestures, facial expressions, and body language can help the ESL learner correctly interpret the spoken language more easily and also leaves an image impression that helps them remember the words.

Top-Down and Bottom-Up Processing

ESL students need to be given opportunities to practice both top-down and bottom-up processing. If they are old enough to understand these concepts, they should be made aware that these are two processes that affect their listening comprehension. In **top-down processing**, the listener refers to **background and global knowledge** to figure out the meaning of a message. For example, when asking an ESL student to perform a task, the steps of the task should be explained and accompanied by a review of the vocabulary terms the student already understands so that the student feels comfortable tackling new steps and new words. The teacher should also allow students to ask questions to verify comprehension. In **bottom-up processing**, the listener figures out the meaning of a message by using "**data**" obtained from what is said. This data includes sounds (stress, rhythm, and intonation), words, and grammatical relationships. All data can be used to make conclusions or interpretations. For example, the listener can develop bottom-up skills by learning how to detect differences in intonation between statements and questions.

Listening Lessons

All students, but especially ESL students, can be taught **listening** through specific training. During listening lessons, the teacher should guide students through three steps:

- **Pre-listening activity**—This establishes the purpose of the lesson and engages students' background knowledge. This activity should ask students to think about and discuss something they already know about the topic. Alternatively, the teacher can provide background information.
- **The listening activity**—This requires the listener to obtain information and then immediately do something with that information. For example, the teacher can review the schedule for the day or the week. In this example, students are being given information about a routine they already know, and need to be able to identify names, tasks, and times.
- **Post-listening activity**—This is an evaluation process that allows students to judge how well they did with the listening task. Other language skills can be included in the activity. For example, this activity could involve asking questions about who will do what according to the classroom schedule (Who is the lunch monitor today?) and could also involve asking students to produce whole sentence replies.

Helping ESL Students Understand Subject Matter

Speaking

To help ESL students better understand subject matter, the following teaching strategies using spoken English can be used:

- **Read aloud** from a textbook, and then ask ESL students to **verbally summarize** what was read. The teacher should assist by providing new words as needed to give students the opportunity to practice vocabulary and speaking skills. The teacher should then read the passage again to students to verify accuracy and details.
- The teacher could ask ESL students to explain why the subject matter is important to them and where they see it fitting into their lives. This verbalization gives them speaking practice and helps them relate to the subject.
- Whenever small group activities are being conducted, ESL students can be placed with **English-speaking students**. It is best to keep the groups to two or three students so that the ESL student will be motivated by the need to be involved. English-speaking students should be encouraged to include ESL students in the group work.

Reading

There are supplemental printed materials that can be used to help ESL students understand subject matter. The following strategies can be used to help ESL students develop English reading skills.

- Make sure all ESL students have a **bilingual dictionary** to use. A thesaurus would also be helpful.
- Try to keep **content area books** written in the ESL students' native languages in the classroom. Students can use them side-by-side with English texts. Textbooks in other languages can be ordered from the school library or obtained from the classroom textbook publisher.
- If a student lacks confidence in his or her ability to read the textbook, the teacher can read a passage to the student and have him or her **verbally summarize** the passage. The teacher should take notes on what the student says and then read them back. These notes can be a substitute, short-form, in-their-own-words textbook that the student can understand.

General Teaching Strategies to Help ESL Students

Some strategies can help students develop more than one important skill. They may involve a combination of speaking, listening, and viewing. Others are mainly classroom management aids. General teaching strategies for ESL students include:

- **Partner** English-speaking students with ESL students as study buddies and ask the English-speaking students to share notes.
- Encourage ESL students to ask **questions** whenever they don't understand something. They should be aware that they don't have to be able to interpret every word of text to understand the concept.
- Dictate **key sentences** related to the content area being taught and ask ESL students to write them down. This gives them practice in listening and writing, and also helps them identify what is important.
- **Alternate** difficult and easy tasks so that ESL students can experience academic success.
- Ask ESL students to **label** objects associated with content areas, such as maps, diagrams, parts of a leaf, or parts of a sentence. This gives students writing and reading experience and helps them remember key vocabulary.

Teaching Reading

Recommendations for Teaching Reading

- Students often benefit from the explicit instruction of new vocabulary. Vocabulary knowledge can be reinforced implicitly by integrating the new words into activities and future texts.
- Reading comprehension can also be improved by explicitly preparing students for reading activities. An example of explicit instruction prior to a reading assignment is to explicitly describe a particular type of plot device that is used in a passage before the students encounter the device in the reading. Guided readings and summaries help prepare a student to comprehend an assigned passage.
- Peer discussions are also known to help improve reading comprehension, as students can help each other develop decoding skills through discussions about the meaning and interpretation of texts.
- Reading comprehension is often affected by students' motivation to read the passage. Teachers should employ motivational strategies, such as frequent assessments or rewards, to keep students engaged when reading.

Guiding the Literacy Instruction of Students

- Throughout the school day, educators should give students explicit instruction and supportive practice in using strategies that have been proven to effectively improve reading comprehension.
- Educators should use a higher quantity and quality of continued, open discussions about the content that students are reading.
- Educators should sustain high standards for students. Students should be expected to be able to answer questions about the text that they read, the vocabulary that they learn, and any applications of the text.
- Educators should work to enhance the degree to which students are motivated to read and are engaged with reading.
- Educators should teach students content knowledge that is essential to their mastery of concepts that are critical to their understanding and success.

Literacy Instruction Strategies to Use Before and During Reading

Instructional activities initiated before students read have a number of purposes:

- To activate the prior knowledge of the students
- To generate questions they may want to ask about the subject and reading before they read
- To discuss the vocabulary words they will encounter in the text when they read it
- To encourage students to make predictions about what they will be reading
- To help students to identify a purpose for their reading

Activities initiated during reading include the following purposes:

- To engage students with the text
- To help students to self-monitor their own reading comprehension
- To teach students how to summarize the text
- To help them integrate new information from the text with their existing knowledge
- To help them make and verify predictions about the text
- To enable them to create graphic organizers to aid comprehension
- To facilitate their use of mental imagery related to the text

Instructional Activities Used After Students Have Read Assigned Text

After students read some text, teachers will initiate various instructional activities to support and evaluate their reading comprehension. Some of the purposes of instructional activities conducted after reading text include the following:

- To have students reflect on the content of the lesson
- To identify where they found this content in the text they read
- To have students consider and study questions the teacher provided to guide their reading and have them give answers to those questions based on what they read and their own prior knowledge
- To have students evaluate the accuracy of predictions they previously made about the text during instructional activities conducted before and during reading
- To have students engage in discussion of the text to express, share, and compare their responses to the text
- To have students summarize or retell the narrative, events, or information they read in the text using their own words, demonstrating comprehension and application.

Instructing Students to Apply Cognitive Strategies

Teachers can follow several steps to teach students how to apply the same cognitive strategies that excellent readers routinely employ to comprehend the text that they read. First, the teacher should give the students **direct instruction** in each cognitive strategy—e.g., inferring, questioning, summarizing, etc.

This direct instruction should include the following:

- The teacher should give the students a definition of the strategy, and explain it.
- The teacher should explain what purpose is served by the strategy during the act of reading.
- The teacher should also identify the most important characteristics of the strategy.
- Then the teacher should give the students concrete examples of the strategy and non-examples (i.e., examples of actions that do not use the strategy).
- Following direct instruction, the teacher should use think-alouds to model the use of the cognitive strategy for students.
- Then the teacher should give the students guided practice in applying the strategy.

"Mindless Reading" Versus Highly Effective Reading

Many students who struggle with reading mistakenly are simply "zoning out" while moving their eyes across the page. This is known as "Mindless Reading." In contrast, effective readers apply cognitive strategies to keep engaged and process the text they read. One strategy that can be employed to help prevent mindless reading is group reading, either aloud or silently. The key to enforcing engagement is to use frequent recaps or comprehension checks. Teachers should encourage discussion between small groups of students reading a passage and should ask challenging and rigorous questions that require paying close attention to the story. Asking students to apply themes or questions about the text to their own life is a good way to keep students engaged, as well.

Readability

Before assigning texts, teachers should evaluate the text's level of readability so they can best set their students up for success. **Readability** refers to a how easily an individual can read a passage. There are several different methods and formulas for evaluating a text's readability. These can be aligned to students' reading levels and inform teachers, parents, and students of which books and materials are the best fit for a student's reading skills. Readability can be determined using factors such as the number of words, syllables per word, and difficult or uncommon words in a passage. Below are a few common algorithms used to determine readability.

FLESCH READING EASE AND GUNNING FOG SCALE LEVEL

The Flesch Reading Ease and Gunning Fog Scale Level methods primarily use syllable count and the length of the sentences in a passage to determine readability. The **Flesch Reading Ease** method is measured on a 100-point scale, with different ranges of scores corresponding to a certain level of education. The Flesch-Kincade Grade Level method converts this score to a grade level, suggesting that a typical student of that grade level can read the passage. The **Gunning Fog Scale Level** method gives a text a score that corresponds to a category of difficulty. Texts that receive a score in the zero to five range are considered readable, scores that range from five to 10 are hard, scores that range from 10 and 15 are difficult, and scores that range from 15 to 20 are very difficult.

DALE-CHALL SCORE

The **Dale-Chall Score** evaluates text based on whether or not the words within it are common or not. This method starts with a set list of words that are considered easy. Scores are given based on the number of words in passage that are not on that list. These scores range from zero to 9.9. Scores equal to or below 4.9 suggest that the passage can be easily read by a typical fourth-grader, while scores exceeding 9.0 suggest that a reader would need to be at a college level to easily read the passage.

FRY READABILITY GRADE LEVEL

The **Fry Readability Grade Level** analyzes a passage based on the number of syllables and sentences per 100 words. These values are documented on a graph, using the two factors as axes. The readability and appropriate grade level of a text are determined by which portions of the graph the text falls under based on its 100-word sample. This method is often completed using multiple 100-word samples for higher accuracy.

READING COMPREHENSION STRATEGIES FOR INFORMATIONAL TEXTS

PAIRED READING STRATEGY TO IDENTIFY MAIN IDEAS AND DETAILS

Students can support one another's comprehension of informational text by working in pairs. Each student silently reads a portion of text. One summarizes the text's main point, and then the other must agree or disagree and explain why until they reach an agreement. Then each person takes a turn at identifying details in the text portion that support the main idea that they have identified. Finally, they repeat each step with their roles reversed. Each pair of students can keep track of the central ideas and supporting details by taking notes in two columns: one for main ideas and the other for the details that support those main ideas.

TEXT CODING

Text coding or text monitoring is recommended as an active reading strategy to support student comprehension of informational texts. As they read, students make text code notations on Post-it Notes or in the margins of the text. Teachers should model text coding for students one or two codes at a time until they have demonstrated all eight codes: A check mark means "I know this." An "X" means "This is not what I expected." An asterisk (*) means "This is important." A question mark means "I have a question about this." Two question marks mean "I am really confused about this." An exclamation point means "I am surprised at this." An "L" means "I have learned something new from this." And RR means "I need to reread this part."

CONNECTIONS AND DISTINCTIONS AMONG ELEMENTS IN TEXT

Students should be able to analyze how an informational text makes connections and distinctions among ideas, events, or individuals, such as by comparing or contrasting them, making analogies between them, or dividing them into categories to show similarities and differences. For example, teachers can help eighth-graders analyze how to divide animals into categories of carnivores, which eat only meat; herbivores, which eat only plants; and omnivores, which eat both meat and plants. Teachers and students can identify the author's comparisons and contrasts of groups. Teachers can help students analyze these processes by supplying sentence frames. For example, "A _____ is a _____, so _____" and "A _____ is a _____ which means _____." The students fill these empty spaces in, creating sentences such as, "A frog is a carnivore, so it eats only meat," and "A rabbit is an herbivore, which means it eats only plants."

Denotative and Connotative Meaning

Similar to literal and figurative language, **denotation** is the literal meaning, or dictionary definition, of a word whereas **connotation** is the feelings or thoughts associated with a word that are not included in its literal definition. For example, "politician" and "statesman" have the same denotation, but in context, "politician" may have a negative connotation while "statesman" may have a positive connotation. Teachers can help students understand positive or negative connotations of words depending on their sentence contexts. For example, the word "challenge" has a positive connotation in this sentence: "Although I finished last, I still accomplished the challenge of running the race." Teachers can give students a multiple-choice game wherein they choose whether "challenge" here means (A) easy, (B) hard, (C) fun, or (D) taking work to overcome. The word "difficult" has a negative connotation in this sentence: "I finished last in the race because it was difficult." Students choose whether "difficult" here means (A) easy, (B) hard, (C) fun, or (D) lengthy. Positive and negative connotations for the same word can also be taught. Consider the following sentence: "When the teacher asked Johnny why he was in the restroom so long, he gave a *smart* answer." In this context, "smart" means disrespectful and carries a negative connotation. But in the sentence, "Johnny was *smart* to return to class from the restroom right away," the same word means wise and carries a positive connotation.

Promoting Student Interest in Reading

When instructing students in the study of literature, it is important to encourage students' interest in literature. This can help students engage in the literature more deeply and better appreciate what they learn about it. Educators can promote students' interest in literature by allowing students to choose what they read. Letting students individually choose or vote on reading materials gives them an opportunity to make choices and gain a sense of responsibility over their education. Students may also gain interest in literature from participating in peer discussions. Giving students the opportunity to share their observations and ideas with each other, and potentially build upon each other's thoughts, also contributes to a sense of responsibility over their learning and education. Students should also be encouraged to appreciate the value of the literature they are reading. If students can relate literature to themselves, the world, history, or other topics and concepts that interest them, they may be better enabled to see the value of what they are reading and its ability to have an impact. Emphasizing text-to-self, text-to-world, and text-to-text relationships equips students to make their own connections with literature, which promotes their interest in literature.

Assignments to Promote Student Interest

Observing relationships between literature and reality can also allow students to see similarities between their observations, their peer's experiences, and various pieces of literature. Many of these similarities are relevant to common human experiences, including emotions, psychology, various relationships, and the stages and progression of life. Once students learn to observe these similarities and themes within literature, they are better equipped to analyze and interpret the function of these elements in a particular work. One way to foster a student's analysis and interest in the work's purpose is to create assignments relevant to the message, plot, or moral of the literature they are studying. These may include analysis essays, student-taught lessons, or interpretive illustrations of concepts or messages. This analysis may be aided by identifying rhetorical and figurative devices in the same work and connecting the use of these devices to the present themes. The application of literary theories and criticism can also reveal the function or relevance of these themes and show a text's treatment of the human experience.

Text Connections and Student Interest

Text-to-self and text-to-world connections also encourage students to understand the personal and societal relevance of a particular work. Students can be encouraged to make text-to-self connections when they can relate the text to their personal lives. This can be facilitated by teaching texts that feature protagonists that are close in age to the students in the class or texts that take place in a familiar region. By teaching or assigning texts that align to current events, teachers can promote students' interest in literature's timeless applicability to world, national, and local events and developments. Alternatively, when teaching texts that do not have characters or events that bear strong resemblance to the students or current events, teachers can still ask students to identify smaller similarities between their lives and the text.

Literature and Student Interest

While students may not choose to read classic British or American literature for leisure, their opinions on assigned readings can inform what they do choose to read on their own. Commonly assigned novels and short stories fall into genres that are still popular today. Students can determine which works they enjoy, consider what genre that work may belong to, and choose their leisurely reading accordingly. For example, *1984* by George Orwell takes place in a dystopian society. This is a common theme in young-adult fiction, so students who enjoyed *1984* may look for novels with similar settings. *Frankenstein* by Mary Shelley is an example of early science fiction, so students who like *Frankenstein* can be encouraged to read other science-fiction novels. These similarities may also be used to pique students' interest in assigned readings by highlighting the similarities between classic literature and contemporary fiction.

Technology and Reading

Students today have considerable access and exposure to technology. Students often use technology for entertainment and social interaction, but technology can also be used and enjoyed in education. Technology can be used to increase students' engagement and interest in literature and to promote their comprehension of the material. Different types of technology can appeal to different students and their learning styles. Games and activities related to literature and lessons make the material interactive and give students an opportunity to see the material applied and presented in an alternative way. Projects and assignments that require students to use technology give students an opportunity to create a unique product and reflect what they valued most about the literature. Technology also allows students to interact with each other and the material outside of class, encouraging their engagement by enabling them to collaborate and make their own connections.

Technology can also promote students' comprehension by presenting literature in various mediums. Many e-books and digital texts integrate tools that allow users to look up definitions, pronunciations, and other information while they are reading without distracting from the text. This promotes comprehension by providing helpful resources that support the reader's comprehension of the text. Audiobooks can also aid in reading comprehension. Some students are more receptive of information they hear, rather than information they read. Students who read a text and listen to a narration of that text simultaneously may be able to focus on the text more deeply and comprehend the information better.

Incorporating Young Adult Literature in the Classroom

Young-adult literature includes a variety of genres and themes. One prominent trend in young-adult literature is plots that take place in dystopian societies in the future. These novels compare to commonly taught novels, such as *1984* by George Orwell, and offer a commentary on the time at which they were written. Many young-adult novels also compare to books like Charles Dickens's *Great Expectations*, which features a young boy growing into adulthood and navigating society and his relationship with others. This is also a common element in several young-adult novels. Many modern young-adult novels also include topics that are valuable for consideration, but are not thoroughly discussed in older works, or are presented in a way that is no longer accurate or accepted. However, young-adult literature is prone to change frequently, as it includes works from a variety of genres and is subject to the trends in the society from which it emerges. The complete body of young-adult literature is very diverse. Some popular examples of young-adult novels include Lois Lowry's *The Giver* (1993), Suzanne Collins's *The Hunger* Games (2008), and Brandon Sanderson's *The Rithmatist* (2013). While these books are often written for teenage readers, the subjects they cover and their popularity give them the potential to be effective educational resources.

Personal Response to the Text

As students read texts, the teacher can promote their connection with the text by guiding their responses. This can include encouraging connections such as text-to-text, text-to-world, or text-to-self. Students can make these connections verbally, in activities like group discussions or oral reports, or in their writing. These activities can be used with any type of text, and may help students connect readings to other subjects or areas of the curriculum. Though they may not do it consciously, students are already making connections as they read. Consciously thinking about these connections and communicating them to others may help students comprehend their reading and increase their interest in the material. Text-to-self connections are particularly effective for helping students form meaning from the text. Each student has unique experiences that may help them relate to different parts of the text or even alter the meaning they derive from the text.

Promoting Respect for Other Cultures through Assigned Reading

Teachers can also promote respect for other cultures and their differences through assigned readings. Literature has been shaped by literary movements from cultures all over the world, providing a diverse volume of world literature. Even within American literature, there is a variety of authors whose works can meet other educational criteria and introduce students to different cultures and ways of thinking within their own country. Having students read these works will inform them of different perspectives on historical periods and events, allowing them to see the experiences and talents of people unlike themselves. Assigning students readings from a variety of world literature, including British literature, will help them understand and respect international diversity. To help students understand and respect national diversity, it is helpful to assign works from literary periods that are sometimes overlooked, such as Native American literature, the Harlem Renaissance, the Dark Romantics, and the Lost Generation. Authors who have given overlooked groups a voice through their writings include Maya Angelou, Mark Twain, Martin Luther King Jr., William Carlos Williams, John Steinbeck, and Amy Tan. Incorporating diverse contemporary literature can also help students respect their peers and community members.

Classroom Participation

Techniques to Ensure Active Listening and Productive Participation

When assigning students to participate in cooperative learning projects or discussions, teachers should consider their **cognitive, emotional, behavioral, and social developmental levels.** If a teacher assigns a topic for age levels younger than the class, students will be bored and unengaged. If the topic assigned is for older age levels, they will be confused, overwhelmed, or lost. Before initiating class or group discussions, teachers should model and explain appropriate behaviors for discussions—particularly for students unfamiliar or inexperienced with group discussions. For example, teachers can demonstrate active listening, including eye contact, affirming or confirming the speaker's message, and restating the speaker's message for confirmation or correction. Teachers should establish **clear ground rules**, such as not interrupting others when they are speaking, not monopolizing the conversation, not engaging in cross-talk, not insulting classmates verbally, and taking turns and waiting for the appropriate time to make a comment. For young children and students with behavioral issues, this would also include refraining from physical contact like hitting, kicking, and biting.

Active Student Listening

Active listening has multiple dimensions. It involves constructing meaning out of what is heard, being reflective and creative in considering and manipulating information, and making competent decisions rich in ideas. The natural properties of speech and thought enable active listening: the typical speed of speaking is roughly 125 words per minute, whereas the estimated speed of thinking is roughly 500 words per minute. Therefore, students have around 375 words per minute of spare time to think about the speech they hear. Students' minds can wander during this extra time, so teachers should instruct them to use the time instead to summarize lecture information mentally—a form of active listening. Listening and learning are both social and reciprocal. They also both allow and require students to process and consider what they hear and stimulate their curiosity about subsequent information.

Incorporating Active Student Listening into Lessons

At the beginning of each day (or class), teachers should clarify the "big picture" and identify the learning objectives incorporated into the day's activities. They should also give students a single word or phrase to summarize the prior day's subject and a single word or phrase to preview the current day's subject. Teachers should not only establish this recall, retrieval, prediction, and planning process as a daily habit, but should also encourage students to develop the same daily habit in their note-taking. Teachers should review main concepts or have students summarize the last lecture's main ideas to make connections with preceding lessons. By encouraging and guiding student listening, teachers supply spoken transitions analogously to those in written research. By cueing students to take notes with questions or summaries at the ends of sections, teachers also help students demonstrate their comprehension.

Using Media to Review

Teachers can allow students to take photos, videos, and audio recordings of lessons to review as needed. To encourage students to reword and recall instructional input, teachers can let students download class outlines from Google Docs. These outlines may include hard-to-spell terminology or vocabulary words, jargon of specific disciplines, and links reminding students to follow up by accessing resources and readings to inform the notes they take. Teachers should give outlines a two-column format: on the right, a wider column with teacher notes, to which students can add, and on the left, a narrower column for students to record notes and questions about previous lectures and reading. Teachers should advise students to take their own notes in similar formats. Students and teachers alike can learn through speaking, writing, listening, and reading when they contribute narratives to supplement visual graphics (photos, concept maps, charts, advance organizers, illustrations, diagrams, etc.) that support the concepts they analyze and explain.

WHOLE-CLASS LEARNING CIRCLES

Forming **whole classes** into learning circles requires students to apply their skills for listening to lectures, synthesizing information, and summarizing the information. Teachers can prepare students by articulating central discussion points; identifying next steps in thought, question forming, analysis, and action; guiding student analysis and construction of meaning from what they have read, observed, and experienced; and asking students questions beginning with "What?" "Why?" and "Now what?"

Basic ground rules for learning circles include:

1. No student interrupts another.
2. Students may skip a turn until others have taken turns, but no student speaks out of turn.
3. Each student has a certain length of time for speaking.
4. Each student starts by restating what was said previously (e.g., summarizing shared points, differing points, missed points, or points not discussed fully).
5. After every student has had one turn, general discussion is open, possibly guided by teacher-provided questions.

PROCEDURES AND GROUND RULES FOR SMALLER GROUPS

Teachers can develop student discussion skills integrating listening, reading, and speaking skills by assigning small discussion groups to tackle assigned problems. Teachers may use established groups, assign new groups, or allow students to form groups of 4-5 students. Teachers can read a text passage, describe a scenario, or pose a question for discussion. They can then give students several minutes to review homework and notes, briefly read new related material, and review essay drafts. Teachers then give each student in each group a specified number of uninterrupted minutes to speak in turn.

After every student has taken a turn, the teacher opens general discussion, setting the following ground rules:

1. Students can only speak about others' ideas.
2. Teachers and classmates can ask students to clarify their ideas, give examples, connect them more closely to what they read, or elaborate.
3. Small groups can summarize overall points for other groups, including shared points, differences, and potential topics they missed.

EDUCATOR TECHNIQUES FOR CLASSROOM DISCUSSIONS

Students who feel comfortable with the teacher and the class are more likely to engage in open discussion. Teachers can encourage student openness and creativity by learning students' names and by posing questions rather than making comments. Lively discussions with all students participating are evidence that students are comfortable. A variety of student answers is evidence that the questioning technique works. When student discussions stray off the subject, learning goals will not be met. Teachers can redirect discussion by restating topics and questions previously announced, and by introducing new questions related to identified topics. When conversation refocuses on stated topics, teachers can identify specified learning goals/objectives students are meeting in their discussion. In most classes, a few students will dominate conversations. Teachers can pose less challenging questions, which can be answered even without preparation, to engage more reticent students, and then graduate to higher-level questions. They can evaluate all students' participation using checklists generated from attendance sheets.

TEACHING STRATEGIES TO ENCOURAGE DISCUSSION

During class discussions, students often contribute erroneous information. Teachers must be tactful in correcting them. If students withdraw from the conversation or cease further contributions, the teacher has not corrected them appropriately. If corrected students continue to contribute, the teacher has succeeded in providing positive reinforcement rather than punishment with the correction. Some ways to do this include acknowledging how the student came to a conclusion but explaining that it does not apply to the current context, or explaining how the student's response might be correct in another situation. Teachers can also provide incentives for students to contribute to class discussions. They may include participation in the syllabus as part of the grade, keep records to tally when each student contributes to a discussion, or assign different students to lead class discussions in turn. These are some ways teachers can evaluate individual student participation in classroom discussions, as well as their own effectiveness in encouraging such participation.

Reducing Intimidation

Students often feel intimidated if "put on the spot" to answer questions without warning. Teachers can put them at ease by allowing time to prepare. They can announce topics and questions for class discussion, giving students five minutes to jot down notes for responses and another five minutes for exchanging and reflecting on notes with classmates before beginning whole-class conversation. Teachers may distribute discussion topics at the end of one class for the next day's conversation or post questions online the night before class. One technique for evaluating discussions is asking students early in the term to write papers about the characteristics of good and bad class discussions, and then discuss what they have written. Teachers then compose a list of classroom discussion goals and give copies to all students. Another technique is an informal survey: ask students midway through the semester to evaluate the overall quality of class discussions. Share responses with the class, and inform them of plans incorporating their feedback to enhance discussions.

Promoting Discussion Outside of Class

Teachers can encourage in-class discussion by promoting group meetings and discussions outside the classroom. Interacting with students outside of class also promotes a sense of community. Teachers can demonstrate to students that they care about them as individuals and about their educational development by asking them about their holiday or summer plans, about how they are feeling during midterm and final exam periods, and about their other classes. Teachers can find online articles related to class material and email or text links to these for review. They can allow time at the beginning of each class for announcements and arrange classroom chairs in a semicircle to encourage conversation. These methods have all been found effective in promoting a sense of community, which in turn encourages class discussions. To address different student learning styles and abilities, teachers can vary the levels and types of questions they ask their students: asking them to give simple information, describe, compare, analyze, justify, compare, generalize, predict, or apply information.